Acclaim for Sister Helen Prejean's

The Death of Innocents

"If death row has a patron saint, it would be Prejean."
—*Los Angeles Times*

"Sister Helen Prejean has done it again—she has written a powerful and poignant book about those whose lives are taken wrongly by our system of criminal justice."
—Cornel West

"Engrossing. . . . Compelling. . . . Prodigiously detailed."
—*The Washington Post Book World*

"Knowledgeable, measured and compassionate. . . . [A] heart-tugging book, replete with well-researched hard facts."
—*Rocky Mountain News*

"Sister Helen Prejean remains the preeminent witness to our most persistent barbarism. Her eloquent testimony on behalf of the condemned and the wrongly convicted—and the example of her fellowship—can inspire all Americans to find a better way."
—Ted Conover

"Chilling. . . . One woman's voice *can* move a nation forward."
—*Providence Journal*

"Impassioned. . . . Moving. . . . Nuanced, off beat. . . . It has much to recommend it."
—*Houston Chronicle*

"Once more Sister Helen enables us to connect on a deeply human level with those on death row. But in *The Death of Innocents* she also explains the seismic change in Catholic teaching on the death penalty. Following Pope John Paul's lead, Catholics everywhere now work for the abolition of this evil." —Bishop Thomas J. Gumbleton, auxiliary bishop, archdiocese of Detroit

"This important and well-written book is a deeply personal, compassionate, searingly honest eyewitness account of the death penalty in America. If you are not outraged by the sheer inhumanity and unfairness of state-sanctioned killing after reading this book, it might be time for you to run for governor of Texas." —Tim Robbins and Susan Sarandon

"It should be read by anyone interested in how this debate plays out." —*New York Law Journal*

Sister Helen Prejean

The Death of Innocents

Sister Helen Prejean is the author of *Dead Man Walking*. She travels extensively, giving, on average, 140 lectures a year, seeking to ignite public discourse on the death penalty. She has appeared on ABC's *World News Tonight*, *60 Minutes*, *Oprah*, NPR, and an NBC special series on capital punishment. She is a member of the Sisters of St. Joseph of Medaille and lives in Louisiana.

Please visit *The Death of Innocents* Web page:
http://www.deathofinnocents.net.

ALSO BY SISTER HELEN PREJEAN

Dead Man Walking

The Death
of Innocents

The Death
of Innocents

An Eyewitness Account of Wrongful Executions

Sister Helen Prejean

VINTAGE BOOKS

A DIVISION OF RANDOM HOUSE, INC.

NEW YORK

FIRST VINTAGE BOOKS EDITION, JANUARY 2006

The Library of Congress has cataloged the Random House edition as follows:
Prejean, Helen.
The death of innocents : an eyewitness account of wrongful executions / Helen Prejean.
p. cm.
1. Capital punishment—United States—Case studies. I. Title.
HV8699.U5P745 2005
364.66'0973—dc22
2004054154

Vintage ISBN-10: 0-679-75948-4
Vintage ISBN-13: 978-0-679-75948-5

Author photograph © www.grantguerrero.com
Book design by Meryl Sussman Levavi

www.vintagebooks.com

Printed in the United States of America
10 9 8 7 6

To Murder Victims' Families for Human Rights,

who show us the way

the earthen vessel may hold the rarest wine

    the handwrought silver goblet—gall

    the tattered cover—words of wisdom

    the gold-edged leaf—the cruelest lie

    stumbling words—love's true oath

    the silver tongue—a razor's edge

    the truth arrives disguised,

    therein the sorrow lies

      —JIMMY GLASS

        EXECUTED IN LOUISIANA, 1987

"Woe to you, scribes. . . . [You] tie up heavy burdens, hard to bear, and lay them on the shoulders of others; but [you] are unwilling to lift a finger to move them . . . blind guides! You strain out a gnat but swallow a camel. . . . [You] have neglected the weightier matters of the law: justice and mercy."

      —JESUS

"When Innocence trembles, it condemns the judge."

      —PUBLIUS SYRUS

        FIRST CENTURY BCE

ACKNOWLEDGMENTS

I have a lot of people to thank for the birth of this book.

My first thanks go to my friend and editor, Jason Epstein, who helped me shape my first book, *Dead Man Walking,* and now this book, five years in the making. I can't think of a better wordsmith on this planet than Jason Epstein, and lucky me, he chose to stay on as my editor after he retired from Random House. This book, which weaves together stories and constitutional arguments, presented a special challenge. I can't imagine writing a book without Jason Epstein. My debt of gratitude to him is beyond measure, my affection for him immense.

Special thanks to my literary agent, Gloria Loomis, who provided the life-giving link to Jason Epstein and Random House. Gloria's savvy ability as an agent has won my admiration, but her fierce commitment to social justice has won my respect and love. Gloria and Jason and the staff at Random House give me renewed hope that publishers and literary folks care about social justice as much as activist nuns do. I count as a peak experience the moment when, seated around a conference table at Random House, editor in chief Daniel Menaker ended a meeting by announcing: "With the publication of *Dead Man Walking,* we opened the national conversation about the death penalty. With *The Death of Innocents,* we're going to catalyze public discourse that will end the death penalty."

I give heartfelt thanks to senior editor Lee Boudreaux and assistant editor Laura Ford; copy editor Sona Vogel; legal adviser Laura Goldin; production manager Richard Elman; the publicity team, headed by Carol Schneider and assisted by Richard Callison and Sally

Marvin; and Gina Centrello, who is giving her wholehearted support to the book. And, of course, my thanks to the enthusiastic sales team, who has pledged to join me on the road to spread this book far and wide.

My heartfelt thanks go to Michael Radelet, who not once, not twice, but three times researched factual content for the myriad end-notes in this book. Mike performed the same painstaking research for *Dead Man,* but this project gave him triple work because the book kept morphing on me. But Mike grumbled only once about the extra work, a worthy grumble if ever there was one. Mike is a writer himself and a great speaker and teacher.

Richard Dieter, who heads the Death Penalty Information Center, also deserves special thanks. He single-handedly read through Chapter 3, "The Machinery of Death," four times, honing the legal arguments and researching court rulings. This chapter bears most of the constitutional arguments, so I needed a lot of help to frame arguments in a way that ordinary folks (like me) can understand.

I'm deeply indebted to generous friends who came to my assistance in the final stages of editing: Rose Vines, who coordinated the work of other editors and who holed up in Montana with me for twelve days to do the final push; Lillie Eyrich, who assisted with legal research; Liz Scott Monaghan and Katy Scott (and Art Scott, who cooked for us during an editing session); Lynn Jensen; Tom Dybdahl; Jason DeParle; and Sister Jane Louise Arbour.

Thanks to the host of lawyer friends and technical experts who read the manuscript and offered advice: Nick Trenticosta, Susana Herrero, Paula Montonye, Denise LeBoeuf, Barry Scheck, Stuart James, Millard Farmer, and Jim Marcus. Lori Urs, whose passion for justice is unquenchable, helped me immeasurably with the Joseph O'Dell narrative. And thanks to Jeff Garis, Jane Henderson, Shari Silberstein, Stephen Zeigler, and Robert Deans, who, on very short notice, researched information.

Great gratitude to all of the people who have provided me with hideaway places to write: the Barker family—Dickie and Charlene, Brett and Melissa, Keith and Stacie, Chris and Kari; Jim and Lin Roscoe; Barbara and Karl Fischer; Scottie and Gerry Scardina; Joe and Joyce Arnona; and, most especially, Franciscan Sisters Marya Grathwohl and Pat Bietsch, fellow nuns and treasured friends, who give me a writing room at Prayer Lodge on the Northern Cheyenne reservation in Montana. I am also deeply indebted to the Northern Cheyenne people, who teach me their traditions and sustain me with their friendship.

Profound thanks to my special assistants: Sister Margaret Maggio, CSJ, Carolyn Clulee, and Emile Netzhammer, who help me at every turn and who provide prayerful support and encouragement. Final thanks to my sister and brother, Mary Ann and Louis, and my religious community, the Sisters of St. Joseph of Medaille, who give me more love and support than I deserve. If it takes a village to raise a child, it surely takes a community to write a book. Now that the book stands poised to be given to the world, what I feel most deeply is humble gratitude.

PREFACE

As in *Dead Man Walking*, this is my eyewitness account of accompanying two men to execution—but with one huge difference: I believe that the two men I tell about here—Dobie Gillis Williams and Joseph Roger O'Dell—were innocent. The courts of appeal didn't see it that way. Once the guilty verdicts were pronounced and death sentences imposed, every court in the land put their seal of approval on the death sentences of these two men without once calling for thorough review of their constitutional claims. The tragic truth is that you as a reader of this book have access to truths about forensic evidence, eyewitnesses, and prosecutorial maneuvers that Dobie's and Joseph's jurors never heard. Not surprisingly, Dobie and Joseph were indigent. It's also no surprise that their defenses at trial were abysmal. In fact, Joseph O'Dell defended himself.

As of September 2004, 117 wrongfully convicted persons have been released from death row. Citizen Innocence Projects, staffed mainly by college student volunteers, have ferreted out evidence and eyewitnesses that liberated the wrongly accused, sometimes only hours away from execution. Dobie and Joseph were not so lucky. And I—my soul seared from watching state governments kill these men—entrust these stories to you. Brace yourself. These stories are going to break your heart. And learning about the court system that allowed the injustices at trial to remain in place might upset you even more.

I used to think that America had the best court system in the world. But now I know differently. Why is it that southern states are (and have always been) the most fervent practitioners of government killing, accounting for over 80 percent of U.S. executions? Why is it that Texas alone accounts for one third of the total number of U.S. executions and, in the latest tally, accounts for fully one half of all state killings in 2004 (as of September 27), while the Northeast, supposedly guided by the same Constitution and Supreme Court guidelines, accounts for only 1 percent of executions? What explains the dramatic regional disparity in the way the death penalty is implemented?

I urge you to stick with me when we come to the constitutional arguments in the third and fourth chapters of this book. It's vitally important that We the People assume ownership of our Constitution and do not leave its interpretation and application solely to attorneys and jurists, even Supreme Court justices. The justices are as prone to ideological bias as anyone else. What's behind Chief Justice Rehnquist's drive to speed up executions ("Let's get on with it!") despite growing evidence of a seriously flawed system? What motivates Justice Antonin Scalia to declare, without shame, that he is a willing part of the "machinery of death"?

When I started out as a young Catholic nun, I had no idea that I would walk this path into America's death chambers. My Catholic faith has been the catalyst to inspire me to follow the way of Jesus, who sided with the poor and dispossessed and despised. In these pages I tackle head-on the spirit of vengeance—a wrongful death can be set right only by killing the perpetrator—that has dominated the religious, political, and legal discourse of our country during the past twenty-five years.

I especially reach out to readers who experience fierce ambivalence about the death penalty (almost everybody): who are outraged at the murder of innocents and want to see their killers pay with their lives, but who also recognize that government bureaucrats can scarcely be trusted to get potholes in the streets filled, much less be allowed to decide who should live and who should die.

This book is only the beginning of the dialogue. At its end you'll find a page of resources, which offers ways to continue the dialogue and—if you're ready—to engage in public action to transform our society.

To young people I say: As you see what happened to Dobie Williams and Joseph O'Dell and see what is going on in our courts, may you be impassioned to devote your lives to soul-size work. I hope what you learn here sets you on fire.

Contents

The Death
of Innocents

ONE • DOBIE GILLIS WILLIAMS

When I first met him I was struck by his name, Dobie Gillis, and then when I heard he had a brother named John Boy, another TV character, I knew for sure his mama must like to watch a lot of TV. Betty Williams, Dobie Williams's mama, is here now in the death house of the Louisiana State Penitentiary, a terrible place for a mama to be. It's January 8, 1999, at 1:00 p.m., and she's here with family members, two of Dobie's lawyers, and me, his spiritual adviser, and we're all waiting it out with Dobie to see if the state is really going to kill him this time.

Dobie's had eleven execution dates since 1985 and close calls in June and November when the state came within a couple of hours of killing him but had to call it off because of last-minute stays of execution. I feel this is it, they're going to get Dobie this time, and I'm praying for courage for him and for his mama and for me, too. I've done this four other times, accompanying men to execution, first with Patrick Sonnier in 1984,[1] walking through this very room on his way to the electric chair, and here we are sitting with Dobie, hoping against hope he won't have to make that walk through this room tonight. His execution by lethal injection is scheduled for 6:30. About five hours to go.

Dobie's death is set to conclude a story that began more than fourteen years before, in the early morning hours of July 8, 1984. It was then that forty-three-year-old Sonja Merritt Knippers was stabbed to death as she sat on the toilet in her bathroom in Many, Louisiana, a small town in north central Louisiana. Mrs. Knippers's husband, Herb, who said he was in the bedroom during the slaying, told investigators that he heard his wife yelling, "A black man is killing me," which led police to round up three black men, Dobie Gillis Williams among them. He was home on a weekend furlough from Camp Beauregard, a minimum-security detention facility, where he was serving a term for burglary. He had been allowed the visit because he was a model prisoner, not prone to violence.

At 2:30 a.m., police officers seized Dobie, asleep on the couch at his grandfather's house, brought him to the police station, and began interrogating him. They told him that they would be there for the rest of the night and all morning and all the next day if need be, until they "got to the bottom of this." Three police officers later testified that Dobie confessed, and at the crime scene investigators found a bloodstain on a bathroom curtain, which the state crime lab declared was consistent in seven categories with Dobie's, and statistically, that combination would occur in only two in one hundred thousand black people. Investigators also found a "dark-pigmented piece of skin" on the brick ledge of the bathroom window, through which the killer supposedly entered and escaped.

Dobie's trial didn't last long. Within one week, the jury was selected, evidence presented, a guilty verdict rendered, and a death sentence imposed.

Now, waiting here in the death house, I pray. *No, God, not Dobie.* I've been visiting him for eight years. He's thirty-eight years old, indigent, has an IQ of 65, well below the score of 70 that indicates mental retardation. He has rheumatoid arthritis. His fingers are gnarled. His left knee is especially bad, and he walks slowly, with labored steps. He has a slight build, keeps his hair cropped close, and wears big glasses, which he says gives him an intellectual look. His low IQ forces him to play catch-up during most conversations, especially if he is in a group.

Earlier today, Warden Burl Cain asked Dobie if he wanted to be rolled to the death chamber in a wheelchair. "Dobie, we'll do it your way, any way you want, so if you want the wheelchair, we'll do that. It might make it easier on you, but if you want to walk, I mean that's okay, too, no matter how long it takes. We'll just go at your pace. If it takes a half hour, whatever it takes, it's up to you, you can have it your way, like at Burger King, have it your way, and we'll do anything you want to do."

Dobie narrowed his eyes. "No way. I'll walk."

Later he says, "Man! Is he crazy? Let them people use a wheelchair on me? Man! No way. No way."

The wheelchair is a sensitive issue. When Dobie got rheumatoid arthritis five years ago, his proud, fit body left him. Some of the guys on the Row started calling him "stiff," and when they'd see a crippled person on TV, there'd be snickers as somebody yelled out, "Who does that remind you of?" Dobie would be silent in his cell.

"I just ignore them," he'd tell me.

I notice how fast and soft and friendly the warden talks to Dobie. Of course he wants Dobie to use the wheelchair. I can tell he wants the process to go quickly so he and the Tactical Unit—the team responsible for the physical details of killing Dobie—can get it over with as soon as possible. Dobie, it is turning out, is proving difficult in several ways. There had been the last-minute stays of execution in June and November, which meant that the Tac team, Mrs. Knippers's family members, the executioner, the support staff, the medical staff, and the ambulance crew that removes the body—all these people had to come back and go through it again, which is hard on everybody. Plus, Dobie rejected the offer to eat his final meal with Warden Cain as two other executed prisoners had done. That must have felt like a slap in the face, because the warden felt he was doing his best to show Christian fellowship to these men before they died.

The meal with the other condemned men—Antonio James and John Brown—had gone well, with clean white tablecloths and the menu and guests selected by the prisoner—lawyer friends and spiritual advisers—along with the guests the warden himself invited—a couple of friendly guards and Chaney Joseph, the governor's attorney (who formulated the state's current death penalty statute and stands ready to block any legal attempt to halt an execution). At these final meals they had all held hands and prayed and sung hymns and eaten and even laughed, and one of these scenes was captured on ABC's *Primetime Live* when a story was done about Antonio James. In the *Primetime* piece, there at the head of the table was Warden Cain, like a father figure, providing the abundance of the last meal—boiled crawfish—making everything as nice and friendly as he could, even though when the meal was done the inevitable protocol would have to be followed and, as warden, he would be obliged to do his job. In the chamber, he'd nod to the executioner to begin injecting the lethal fluids into the arm of the man whose hand he was holding and with whom he was praying.

The warden is fond of quoting the Bible, and the verse he quotes to justify state executions is Paul's Epistle to the Romans, chapter 13, which states that civil authority is "the servant of God to execute wrath on the wrongdoer." Yes, this distasteful task laid on his shoulders is backed up by God's word, which he tries hard to follow because he takes very seriously the eternal salvation of every man in this prison entrusted to his care. Warden Cain would do anything to avoid carrying out the death penalty, but it goes with the territory of being warden, and he likes being warden and is only a few years from retirement. So he goes along reluctantly and tries to be as nice to the condemned and their families as he can.

He could do what Donald Cabana, the former warden of Parchman Penitentiary in Mississippi, did. Warden Cabana quit his job because his conscience wouldn't allow him to participate in executions. In his book, *Death at Midnight: The Confession of an Executioner,* he tells of presiding over the execution of two men in the gas chamber at Parchman. The second one, that of Connie Ray Evans, really got to Cabana because he liked the man, and they talked often and long. He tried truthfully to answer Connie Ray's questions about how best to deal with the gas when it came, telling him to breathe deep, that it would be over faster that way.[2] Then, after watching the dying man gasp for breath and twitch and strain against the straps in the chair, Warden Cabana quit the job, and today he gives lectures against the death penalty to anyone who will listen.

Warden Cain could choose to do that. He has confided to one of Dobie's defense attorneys that he draws the line when it comes to women. Louisiana has one woman on death row, Antoinette Frank, and the warden says, no, he just couldn't execute a woman, that he'll quit before he does that. I wonder if he realizes that he's the first trigger of the machinery of death—he nods and a man dies. The death certificate states the true nature of the deed: "Cause of death: homicide." Maybe there's a qualifying word, "legal," but it's homicide all the same.

When Dobie turned down the warden's invitation to share his last meal, he said, "I ain't going to eat with those people. It's not like, you know, *real* fellowship. When they finish eating they're going to help kill me." He is the first one up for execution who's turned down the warden's invitation, and I've heard through the prison grapevine that the men on the Row respect him for it.

We're all sitting around a table with Dobie in the death house visiting room: Jean Walker, Dobie's childhood sweetheart; his mama; his aunt Royce; his brother Patrick; his four-year-old nephew, Antonio; two lawyer friends, Carol Kolinchak and Paula Montonye; and me. Dobie's mama has her Bible open and puts her hand on it, saying, "No, not this time, either, they're not going to kill you, Dobie, because in Jesus's name I've claimed the victory, oh yes, in faith I claim the victory because God's in charge, not man, God is the lord of life and death, and in Him is the victory, and you must believe, Dobie, you must trust, as the psalm says, Oh, God, you are my rock. Do you believe, Dobie, are you trusting God to bring you through this? Do you have faith?"

Her words are strong and urgent, and they shore her up against this dark and dreadful process. She is trying to infuse the spiritual strength she feels into her son, who says softly, "Yeah, Mama, I believe."

"Say it like you mean it, Dobie, say it with conviction."

"Yeah, Mama, I believe, I do."

Dobie sits close to Jean, now back in his life after twenty or so years. She's declared herself "strong in the Lord" and has her husband's approval for these visits. She wants Dobie to be "strong in the Lord," too. She heard about Dobie's pending execution and reappeared in his life a few weeks before his June death date some eight months ago, and he can't stop touching her. During earlier visits in the death row visiting room—not now—he was like a playful teenage boy, sitting close to her, pinching her arms, thumping her head, teasing her, coaxing, telling her how cute her smile and her eyes were. When his mama had enough of it and told him to leave her alone, he smiled and said, "I just like to pick at her." His mama would open the Bible, read a passage, and press him for the meaning. Sometimes she would read lengthy passages and Dobie would say, "Not so long, Mama. Pick a short one. I just want to visit."

My faith doesn't give me the same assurance Dobie's mama feels that he won't be killed tonight. I'm praying that God will give him the strength and the courage he needs to overcome fear. Dobie's been telling me how the fear eats at him. He was glad when Jean brought him a black baseball cap with the words of Isaiah, "Fear Not," embroidered in white letters on the front. Prison rules forbid prisoners to wear hats with any sort of logo, but the guards let the "Fear Not" hat slide. Dobie's worn it for three solid weeks except in the shower, and he wanted badly to wear the hat here in the death house, but the guards took it away when he was brought in at 9:30 this morning. "Man," he says, stretching out the last part of the word, "mannnn, they won't even let me have my hat." It's one more disappointment, but he tucks it somewhere inside, because after fourteen years of living in the "waiting to die" place, he's used to holding himself in check and not wishing too hard for anything.

Dobie is sitting at the end of the table with his back to the window, through which you can see one of the two guards with automatic weapons guarding the front door. With the lagoon outside and the flowers in pots near the front entrance, you'd never know this is a building where people are put to death. And when you're inside, all you see is a room with tables and chairs, two vending machines, and at the far end a white metal door. Behind this door, always kept locked, is the black cushioned gurney and the witness room with two rows of plastic chairs. Everything is neat and painted fresh and clean, the gray floor tiles polished and gleaming. The warden has had two large murals painted on the walls of this room, one of Elijah being taken up to heaven in a fiery chariot and the other of Daniel in the lion's den, the lions with yellow, glinting eyes and Daniel looking upward toward an opening from which heavenly light pours. In the scripture stories, both men escaped death. Elijah was taken up to heaven alive in the chariot, and Daniel, through God's power, persuaded the lions not to eat him. I sense in the murals an effort to make this a holy place, a place that's not really so bad, because here you get to go to God.

This is a place where everything is run by protocol. Each step of the execution process has been carefully chiseled out. "Here's what we do if he goes peacefully. Here's what we do if he fights us. Okay, now, when we get in the room, I strap the legs, and you, the chest, and you, the right arm." Everybody knows his part in the ritual. The Tac team has practiced over and over, so when it comes to the real thing, they can do what they have to do. Plus, they're bolstered by the law, by general popular support for the death penalty, and by the knowledge that all the courts in the land and the U.S. Congress say it's constitutional to do the deed they'll be doing tonight. Sometimes even the prison chaplains give their blessing to the act, backing it up, of course, with a quote from the Bible.

Dobie's family will have to leave him at 3:00 p.m. It's 1:45, and I want to give them some privacy, so I stand away from the visiting table over by the lion's den mural. A guard is standing near me. We're close to the wall, looking straight into the yellow eyes of one of the lions, our backs to Dobie and his family. The guard tells me he's been here for every one of the twenty or so executions since 1983. He jabs his thumb toward the visiting table and whispers, "We got to get rid of the death penalty once and for all, because look who's in here. It's always families like this."

There's a tight, cold band in my stomach, the feeling of "Oh no, not again, they're doing it again." My stomach always knows about executions ahead of my brain. Having accompanied four other men through this ordeal doesn't make it easier. More predictable, but not easier. And harder to take, because now I know so much about the death penalty, and one of the things I know is that innocent people get thrown onto death row along with the guilty.

When I first started visiting the condemned in 1982, I presumed the guilt of everyone on death row. I thought that an innocent person on death row would be a pure anomaly, a fluke. Not with all the extensive court reviews and appeals. Now, after working intimately with so many of the condemned and their attorneys, I know a lot better how the criminal justice system operates and how innocent people can end up on death row. Now I know that 95 percent of the justice an accused person can expect to get in the criminal justice system must happen at trial. Because once the "raw stuff" of forensic evidence, eyewitness accounts, police reports, expert witnesses, and alibis is presented and decided upon by a jury, chances are no court will ever allow it to be looked at again. With so much in the balance as you go to trial, you better have a skilled, energetic lawyer who thoroughly knows the law and how to conduct an exhaustive investigation and is aggressive enough to get hold of the *original* police report with its fresh, uncensored reporting of facts and eyewitness accounts.

Honorable people have disagreed about the justice of executing the guilty, but can anyone argue about the justice of executing the innocent? And can anyone doubt, after the revelations of the past five years, that we do it all the time?

No, God, not Dobie.

Inside my soul, I'm trying to find a rock to stand on.

Jesus, be here now. You went through the agony of execution. Please help Dobie.

The prayer is like breathing, and my soul steadies. At least for now Dobie is alive and visiting with his mama, and they are together and okay. Just for now. Just for the moment. In the death house I've learned to dwell in the present because the strength comes that way. I know not to take on the horror ahead of time. *My grace is sufficient for you.* When the family leaves at 3:00, I'll be close by to help Dobie take on the rest of this day as it comes. My soul is poised. I'll talk to him, affirm his life, thank him for the gift he is, pray with him, face the fear head-on, face it, deal with it. And I'll call him forth, summon him: "Dobie, how are you doing? What are you feeling now?" The enormity of the death that is about to happen is so great that it is easy to feel engulfed and muted and paralyzed. In words there is life, there is communion, there is shared courage.

Meanwhile, silently around us in this room, others are poised for what is about to take place. The media and witnesses will soon be gathering in a building near here. The executioner, the technician who will administer the lethal dose, is surely already nearby, organizing the vials of pancuronium bromide, which will stop Dobie's breathing; the potassium chloride, which will put him into cardiac arrest; and the vial of sodium pentothal, given first, which will put Dobie to sleep.

In the room where the witnesses are gathering, there are refreshments and the buzz of people talking and some official or other going around getting people to sign the witness agreements. I'm amazed at how banal the steps are to kill a human being, and I'm amazed at how polite and considerate the warden and guards are. Southern hospitality is a real thing in Louisiana. Even the big deal made about the last meal is genuine in a state where food is given priority. This is the death house, where killing is done by quiet-spoken, polite people, who first serve you a fine meal and pray with you before they kill you.

I notice that Shirley Coody is sitting over at the food-serving table near the Elijah mural. She was here in June and November, too, when Dobie came within an hour of being killed. Her face shows her distress over what is going on in this room today. It was her ex-husband, Major Kendall Coody, supervisor of death row, who, after participating in five executions, called me into his office and said he couldn't do it anymore, that he had to quit. And over these sixteen years he's the only person I've ever met, other than Warden Cabana, who quit his death-dealing job because of his conscience. I notice that even though Shirley Coody has "Major" in front of her name, she won't be participating in the execution of Dobie tonight. No woman is ever part of the Tac team, a job that may require physical force to subdue a noncooperative prisoner. Her obvious role here is to show kindness to this little family, offer them food and drink, talk to them gently.

It's a shame that someone like her, who has such compassion for people, is made to play her part in this death process, even in a peripheral way. The reason she's even here at all is that the death house happens to be part of the camp she supervises, Camp F. Normally this room is used for prisoners' visits with family and friends. That's why the vending machines are here. What goes through Shirley Coody's heart as she watches mothers hold their sons close for the last time? In November, when Dobie came so close to dying, I noticed that her eyes welled with tears when Betty and the family said good-bye. And earlier, in June, when the stay came just as Dobie's last meal was being served, Shirley Coody was one of the guards he invited to come and eat what had to be the most celebratory meal of fried shrimp and catfish of all time. I'll never forget the sight of Dobie walking out of this place of death—alive man walking—right through the front door under the EXIT sign, and behind him, Sergeant Lee Henry, carrying three boxes of leftovers from Dobie's "last" meal, to be shared with the guys on the Row, who were about to be drop-jawed with surprise at the sight of Dobie walking onto the tier.

. . .

Sonja Knippers was stabbed eight times in her back, neck, and chest, her blood splattering over the wall, floor, and window curtain. I can scarcely imagine what terror and pain she must have felt in the last moments of her life and what agony her three children must go through when they imagine and reimagine how their mother died. Who can blame them for wanting to see Dobie die? I met some of them at a court hearing for Dobie in 1991. I approached them, seated there in the courtroom, told them I was Dobie's spiritual adviser, and offered to help them any way I could. One of the daughters, a young woman in her twenties, asked me, "Has he told you why he killed our mother?" I had to be honest. I said I was just learning about the case, but what I knew made me question whether Dobie had killed her mother. She stiffened. "We won't be needing your help," she said, and turned away.

I'm not surprised she turned away. When I first began visiting death row inmates I avoided the victims' families, a terrible mistake I promised never to repeat. Nine times out of ten these families don't want to have anything to do with me, but you never know. There's that one in ten, such as Lloyd LeBlanc, whose son was murdered by Patrick Sonnier and his brother, two of the men I visited in prison; and he wanted very much to see me. He had said to me, "Sister, where have you been? I've had no one to talk to." But most of the victims' families I have been able to help are not those affected by the crimes of the men I counsel on death row. Almost always, those families see me as the enemy.

The *Sabine Index,* the Many, Louisiana, weekly newspaper, in its front-page articles about the Knippers murder and the ensuing fourteen-year legal struggle to bring Dobie to execution, was guided by the prosecution's version of events and gave ample coverage to any statement or commentary the district attorney wished to make about the case. This week's edition, in the final countdown to Dobie's execution, gives a summary of the case, a version of events that essentially recapitulates the prosecution's presentation to the jury. It is a story that has already been presented numerous times to the people of Many:

> How Dobie, home on leave for the Fourth of July weekend, entered Sonya and Herbert Knippers's Esso Drive home on July 8, 1984. How he hid,

apparently nude, behind a bathroom door, and confronted Mrs. Knippers when she left the living-room couch (she had been reading and dozing there) to use the bathroom at 12:48 a.m. How he slammed the door behind Mrs. Knippers, stabbed her repeatedly as she screamed, and then escaped through the bathroom window. Mr. Knippers, sleeping in the bedroom, is reported to have been awakened by his wife's cries and to have helped her from the bathroom to the living-room couch, where she died. Evidence gathered at the scene and elsewhere helped lead to Dobie's conviction, the *Index* reports: "a black pigmented piece of skin and a pubic hair, found on the brick window ledge . . . a blood-soaked curtain. . . . [S]crapes on [Dobie's] legs and a puncture wound" as well as a bloody T-shirt found stashed near the house where Dobie was staying. "By 5:30 a.m.," the paper says, "Williams had allegedly confessed to the crime on a tape recording. Soon after, though, it was discovered that the recorder had not been properly used . . . and there was no recording."

Actually, there was no blood on the T-shirt. What appeared to be the most damning evidence against Dobie was the bloodstain on the curtain. The last-minute stay of execution Dobie received in November 1998 was to allow for DNA testing of that bloodstain. DNA testing had not been available at the time of Dobie's original trial, but I'm not convinced that fact alone motivated District Attorney Don Burkett to stop Dobie's execution so that DNA testing could be done. I think Burkett was upset by the report he saw of a top-notch bloodstain expert, Stuart James, whose analysis of the evidence seriously questioned Burkett's outrageously contrived scenario of how Dobie supposedly killed Sonja Knippers. (James's critique is presented in detail later in this chapter.) At trial, Dobie's defense attorney had failed to get independent forensic testing done, and this allowed Burkett's version of the crime to go uncontested for thirteen years. That is, until Dobie's appellate defense team—their backs against a wall in the courts, their client about to die—hired Stuart James to study the forensic evidence to see if it might point to

Dobie's innocence, or at least raise substantive questions about his guilt. Faced with James's critical analysis of bloodstains, which showed that Dobie could not possibly have entered and exited through the tiny bathroom window, as he had argued (the window fully opened measured eleven inches high and one foot eight inches wide), Burkett agreed to the DNA testing. Although James's report had been shown only to him and not to the public, Burkett must have known that Dobie's defense could easily make it public. The all-white jury had readily believed his scenario, but what would the general public think?

Whatever his motivation, Burkett's last-minute call for DNA testing was a decent and fair-minded act. He could have let the execution proceed, declared the case closed, and then ordered the destruction of evidence—including DNA—rendered extraneous by the execution. My own hunch is that Burkett must have been shaken by Stuart James's analysis, which so strongly contradicted his own. I wonder if he allowed the DNA testing because he knew that if a scientifically accurate test such as DNA proved to be a "match" with Dobie's blood on the curtain, that fact alone would seal Dobie's guilt in the minds of most people (maybe in his own mind as well). But as a prosecutor, Burkett must have known that even DNA confirmation that Dobie's blood had been found at the scene of the murder was still only circumstantial evidence. He well knew that to successfully argue proof of guilt beyond reasonable doubt, the prosecution must present a scenario of the crime that is *consistent with* the "story" the evidence tells.[3]

The power to choose the laboratory to conduct the DNA testing was in Burkett's hands, and he selected GeneScreen Laboratory in Dallas. He also chose to bar Dobie's defense from conducting simultaneous testing by experts of their choice or to have a representative present to observe the testing at GeneScreen. Defense attorney Nick Trenticosta had to go along with the prosecutor's decision. "What else could I do?" Nick later told me. "In just a few hours they were going to kill Dobie unless the prosecution called for a stay, so I wasn't in any kind of position to demand fair terms for the testing. I figured that if Burkett would stay the execution, then maybe later he and I could work out a more equitable arrangement for testing." Nick wasn't particularly happy about the choice of GeneScreen, but given the imminence of Dobie's death, he didn't have time to research the lab's reputation among experts in the field. A seasoned capital litigator, Nick knew not to push Burkett too hard. Lawyers—like doctors, out to save lives—have their own kind of Hippocratic oath. Doctors vow: "First, do no harm." Capital defense lawyers vow: "First, don't let them kill your client."

On December 1, 1998, GeneScreen Laboratory sent its much awaited report to Burkett's office. Their DNA analysis of the blood sample had led them to conclude that the sample on the curtain and Dobie's blood matched. Burkett immediately released the results of the GeneScreen report to the media and declared that the most advanced scientific technology of the day had now confirmed beyond doubt what the state had contended all along—that Dobie Gillis Williams was guilty of the murder of Sonja Knippers. A day or two later, Burkett requested a new execution date for Dobie, and a Louisiana judge readily obliged, setting the date five weeks away on January 8, 1999. It was the eleventh date of execution set for Dobie during his fourteen years on death row.

As soon as Nick and his team heard of the GeneScreen report, they scrambled desperately to find DNA experts to critique it—free of charge. Like so many other Louisiana criminal defense lawyers whose clients are poor, Nick always struggles for funds to defend his clients. Louisiana judges are notorious for denying defense requests for expert witnesses and forensic testing. But Nick found Susana Herrero, a criminal investigator in Seattle, who worked with some of the leading DNA experts in the country, among them lawyer Barry Scheck, founder of the Innocence Project, Edward Blake of Forensic Science Associates in Richmond, California, and Randell Libby, a molecular geneticist at the University of Washington School of Medicine. For Nick, recruiting DNA experts was a minor challenge compared with the other huge problem he faced. Burkett allowed him access only to the conclusions of GeneScreen's analysis, not its case file, which contained photographs of the actual tests and the technicians' bench notes. Without that raw data, even the best DNA experts he might recruit would have nothing to analyze. Not only had Burkett refused to allow Dobie's defense to conduct independent DNA analysis of the blood evidence or to at least have a representative present during GeneScreen's testing (when only one sample of evidence exists, Nick believes, fairness dictates that both prosecution and defense be present during the testing), but he continued to block Nick from the GeneScreen raw data until January 5, three days before Dobie's scheduled execution. As soon as Nick got his hands on the data, he sent it immediately to Blake and Libby and several other experts. All of them found serious problems with GeneScreen's work: sloppy technique, poor quality controls, subjective interpretation. On one particular set of tests called STR gels, which line up two ladders of chromosomes to compare them, the gels had been applied to the ladders so unevenly that it was impossible to measure and compare them. In the same STR test, despite the fact that one in four of the controls failed, the lab relied on the results and drew conclusions. Messy technique means inconclusive results, the experts said. Consequently, none of the experts agreed with the lab's conclusion that the blood sample on the curtain "matched" Dobie's blood. They said the tests should be conducted again, which Burkett refused to have done.

Interestingly, one of the tests that uses polymarkers to line up genetic components or alleles produced a "rogue" allele that could not be accounted for as coming from Dobie or the victim; yet GeneScreen simply glided over this without comment.

But it all came too late. There simply wasn't time to digest the problems and file a motion for retesting of the evidence. Despite the fact that Barry Scheck phoned him and implored him to allow retesting, Burkett simply said that experts always tend to disagree. He was going along with the opinion of the experts at GeneScreen.

And now here we are on January 8 with Dobie in the death house for the third time. I can't shake the feeling that Dobie is going to be killed tonight. Nick and the defense team have nowhere else to go with his case. No court will grant a hearing, and the Louisiana Board of Pardons and Paroles, appointed by pro–death penalty governor Mike Foster, has never yet granted clemency to anyone condemned to death.

Dobie has said all along that he's innocent, and I have a lot of questions about his trial. I've talked with Paula Montonye, a member of the defense team, and learned a few details about the startling contradictions between the state's case and the forensic evidence recently uncovered by Stuart James's forensic analysis. I learn that there is no audio or visual recording of Dobie's (unsigned) confession and that jurors heard conflicting versions of this alleged confession by police officers who claimed they heard him confess. I also learn that Dobie's original lawyer permitted, without objection, an all-white jury to be seated and did not order an independent analysis of the forensic evidence. I oppose the execution of all human beings, even those guilty of horrendous crimes. But Dobie?

Betty Williams doesn't bite her tongue. "They got Dobie because he's a black man and Mrs. Knippers was a white woman. From the git-go they just all presumed a black man did it, and so that's all they ever went after."

Of course, this is Dobie's mama talking. Isn't this what any mother whose child is in danger does? Protest her child's innocence no matter what the evidence?

But more and more now, I am coming to believe the mothers.

Recently, we have been witness to astounding admissions of error by state and federal courts forced to free 117 wrongly convicted people from death row since 1973, and the number keeps growing.[4] Seven Louisiana death row inmates have been found to be innocent over the past six years (as of September 2004). Illinois alone has had to free 13 such people, some under sentence of death for eight, ten, fifteen years, which in the year 2000 led the governor to enact a moratorium on executions. Some innocent persons were freed because of DNA evidence, others because committed citizens and lawyers were finally able to expose suppressed exculpatory evidence, outrageous testimonies of jailhouse snitches, falsified police reports, or evidence of "coached" eyewitnesses. In Illinois, Anthony Porter, two days away from execution, was freed because journalism students from Northwestern University dismantled the case against him and exposed the real murderer.

In 1997, the American Bar Association, many of whose members support the death penalty in principle, found such rank unfairness in the application of the death penalty that they called for a moratorium. It was concern about "due process" and "equal justice under the law," so palpably absent in the case of many indigent and minority defendants, that persuaded the ABA to pass its resolution. Nobody knows better than lawyers what kind of justice gets meted out in the courts. They know the difference in treatment given the O.J.'s of the world in contrast with the NoJ.'s, forced to accept overworked, underfunded, or inept attorneys to defend them.

Brady v. Maryland in 1963 requires prosecutors to turn over evidence that could be favorable to the accused, but the requirement has no teeth.[5] Who knows how much evidence unfavorable to the prosecutor's case simply disappears or is conveniently not brought up? Working closely with police, prosecutors are privy to such information, but turning it over to the defense seems a more or less voluntary action that requires a huge degree of integrity on the prosecution's part. Defense attorneys have no way of knowing what is being withheld from them, nor do they have an assured way of getting such information from prosecutors, who suffer virtually no penalty for withholding it. Sometimes a fluke or stroke of luck turns up the concealed information, but such findings seem to be hit-or-miss, mostly miss, and require a scrappy, energetic, leave-no-stone-unturned defense attorney. Of the more than 500 documented cases in which innocent people have been convicted of homicide in the past century, including 175 or so where the defendant was sentenced to death, "prosecutorial misconduct" is one of the most frequent causes of miscarriage of justice.[6]

But what about Dobie Gillis Williams? Is he an innocent man about to be executed?

It took the jury a little over two hours to find Dobie Williams guilty of the murder of Sonja M. Knippers. None questioned the scenario of the crime that Burkett presented to them, a scenario that seemed to match the forensic evidence—bloodstains, knife, skin, hair—found at the scene. This scenario had Dobie crawling through the Knipperses' bathroom window, waiting behind the door, and stabbing his victim as she sat on the toilet; then, in his hasty exit out of the window, he left a drop of his blood on the curtain and skin and hair on the windowsill. And if anyone on the jury had a trace of doubt about Dobie's guilt, there was his confession. Police officers testified that he admitted he had killed Sonja Knippers in the early morning of July 8, 1984. What more did a jury need? They voted unanimously for guilt and unanimously for death.

Dobie's defense counsel, Michael Bonnette, couldn't stop the tide unleashed against his client. To retain Bonnette's services, Dobie's family had cobbled together $10,000, which took some doing, with uncles and aunts and Dobie's mama putting in what they could. Betty said the family wanted an African American to defend Dobie. They knew he'd appreciate how treacherous Dobie's situation was—a young black man accused of killing a white woman—and use all his lawyerly skills to fight hard for Dobie.

Unfortunately, they made the wrong choice. Bonnette not only lost this case but has since been disbarred for unethical practices in other cases.

The Williamses lived in the black section of Many for years. Their small house, which sat on cinder blocks, was literally on the wrong side of the tracks, in a section without paved roads or side-walks.

They knew all too well how things worked in the town. Their kids knew the "nigger" taunts and the fights in school. And they all knew the stores, eating places, lounges, and churches where, as black people, they felt welcome and where they didn't. And in the courts and district attorney offices, the black people of Many, like those in most small towns in Louisiana, knew that should they ever run afoul of the law, they would face white judges and white district attorneys and predominantly white jurors. Plus, they knew that all or almost all of the people in the local media were white, including editors and reporters for the town's weekly newspaper, the *Sabine Index*. When the Williams family opened the *Index* and read about social happen-ings in the town, they were not surprised that most of the stories were about white people. When black people were in the news, it usually meant they were in some sort of trouble. And Dobie, accused of the murder of a white woman as reported on the front page of the *Index,* was in *big* trouble.

Betty Williams said about the *Index*'s account: "They always give the DA's side. They never interviewed me or any of our family to get our side of the story." The family's side of the story was that Dobie was at his grandfather's house when the murder happened and the evidence against him was circumstantial or "outright lies."

"They just zeroed in on Dobie and never checked out any other suspects, and all those law enforcement folks just took whatever Mr. Knippers said as Gospel truth and went with that, including his ver-sion that his wife in her dying words told him a black man was killing her and that he escaped out of the bathroom window." Betty thinks that's the most preposterous thing she ever heard. "You tell me how on God's green earth could any dying person, about to face the judg-ment throne of God, waste their last breaths saying stuff like that about what race a person was or what window he crawled out of. That sounds like somebody in a murder mystery book, giving those last little clues about the murderer, not somebody ready to meet God and step into eternity. Going after Dobie, an innocent man, that don't honor that poor woman."

Dobie's trial began May 13, 1985. An all-white jury, composed of nine women and three men, was selected in a day and a half. During the jury selection, the small pool of black people called for duty was easily dismissed by District Attorney Burkett by the "strikes" allowed him, which meant that he could dismiss possible jurors without giving a reason. Dobie's lawyer, Bonnette, had twelve such strikes, but with the overwhelming number of white jury candidates, he couldn't dismiss them all; and he raised no formal objection as the all-white jury was seated for the trial. Later, in appeals to higher courts filed on Dobie's behalf, Bonnette's failure to raise a formal objection to the racial composition of the jury and the grand jury that indicted him would be a pivotal factor in deciding Dobie's fate.

Evidence and arguments by prosecution and defense took place in three and a half days, and by day five the jury unanimously found Dobie guilty. The *Index* ran the story of the verdict on its front page, featuring a large photo of the Grant Parish Courthouse in Colfax Parish, where because of a change of venue the trial was held. A caption stated that "the Many black" had been found guilty.

The Knipperses lived in a half duplex owned by the Sabine Housing Authority. They had been married for almost twenty-six years and spent most of them in Many, where Herb Knippers worked for his cousin as an auto parts salesman and Sonja Knippers did the best she could at keeping house, despite the fact that she suffered from a bad back and had to lie down frequently, according to her husband. Their two daughters were married and lived nearby, and their son, Monty, was fifteen and lived at home.

Herb was the only other person home the night she was stabbed to death in her bathroom. At the trial, "tears rolling down his cheeks" and "phrases rolling from his mouth," as the *Index* reported, Herbert Knippers gave his account of the murder. He was sleeping, he said, in the bedroom and was awakened by a loud scream and "the awfullest bunch of bumping and knocking and banging and screaming and hollering," and he heard his wife yelling, "No, don't. . . .

Don't hurt me. Don't kill me. Don't kill me. Don't kill me. . . . This black man is killing me, help me." He said he had backed up to run against the locked bathroom door and then it "popped open," and his wife emerged, bleeding, and said, "A black man has killed me." Then she described her assailant's exit route: "He went through the bathroom window." Those were her last words, Knippers said. He helped her to the couch and immediately called for help.

When the police picked up Dobie, they noticed he had abrasions on both legs, which they thought could have been caused by a hasty exit out the bathroom window. The time of Sonja Knippers's death was put at 12:45 a.m. by Dr. Clarence Poinboeuf, the coroner, though the record reveals that in his original report he had written 11:45 p.m. as the approximate time of death, then later changed it.

Dobie always maintained that after drinking at Fred Harris's store, he left to walk home around 11:30 p.m., arrived at his grandfather's house around 11:45 p.m., and was let into the house by his sister Cheryl. He felt "intoxicated and sick" from the drinking, he said. He took a bath and then made a telephone call to Debbie Sloan, his girlfriend, but her cousin answered the phone and said Debbie wasn't home.

Cheryl would later testify that he got home at 11:45. Johnny Sloan, Debbie's cousin, would testify that he answered the phone when Dobie called at 11:45 and told him Debbie was not at home. Dobie's uncle Samuel, who lived in the house, would also testify that Dobie arrived home between 11:30 and midnight. Dobie said he went to sleep on the living room couch until he was awakened by two police officers, "shining a flashlight up and down my body."

But Clyde Gosey, an acquaintance of Dobie's, would contradict all four of them by testifying that he had seen Dobie near the Knipperses' house, which is less than a mile from Dobie's grandfather's, sometime around 11:30 or 11:40 p.m.

After Dobie's two-and-a-half-hour interrogation in the Sabine Sheriff's Office, police officers said he confessed to murdering Sonja Knippers. His alleged confession didn't reveal how he had gotten into the house or what his motive was other than he had "been drinking," but he supposedly said he had found a knife on the back of the commode after he got into the bathroom, then waited behind the bathroom door, then stabbed Sonja Knippers and fled through the bathroom window, dropping the knife in the backyard as he ran.

After the interrogation, investigators went to the Knipperses' house and found a knife lying in the grass in the backyard about thirty feet from the bathroom window. Near the knife they also found a left glove and, under the bathroom window, two plastic milk crates. And there was the bloody curtain, with that one spot the crime lab would say matched Dobie's blood type.

Dobie did not sign a written confession, and there was no tape of his confessing. The three police officers who had conducted the questioning—Jimmy Kinney, Joe R. Byles, and James D. McComic—gave conflicting testimonies but agreed that Dobie had confessed. Normally courts rule out such testimony as "hearsay," but an exception is made for police. So one officer was allowed to say that Dobie's sister Cheryl originally told him that Dobie didn't get home until around 1:00 a.m. despite her testimony that Dobie had returned home around 11:45 p.m.

In court, Herb Knippers readily identified a steak knife with a wooden handle, which the state presented in evidence as the murder weapon. He said he knew the knife very well because earlier in the afternoon of the murder he had used it to cut up chicken and seasonings for gumbo. He remembered that he had washed the knife and left it on the drainboard in the kitchen. But then he said to the police and later in court that possibly he might have put the knife on the back of the commode when he went to wash his face in the bathroom while making the gumbo. But, no, he testified, he was sure he had left it on the drainboard in the kitchen.

Exactly where Dobie had allegedly picked up the knife was a source of some confusion, because, the officers reported, he had first said that he walked to the kitchen, got the knife, then went back to the bathroom to wait. But both McComic and Kinney said they had stopped him and said they couldn't buy that explanation, because Dobie would have had to tiptoe past Mrs. Knippers sleeping on the couch in the living room to get to the kitchen. Then the officers said Dobie changed his story, saying that he had picked up the knife from the back of the commode.

To add to the confusion, the prosecution contended that the window screen had been cut from the outside by the killer, which presupposed a knife or a weapon of some kind. Why, then, would the murderer look for a knife in the Knipperses' house if he already had one?

There were other contradictions. For instance, Kinney testified that Dobie said, "I walked halfway down the hall and I looked and saw her laying on the couch. Then I went back to the bathroom. . . ." Then Byles testified that Dobie said he looked through the bathroom door and saw Mrs. Knippers sleeping on the couch, but later investigators found out that the couch in the living room can't be seen from the bathroom door. So they confronted Dobie about that, too, and, once again, they alleged, he changed his version of events.

Dobie's defense attorney, Michael Bonnette, in his cross-examination of the officers, pressed them on the way the confession had been obtained, taking Dobie in the middle of the night and questioning him over and over, feeding him information. Bonnette did get the officers to acknowledge two crucial pieces of information about the crime they had relayed to Dobie—that the victim had been stabbed and that the crime had taken place in the bathroom. Perhaps they had also pieced things together for him: If there was a stabbing, there had to be a knife—so where was the knife? And how did he enter and leave the apartment? Didn't he leave through the bathroom window? Didn't it have to be the bathroom window, since that was what Mr. Knippers reported his dying wife had said?

Bonnette knew the tape would reveal the way information was fed and coercion used, such as threatening a penalty of death unless Dobie confessed.

But there was no tape, so it was Bonnette's critical questioning against the credibility of local police, shored up by DA Burkett, who assured the jury that the three law enforcement officers "certainly would have no reason other than to tell you actually what was said." He asked the jury to keep in mind that these men had been roused in the middle of the night, and all in all, he thought they deserved "hats off."

There were other problems in the forensic evidence that Burkett had to address. How could it be that the knife identified as the murder weapon didn't have a speck of blood on it—the victim's blood or animal blood (Knippers said he had cut up chicken while cooking gumbo)—not even under the wooden handle? And how could he explain that no trace of the victim's blood could be found on Dobie's clothes—his blue jeans, his shirt, or his shoes? Given the blood splattered everywhere in the bathroom, how could a killer lean over the victim, stab her, and not get any of her blood on him? The absence of Mrs. Knippers's blood on Dobie's shirt seemed especially problematic, because every article about the crime published in the *Index*—as Betty Williams was quick to point out—invariably included a "rolled up bloody shirt" as part of the incriminating evidence against Dobie. Finally, however, when the hard evidence was in, the crime lab reported that there was no blood on the shirt.

But Burkett called on the testimonies of two coroners—Clarence Poinboeuf and George McCormick—to interpret the bloodstain evidence to the jury. Poinboeuf said that the knife, the alleged murder weapon (for which the crime lab gave no report on fingerprints), had lain all night in the grass and had been covered by dew, which he thought could have washed off the blood. And McCormick explained that it was highly possible the assailant would have none of the victim's blood on him because, in his opinion, the bloodstains on the bathroom wall and curtain were "wiped" blood, not "splashed" blood, which occurred when the victim stood up, fell against the wall, and grabbed the curtain. So, since the blood didn't "splash," none of it got onto the killer. McCormick also explained that because Mrs. Knippers was stabbed mostly in her back as she sat, slumped over, on the toilet, the blood tended to pool inside her nightgown and would not therefore have spurted onto the murderer's clothing. Even the jugular vein, severed in the victim's neck during the stabbing, would tend not to spurt blood, McCormick explained, because a vein, not an artery, had been severed, and veins don't spurt blood the way arteries do.

Years later, forensic expert Stuart James would be aghast at this peculiar explanation. But his expertise was not available at Dobie's trial.

McCormick also testified that he examined the scrapes on Dobie's legs and found that such scrapes did, in fact, correlate with the type of scrape across a "fixed object" such as a brick window ledge. McCormick examined the photograph of the window ledge and said that in his opinion it did seem to reveal a piece of "darkly pigmented" skin about the size that might have come from the scrapes on Dobie's legs. Such scrapes, he surmised, also seemed to indicate that Dobie could not have had his pants on when he crawled in and out of the window. McCormick also examined what he called a "puncture" wound in the web of Dobie's left hand between his thumb and forefinger and testified that such a wound might have been received during the stabbing. The scrapes and puncture wound seemed fresh, McCormick said, and could account for Dobie's blood on the curtain.

So Burkett told the jury that Dobie "apparently was either nude at the time he went in the window or he took his clothes off after he got inside and placed them back outside." Which posed an interesting scenario: A young black man enters a white person's home nude and unarmed, finds a fortuitous weapon, and waits behind the bathroom door for his victim—or someone—to appear. (Who knows whether or not the husband might come into the bathroom first, and what then?)

But remember the size of the bathroom window, through which the killer supposedly entered and exited—one foot eight inches by eleven inches. Mr. Knippers testified that the lock on the window was broken, but that neither he nor his wife worried about it, because "it was so small . . . [and] high up off the ground."

It was a version of events that might have strained credulity too far for even an impressionable jury, but support came in the testimony of Ted Delacerda, the chief investigator, whom Burkett now called to the stand. Delacerda, larger in weight and build than Dobie, swore that he himself had scrambled headlong out of that window and done it in seven seconds. The word was that there was a videotape that documented Delacerda's speedy exit. However, the tape never surfaced, nor was it presented to the jury.

With such a mind-stretching escape scenario, what helped seal Dobie's guilty verdict was that drop of blood that stained the window curtain—the one that laboratory analysis had identified as highly consistent with Dobie's.

The blood on the curtain at least placed Dobie at the scene of the crime, Burkett insisted, and in his closing argument, he claimed that the various pieces of evidence—the blood on the curtain, the skin and hair on the ledge, the fresh scrapes on Dobie's legs, the puncture wound in his hand, the murder weapon found at the scene of the crime—when taken together pointed to Dobie Williams as the killer.

His demonstration of culpability done, DA Burkett faced one final challenge: to persuade the jury to sentence Dobie Williams to death. Finding Dobie guilty of murder wasn't enough. For first-degree murder, the Louisiana statute demanded an additional "aggravating" circumstance—namely, the commission of another felony in the course of the murder. Burkett explained to the jury that "aggravated burglary" was involved in this murder. And where was the evidence of burglary? Were valuable objects missing from the Knipperses' house? Were dresser drawers opened and possessions askew in the assailant's search for valuables? Burkett explained that "aggravated burglary," according to Louisiana law, is "unauthorized entry of an inhabited dwelling with the specific intent to commit felony or theft." So, with intent to commit felony included in the definition, evidence of burglary per se was not needed, Burkett explained. He argued that the stabbing, itself a felony, in this case was accompanied by the additional aggravating circumstance of another felony—namely, Dobie's unlawful entrance and use of a weapon. The argument was highly circuitous, but the jury seemed amenable to the logic. Burkett argued, "We don't know exactly what felony Dobie Gillis Williams intended to commit when he entered the residence that night. Maybe he intended to do just what he did, and that's kill somebody. Maybe he intended to rape somebody. Maybe he intended to rob somebody. But there is no doubt he didn't enter to give his greetings and see how the Knippers family was getting along that particular night. He did it with a specific intent—when I say 'did it,' entered the building with specific intent to commit a felony and in fact did commit a felony. He murdered someone. . . . He is either guilty of first-degree murder or he is not guilty of anything."

The jury found him guilty of first-degree murder.

Mrs. Knippers's murder was the first homicide case Burkett had faced after he was elected district attorney of Sabine Parish. It was a high-profile case. Here was a white woman, killed in the bathroom of her own home, whose dying words (according to her husband) were, "A black man killed me." And while aggravated rape was never proved against Dobie (the laboratory report showed that Sonja Knippers hadn't been raped), suspicion was palpable, especially since the killer was thought to be nude and the pictures of the victim showed her underwear down "between her buttocks and her knees," as Dr. McCormick pointed out to the jurors. The Many community was traumatized, and Burkett devoted himself untiringly not only to the investigation and trial, but also to the fourteen years of appeals that followed.

State and federal courts that reviewed Dobie's case did not seem to believe that Dobie's constitutional right to an "impartial jury" was in any way compromised by the all-white jury chosen to render judgment on his life, nor were they troubled by the fact that the grand jury in Sabine Parish had never had a black foreperson since the days of Reconstruction, even though the population of Sabine itself is more than 27 percent black. Why were black people always excluded from serving as forepersons? The Louisiana Supreme Court ordered a hearing to look into the Sabine Parish grand jury selection process. And what did the hearing show? That something of a "good ol' boys" club existed in the town. Judges, district attorneys, and most law enforcement officials were invariably white, and the process they followed for selecting grand jury members was pretty casual, with the community leaders offering names of people they knew—who, of course, were other white people. The result, not surprisingly, was that few black people even made it onto the grand jury, much less as foreperson. When a writ of appeal came to the Fifth Circuit Court of Appeals to review this process, did they agree that there was a pattern of racial discrimination?

They refused to examine it. Dobie's lawyer, they said, had failed to raise an objection to the racial composition of the grand jury.

Back in 1982, when I was making my first visits to death row, I found out that judges wear procedural gloves. No matter how "crying for justice" an issue might be, if you don't go through the correct procedure, you're out of luck. Executions have taken place after writs were denied because defense attorneys filed the writ one day late or typed the wrong title of the motion.[7] "We are a court of laws, not justice," U.S. Court of Appeals judge Learned Hand once said. Laws get interpreted and parlayed into procedures, which can become so rigid that they prevent justices from touching the quick of the issue, and that's where the legal gloves come in. I remember how shocked I was when I first discovered this procedure-over-justice mentality, even in life-and-death cases. I learned early on that an inept lawyer can get you killed.

Only within the past year have Dobie's lawyers hired Stuart James to examine the evidence against him. It's too late, of course, thirteen years after trial and conviction, to get any court to grant an evidentiary hearing on guilt or innocence. Most states, including Louisiana, have severe statutes of limitations on such hearings, so Dobie's appeals lawyers have been concentrating on constitutional issues, which are narrow in scope, to save Dobie's life. In effect, his guilt was decided when the jury in Colfax found him guilty. It was up to Bonnette to file an appeal with the state court after the verdict was handed down, but he had no experience with postconviction appeals. Plus, he had severely limited issues for such appeals because he had not raised the right kinds of objections during the trial itself.

Some months before Dobie's scheduled execution in June 1998, Paula Montonye, the public defender from Connecticut working with Nick Trenticosta at the Loyola Death Penalty Resource Center in New Orleans, begins to focus her energies on Dobie's case. She's fiery and fresh and determined not to see Dobie die. "He was washing through the appeals courts, which kept deciding against him on one issue after another, and there was nowhere else to go but into innocence," she said. Of course, that is just what Dobie has been telling us all along—that he is innocent.

She goes back to Many, talks to people, and persuades the defense team to hire Stuart James, whose specialty is bloodstain evidence. For the first time, someone representing Dobie's interest examines the forensic evidence, an essential step any decent defense attorney should do for his or her client, but one that Bonnette failed to do. And because he had no independent examination of forensic evidence to call upon, all Bonnette could do was raise his own commonsense questions and try to point out inconsistencies in the prosecution's experts' interpretation of the evidence—a weak and ineffective endeavor with disastrous consequences for Dobie.

When Stuart James's investigation is done, Paula arranges for us to meet. I go over to the Loyola Death Penalty Resource Center, and we get cold drinks and sit around a table to talk. Stuart James, it turns out, literally wrote the book on this sort of thing. He is a coauthor of *Interpretation of Bloodstain Evidence at Crime Scenes,* which is in its second edition. He is in his late fifties, thin, balding, low-key, and very precise.

His report sits on the table in front of him. I feel edgy, on the precipice of something big. Until now I haven't pushed much to find out about Dobie's guilt or innocence. I never do. I don't believe that the government should be put in charge of killing anybody, even those proven guilty of terrible crimes. In the eight years I've been visiting Dobie, he has maintained his innocence, and at times certain parts of the evidence would come up—the shirt he took off because it had liquor on it, the cut on his hand from the lawn mower and how he had gone into the house to put some alcohol on it, the scrapes on his legs from football at Camp Beauregard. Mostly I just let him talk, ask him to explain some things in more detail, but I don't delve much into forensic evidence or other details of the case, trusting that the good and committed lawyers handling his appeals are doing all they can. With them, I have been hoping that the constitutional issues in his case, which seem substantive to me—the racial composition of the jury and grand jury and the ineffectiveness of Dobie's defense counsel—would be enough for the courts to overturn his death sentence and grant him a new trial. But we're coming to the end, and more and more now, the courts are turning him down, especially the Fifth Circuit Court of Appeals, arguably the harshest appeals court in the country, which upholds almost every death sentence presented to it.

In our meeting, Stuart is visibly upset over Dobie's imminent execution, and he starts in right away about what he learned from the bloodstain evidence, laying out photographs of the bathroom scene on the table and pointing out the blood on the wall under the window. He tells us that the blood clearly is impact spatter, not wiped blood (as the prosecution's expert contended), and he points out the copious amount, which would suggest the attacker would have some of Mrs. Knippers's blood on him, especially on his hands, from wielding a knife in eight different thrusts. Yet we know no blood whatsoever was found on Dobie's clothes, nor is there a palm print or fingerprint on the windowsill as he, supposedly, lifted himself out of the window. Nor is there any kind of alteration of bloodstains under the windowsill where his feet and legs would have rubbed as he hoisted himself through. He'd have to be some kind of trained gymnast to spring from a standing position through such a small window without leaving even a fingerprint. But even supposing such a gymnast scenario, there are no footprints in the bathroom or outside the window, either.

All of this leads Stuart to conclude that the killer did not exit through the bathroom window and must have gone out through the bathroom door.

Paula picks up on the absence of footprints at the scene. She wonders why the prosecution would propose the absurd scenario that Dobie had exited through the window. To do that, she reasons, he would have had to stand on the toilet on which his victim was still seated, because they found no prints of any kind on the toilet seat. And the idea that Dobie could have sprung from the floor out of that incredibly small window in so short a time was even more absurd. . . . "That's the craziest thing I ever heard," she says.

Stuart also notices in the crime scene photographs that the small articles on the back of the toilet appear undisturbed. That's odd, he says, since the murder happened while the victim was seated on the toilet. Stuart tells us that there had to be a vigorous struggle from such a violent attack, and add to that that the assailant exited through the bathroom while Mrs. Knippers sat on the toilet—well, how can you have all that physical activity without turning over even one little knickknack on the back of the toilet?

Paula interjects to say that Mr. Knippers seemed to indicate all the physical activity going on when at the trial he talked about all the "knocking, bumping, screaming, and hollering" going on.

"No way are you going to have that kind of activity and all the knickknacks in place," Stuart says. "It's very strange."

And the blood on the curtain identified as Dobie's blood?

Stuart explains that when he examined the spot of blood said to be Dobie's, he noticed that it saturated the curtain. He points out that such a saturated stain would have to come from a wound on Dobie's body that was actively bleeding, and which wound was that? Certainly not the superficial wound in the web of his left hand. Stuart goes on to say that it was never really explained at trial exactly how this so-called puncture wound in Dobie's hand was received, only some casual assumption that he *must* have inflicted it on himself when he was stabbing his victim. Betty Williams later told me that Dobie cut his hand when he mowed her lawn, her father's lawn, and her brother's lawn, all on the day of the murder. Betty said her dad and sister were there and remembered Dobie asking for some alcohol to clean the wound.

But even if there wasn't another explanation for the cut, it penetrated only the outer skin and fat in the web of the hand. Stuart says that when he magnified the photo of the hand wound, he saw how superficial it was, more like a shaving nick than a puncture wound, so he feels certain that the drop of blood that saturated a spot on the curtain couldn't have come from the wound in Dobie's hand. He also wonders how a wound capable of saturating the curtain left no bloodstains on Dobie's clothing, especially inside or near the pockets, which is where, he says, you frequently find it. Assuming that he puts his clothing on again after he leaves the bathroom, Stuart says, wouldn't you expect that his hands touching his pants or his shirt would get some of that blood on his clothes somewhere?

Stuart also questions whether such a clear-cut drop of blood could have saturated the curtain by Dobie scraping against it in an effort to squeeze through the tiny window opening. He'd be brushing against the curtain, which would leave a bloodstain other than the kind that's here, more of a brushed-against stain than such a well-defined droplet, he explains. Plus, he's bothered by how the five blood samples were selected from only a particular section of the sheer set of bathroom curtains, located on the inside, even though crime scene photographs indicate blood on the outer curtains. Usually, random samples are taken from various sections of fabrics, not all from one concentrated area, Stuart explains. He also asks why only the sheer curtains were collected as evidence, not the other curtains as well, since both contained bloodstains. According to the crime laboratory report, blood in an area designated T-2, on the left edge of the sheer curtain, was the same type as Dobie's. Four blood samples from areas designated as T-1, T-3, T-4, and T-5 matched Mrs. Knippers's blood type.

As Stuart talks about the blood samples, I remember Betty Williams's question about one bloodstain that laboratory analysis showed did not match Dobie's or Mrs. Knippers's blood. "How come they didn't do anything with that drop of blood and who it might lead to? They just pushed it aside because they knew it didn't fit in with the case they were conspiring against Dobie."

And the scrapes on Dobie's legs? Could they possibly explain Dobie's blood on the curtain? I ask Stuart James.

"Two problems," he says.

The first problem is that according to trial testimony, Dobie supposedly scraped his shins on the bricks of the window ledge on his way *out* of the window—an exit, the prosecution contended, that was *headfirst*. So how did he get blood on the curtains, which were *inside* the window, from legs that hadn't yet been scraped on the window ledge outside?

The second problem, Stuart says, is that the kind of saturated bloodstain that is so clearly delineated couldn't have been obtained from the scratches on Dobie's leg brushing against cloth. There are bloodstains on the inside of Dobie's blue jeans from some cuts, Stuart says, but he couldn't tell from the photos whether or not the abrasions were fresh, which the prosecution had claimed. A lot of things are missing, Stuart says, such as the videotape that supposedly would have shown fresh abrasions.

(That makes three tapes not available for viewing: the one of Dobie's alleged confession, one of Officer Ted Delacerda's headlong high jump out of that window, and now this.)

Dobie said that when he got to his grandfather's house that night, he took a bath. Sometimes bathing can remove scabs, which might account for the bleeding inside the jeans. It may have been seepage, a type of bleeding that comes from wounds that are not fresh, but without a closer examination Stuart couldn't really tell. Regardless, he says, even fresh scrapes on Dobie's legs wouldn't explain the droplet saturating the curtain. Again, he says, as with Dobie's hand, this would be a brushed-against kind of stain.

He concludes his report by making several recommendations for further testing, which he said could still be done. One recommendation was for further forensic examination of the photographs to determine the freshness of the scratches on Dobie's legs. Another was DNA testing of the other bloodstains on the curtain. If the small bloodstain selected for testing had come from a bleeding wound, then in all likelihood such a wound would have bled not onto only one spot on the curtain, but on other parts as well. So why not collect other samples for DNA testing, which was far more accurate and required only a microscopic amount of evidence, no matter how old? This DNA testing is possible even fourteen years later, in 1998, Stuart says, especially since the defense conducted no independent forensic testing at the time of the trial.

Paula insists that the further testing should be done by the defense as well as the prosecution, so Dobie's interests would be protected.

Stuart says he's deeply disturbed by the case because so much of the interpretation of the forensic evidence that the prosecution presented to the jury was erroneous or contrived. It raises serious questions about Dobie Williams's conviction for murder.

And the dark-pigmented skin the prosecution said they found on the window ledge?

"I never saw it," Stuart says. It disappeared from the plastic tube in the crime laboratory where it was brought for testing. Nor was it ever confirmed as human skin when the lab tested it.

Paula brings up another "curious thing" about the bloodstains. Some of Mrs. Knippers's blood made its way outside the bathroom and was found on one of the plastic milk crates on the ground under the bathroom window. She wonders how it got there. The curtain covered the window, she says, so it's very improbable that blood could have spattered through the curtain and onto the crate. "And as for Dobie's hands putting the blood there, I mean, how could he have blood on his hands to get on the milk crate if he didn't have blood on his hands to get it onto his own clothes?"

Stuart, getting back to the skin and hair evidence, which was supposedly in a tube from the crime lab, says that only a piece of hair remains, but hair comparisons, he says, are not enough to positively identify someone.

"When you attack the scientific evidence that the prosecution presented piece by piece," Stuart says, "the case against Dobie comes down like a flimsy pyramid." As he's talking, he gets drawn into another crime scene detail that puzzled him. The curtains are delicate fabric, hanging on a lightweight rod, like the kind you get at Wal-Mart, he says. There's a photograph from the crime scene showing those curtains hanging there as if no activity ever took place. But how could such curtains withstand Mrs. Knippers standing up and grabbing them, which the bloodstains suggest she did? How could the murderer struggle in and out of that very small window, close enough to the curtains to leave some of his blood on them, and yet not disturb them? "That's as strange as the undisturbed knickknacks on the back of the toilet," Stuart says.

Paula says she thinks it's just as bizarre that one of the state's experts proposed that overnight dew could have washed the knife, supposedly the murder weapon, clean of blood. "It should never have been presented to the jury as evidence. There was absolutely no physical evidence to link that knife to the crime," she says, "not even a molecule of blood underneath the wooden handle of the knife when they took the knife apart in the lab. No animal blood, either, if it was supposed to be the knife Mr. Knippers used to cut up chicken for gumbo."

But what about the glove? Could its use during the crime account for the lack of blood on the knife? Stuart says that no blood was found on either the outside or the inside of the glove. "It, too, was irrelevant," Paula says.

What about overnight dew washing all the blood off the knife? Stuart says that in his twenty-plus years of forensic work, he's never heard of such a thing. "Dew *settles* on things, it doesn't *wash* things, especially under the wooden handle where blood would tend to collect during a stabbing of this kind," he says. He calls such far-fetched interpretations of evidence "forensic cartoons."

Although I'm no attorney, much less a forensic expert, I have enough common sense to know that emotionally, at least, it's a great deal easier for the prosecution to make its case to the jury when there is a murder weapon to exhibit. I also think that if Dobie had had Paula Montonye as his original defense attorney, he wouldn't be sitting on death row now.

This all leads me to ask about the knife's location when Dobie supposedly picked it up. How could Dobie have picked up the knife in the bathroom when Herbert Knippers clearly said that he left it on the drainboard in the kitchen?

"Innuendo," Paula says. During Mr. Knippers's testimony, at one point he said that "perhaps" he "might" have brought the knife into the bathroom when he went to wash his face while cutting up onions. That sticks in the jury's mind, Paula says. And even though Mr. Knippers changed his mind about that, saying, no, he's sure he must have left it in the kitchen, "knife in the bathroom" has become part of the scenario. Then, when you have Dobie supposedly confessing that he got the knife in the bathroom, it fits the scenario perfectly. For the prosecution's version of the crime to make sense, the knife had to be in the bathroom, because you sure can't have Dobie walking past Mrs. Knippers on the couch to get a knife in the kitchen.

It takes a sharp defense attorney to expose what is fact and what is innuendo, Paula says. Mrs. Knippers's underwear pulled down was another example of the prosecution's use of innuendo. They used it to insinuate attempted rape, though when someone's sitting on a toilet, where else is a person's underwear going to be?

It's devastating to hear what Stuart and Paula are saying.

I think of Dobie going through his trial, forced to listen to the case mounted against him. He must have felt swallowed up, buried. He told me that during the trial he would be so depressed at the end of each day that all he could do was go to his cell and sleep. Dobie says Bonnette kept telling him, "Everything's gonna be all right." I'm angry now at Bonnette. He took that $10,000 from Dobie's family and didn't even hire a forensic expert to examine the evidence. I used to think that courts were the place where everybody could come and all the sides of truth could be sounded out and debated. Now I know better.

There's one more piece to Stuart's findings. He's troubled about what the police did not examine. Like Herb Knippers's clothing. It's important to systematically exclude everyone who had contact with the victim, Stuart says. This is basic investigative procedure. But the husband's clothes seem to just disappear. There is no record that they were ever examined. He was an active part of the scenario, and he had contact with the victim before and after her death. It is a radical departure from procedure to automatically exclude him and not examine any physical evidence connected with him.

The job of any decent criminal investigator is to consider every possible scenario of a crime.

Stuart points out that it's standard criminal procedure to first rule out the husband as a suspect when his spouse has been violently attacked, especially when the violence happens in the couple's own home. Stuart has also been taken aback by what he calls a "huge omission" in the state's investigative procedure—although the living room was an important part of the crime scene, none of the furniture or objects there were retained for examination, not the couch and pillows on which Mrs. Knippers lay or the book that sat open by her body.

Trace evidence, such as blood, hairs, and fibers, could have been transferred from Mrs. Knippers's body and nightgown onto Mr. Knippers's clothes, the couch, and the pillows. They could have held important information to include or exclude suspects.

Stuart's long list of inconsistencies strengthens the claims Betty Williams had been making all along—that the investigation into Mrs.

Knippers's murder was flawed from the start. Betty remembers the morning four police officers knocked on her door, looking for Dobie. It was 2:30 a.m., just a few hours after the murder. Betty sent them to her father's house next door, where they picked up Dobie.

When Dobie didn't come home the next day, Betty called the police. She said they told her Dobie might be a witness to something, maybe a stabbing.

"The officers never did tell me what had happened. They never did tell me that Dobie was being accused of killing Mrs. Knippers," Betty said. "They never counted us."

From that first night, Betty said she witnessed a host of problems with the investigation. The police brought tracking dogs to her father's house shortly after the murder, presumably to sniff out any traces of Mrs. Knippers's blood. "My brother Bobby was watching those dogs. I was looking out of my door at them," Betty told me. "We never did see the dogs move or scent when they took them off of the back of the truck. The dogs just sat there. They never, never, never moved."

And there Betty sat, on her front stoop, in the courthouse, in the death house, watching injustice after injustice inflicted upon her son, with no power to stop it.

"Dobie was convicted the night the officers picked him up. He was proved guilty, and he was never proved innocent. Dobie never had a chance. They never gave him a chance."

It's too late to do anything now, too late to save Dobie's life. Dobie says he was drinking cognac and beer with friends at Fred Harris's store until about 11:30, when he started feeling sick and headed home. What amazes me is that every time he tells the story, I can see how bad he feels that he disobeyed his mama that night. He had promised her he wouldn't drink when he came home, and there he was, disobeying her, knowing that it was "always a bad thing" when he didn't listen to his mama. Whenever he talks of that July night, he says, "Man, I knew I should have listened to Mama." Obedience to her had always given him protection. Once she had even saved him by coming straight into the bedroom, where he was sleeping with a woman, and pulling him right out of bed. "Son, get your pants on. This lady's husband is coming with a shotgun straight over here right this very minute."

He knows, of course, that what is happening to him is entirely disproportionate. He knows that, but what seems to gnaw at him most is knowing that he let his mama down, and now all this trouble is coming down on her and him and his whole family. All because he was so stupid as to go to Fred Harris's store that night to drink beer and sweet cognac that made him sick as a dog. "Man," he says, shaking his head, "man, why did I have to go and do that?" His mama isn't letting him forget it, either. Sometimes during visits the two of them return to the subject of his disobedience, she with fresh wrath, he with fresh remorse. It's something deep between them, and it never entirely goes away.

We're in the death house, and it's close to 3:00 p.m. Three and a half hours before execution. It's almost time for the family to leave. I've joined Dobie and the others around the table. Betty Williams is saying, "The proof is in the blood." Dobie's aunt Royce says that a few days ago she got a "warm feeling" through her body, and Betty says that warm feeling is good news for Dobie and healing for her. She says she, too, felt the Holy Spirit, "first here," and she points to her stomach; "then here," her two sides; and "out here," the top of her head. She explains that the number "three" is always a good sign. "This is Dobie's third date; the last reprieve he got was for fifteen days, that's three sets of five; and the Bible says it takes three witnesses.

"Sister Prejean, what's God telling you about Dobie?"

The question is squarely to me, because Betty's been aware that every time she has talked about Dobie's being spared, I've been silent. She wonders what God is telling me, and I answer her that whatever happens, even if Dobie is killed, I believe God's strength and love will be with him. I say that Jesus, too, agonized and asked to be spared from death before he was executed but had entrusted his life into the hands of his loving Father.

Dobie is looking hard at me as I say this. There had been considerable family discussion about whether he was "saved." When family members talked to him on the phone, especially his uncle Bobby, they kept asking him, "Dobie, are you saved? Have you taken the Lord Jesus Christ as your savior?" Dobie didn't know how to answer. The words confused him. He'd talk to me about it, and I'd tell him what I thought about faith—you so believe in Jesus that you shape your thoughts and actions to his way of seeing and doing things, especially the way he reached out and loved everyone, even outcasts, even his enemies. Hadn't Jesus emphasized that it's not those who make an outward protestation of their faith, saying, "Lord, Lord," who know liberation and redemption, but those who carry out God's will in their lives? I pointed then to ways I saw him living out his Christian faith—the way he was patiently enduring all the years on death row, especially with arthritis; the kindness he showed his fellow prisoners, never trying to con anybody, always ready to share treats and cigarettes when he had a supply and others didn't; the way he practiced integrity and truthfulness, unwaveringly maintaining his innocence even as he protested the injustice done him, yet without bitterness or a spirit of vindictiveness. And I showed him how he was using his imprisonment to deepen his spiritual life— praying, reading his Bible, attending days of spiritual reflection offered at the prison.

Dobie wearied of the endless conversations about whether he was "saved" and finally called it all to a halt, saying, "Am I saved? Yeah, I'm saved. Sister Helen says I'm saved." That made Betty laugh, and she told me that in many ways I was the mother to Dobie that she couldn't be.

"No, Betty, no, no," I'd counter, "I'm his sister. He only has one mother."

Betty Williams had a rough life, first in her own childhood, then with men, all of which drew her children into a whirlpool of violence and chaos. Once, during an altercation with Dobie's father, she seized his gun and aimed it at him. He swept up two-year-old Dobie and held him out as a living shield.

His father soon left, but things didn't get better for Betty and her family. When Dobie was twelve years old, he found himself being put on a train to Kansas City with his brother Zeno. They were going to live with their father for a while because of the escalating violence at home. Dobie was older and stronger then and had begun to take on his mother's current boyfriend. He once told me how he and his brother cried as the train moved them farther and farther away from their mother and home and everybody they knew. "We didn't understand why Mama was sending us away." In Kansas City, Dobie got involved in gangs, did drugs, barely survived in school. After he had a fight with his stepsister, who stabbed him with scissors, Betty sent for the boys. Dobie was struggling with depression. Twice he tried to commit suicide.

"I guess you could say Dobie was an abused child," Betty once told me. Of her seven children, two of the boys are diagnosed schizophrenics, on heavy medication, and in and out of mental institutions and jails. Before Dobie got so close to execution, I think Betty had some comfort that on death row, at least he was safe and cared for. She has said more than once that if Dobie had stayed on the streets, he'd be dead.

She's turned to church life at King's Chapel, a small African Methodist Episcopal community, to hold her own life and her family's life together. Religion—with its regular rhythm of worship, Bible study, and community involvement—helps inspire and strengthen her spirit and gives her family's life purpose and cohesion. When I lived in the St. Thomas Housing Project in New Orleans, I saw the important role that religion could play in the midst of all the chaos and craziness of guns, drugs, poverty, and hopelessness. I also came to appreciate the strictness of a clear moral code: *God says do this; the devil says do that.* Lack of clear boundaries or discipline could mean death, especially for young men. Mothers in St. Thomas knew that a child involved in the church had a better chance of survival.

The clock says 2:50. Around the table with Dobie, we hold hands and Betty leads the prayer. The mood is somber until Dobie's four-year-old nephew, Antonio, asks Betty to sing "Oh Happy Day," which is his favorite, and she launches full throttle into the hymn, confident from singing in many a church gathering. We become the background chorus, echoing, "Oh happy day . . . ," as she makes her way through the verses about Jesus walking this earth, preaching the good news of salvation, and healing the people. The song makes Antonio happy; smiling, he looks up at his grandmother, who knows the whole hymn by heart and can sing it with a strong voice. His little voice pipes in now and then on the chorus, but mostly he just swings his feet in the chair and smiles. Dobie has his head down and is holding tight to Jean's hand. I look past Betty to the white metal door and see that Major Coody has her head down and is praying, too, with Elijah behind her being swept into heaven, the trail of his long white robe curling behind him.

Little Antonio has been in this place twice before, kissed his uncle Dobie good-bye twice before, and he's about to do it again.

Warden Cain comes into the room and asks, "How's everybody doing?" He says he's been driving around the prison, checking on the duck population. Permits are given to go duck hunting and fishing here. "Didn't see many ducks," he says. "Nothing much is happening today. In this place you can have all hell break loose with everything happening or a day like today with nothing happening."

Nothing happening, give or take a man about to be killed.

"We've had a fine visit, Warden," Betty says to him, "and we just want to thank you for the kindness and dignity you've shown us, but I know it here"—and she points to her heart—"Jesus has saved him twice and he's going to do it again." She turns to her son and tries once more to infuse her faith into him. "Believe now, Dobie. Stand on the Lord, who is your rock."

Dobie says, "I believe, Mama." He can barely talk because he knows they're all leaving now, and he clings to Jean's hand.

The warden is talking soft and fast and friendly again. "Now it's about time for y'all to leave. Now be strong. We're all in this and have to do our part. It's best for Dobie if you're strong and not crying and broken up. He's strong. See? God's with him. It's like Shakespeare says, all the world's a stage, and each of us has a role to play, and we're all just playing our appointed roles in the scheme of things, which is in God's hands, and I'm playing my role and you're playing yours." He tells them that some guards are going to take them to Camp C, where they can wait it out, just as they did before. Aunt Royce asks if a TV will be there so they can hear the news, and the warden assures her there will be a TV, even with cable and plenty of food and drinks and everything they need. They know the scene; they've been there twice before.

I'm grateful to the warden for his kindness to Dobie's family. In other prisons, such as San Quentin, the families of the condemned cannot be close like this before an execution. When the warden and I have a chance to talk together, I thank him for the dignity he shows these families. It's one of his good traits. He was the first warden at Angola to allow contact visits for death row inmates, not just immediately before execution, but regularly. In earlier days, I watched Robert Willie's mama and brothers visit him for the last time and not be allowed a good-bye hug. Visions of mamas and sons in this death house are flowing through me now, and I again see Willie Celestine's mama reaching up to give him a quick kiss on the cheek before she hurried, almost ran, out of this building, telling me afterward, "If I had put my arms around my boy, no guard could have pried my arms loose."

Everybody's standing up to leave. There's the sound of people moving and chairs scraping across the floor. Antonio, tired of sitting still so long, takes a run toward the door. "Hug your uncle Dobie," Royce tells him, and he turns back to Dobie for his hug. Warden Cain tells Antonio that he should ask his uncle Dobie for a Snickers bar because his uncle has a "big old supply" and all Antonio has to do is ask him. So the bestowal of a Snickers gets in the mix of the final leaving, and I wonder how much of this Antonio will remember when he's a grown man. Little kids and death houses don't mix. Dobie holds him in his arms for such a long hug that Antonio starts wiggling away, ready to move out of this sad, serious place, ready for Camp C, where there will be a TV and plenty of good food and cold drinks. Dobie hugs each one, especially his mama. He hugs his mama three times. They had a little tiff earlier in the afternoon, when she repeated something about him that other people said and he said, "Mama, you always put me down." He became angry and was still getting over it. When he hugs her, he tells her he's sorry he got mad and that he loves her. She answers, "It's all right, Dobie, it's all right," and shores him up with a scripture passage that she wants him to read after they leave: "Though I walk through the valley of darkness, I fear no evil, for Thou art with me."

Everybody's strong.

Everybody leaves.

Dobie stands by the window and watches his family walk past the guards with the automatic rifles and climb into the white van that will take them to Camp C. I rush to his side along with Carol Kolinchak and Paula Montonye. We put our arms around him, holding him tight around the waist and shoulders, and wave to his family as the van pulls away. I know he is seeing his family for the last time. It's up to us now.

I get very active, talking to him, telling him what a good human being he is and that Jesus is very close to him and will give him all the strength he needs. Paula says what a good family he has and how lucky he is to have them. Carol says she feels honored to be with him now, tells him what a privilege it's been for her to work on his case, and says how much she's come to care for him and respect him as a person. We have all moved into a mode of initiating, comforting, strengthening, not letting his spirit go slack.

A guard approaches Dobie and says he'll have to go to his cell now. Across the foyer and hallway, out of sight of this room, there are four holding cells, and Dobie will be placed in the first. I know the cell very well. In it sat three others I have accompanied to execution: Patrick Sonnier, Robert Willie, and Willie Celestine. Once Dobie's inside the cell, the guard informs us, we'll be able to sit right outside it to visit. For now I let it happen, but as soon as Dobie is settled, I go to the officer in charge and ask him to explain to Warden Cain that it's hard for us to hold Dobie's hands in the cell because of his arthritis, that he can't stretch his arms; it's too painful, so could the warden let him sit outside the cell so he can be near us and we can touch him?

I'm well aware that all these special permissions, a break from the regular protocol, are a pain to the warden. The last time, when Dobie came so close to execution, the warden said that all the special visits, the trouble involved in getting transportation for everyone, was killing him. He said this in front of Dobie and the lawyers and me, and I couldn't let it pass. "Killing you?" I asked, touching him on the shoulder. "Killing you?" So here goes another special permission, but I absolutely know we need to be close to Dobie to touch him in these, his last hours. I think of how Jesus, in the agonizing moments before his death, asked his disciples to watch and pray with him, but they all went to sleep.

A short while later, word comes from the warden that Dobie can visit with us outside the cell. Just until 4:30, then he has to go back in. Sergeant Henry, whom Dobie likes, is the guard chosen to be with him inside the holding cell section. When Paula, Carol, and I go through the metal door and enter the cell area, Sergeant Henry has the TV tuned to *The Jerry Springer Show*. I ask Dobie if he wants the TV on, that it might be a little hard for us to talk. He doesn't care, he says, and it's okay with him if Sergeant Henry wants to watch it. So I help Sergeant Henry move the TV away from the front of the cell, and he lowers the sound, saying, "It helps me keep my mind off things."

Dobie opens a pack of Camel cigarettes. "Hey, a big-time Camel man," I tease. He usually smokes cheaper Bugler cigarettes, rolling his own, as do most indigent prisoners here.

"Might as well," he says. "Trying to use up the money in my account. Can't spend it all.

"Hey, look at this." He sees he's been trying to open the cigarettes from the bottom of the pack. "No wonder it's so hard." His fingers are so crippled, he can't even open a flip-top can. I offer to open the cigarettes, and he hands them to me. I hit the edge of the pack against my hand and a few cigarettes come out, and Paula teases, "Hey, Dobe, this must be a smoking nun. Look how she handles these cigs like a pro, huh?"

"I taught her how to roll one."

"I didn't do too well," I say. "The first was very fat and loose, and the second was very tight and skinny." Dobie smiles.

He has only a couple of hours to live, and we are talking about rolling cigarettes. We're letting the conversation go anywhere it wants. We're talking about everything. What are the best things to talk about before you die? I remember that Patrick Sonnier and I talked about God, death, love, remorse, forgiveness, his daughter Star's karate lessons, and how his mama made venison stew.

Dobie is not in a hospital dying of some disease, with his life energies and faculties fading. He's fully alive, has his full energy and emotions and consciousness. It makes his coming death impossible to comprehend. I know not to think ahead. I know that my strength is tied to his strength. I know that I am hanging by a thread of moral courage. If he comes apart emotionally, so will I. I know not to think of his being killed in just a few hours because I don't have God's grace for what lies ahead. But the grace is here now, and we are all abiding in this grace, which shores us up and links us closely to one another.

Dobie has a sack of mail at his feet. He has been getting letters from all over the world since the BBC aired two documentaries on him. He made some good friends, Liesel Evans and Carmel Lonergan, while doing that documentary. They're two charming British women who came over several times to do the filming. They got to know Dobie and to care about him. Their letters and visits have cheered him immensely. It really helps that they're women. He loves the company of women, is most himself with women, and look, here are three women with him now in his last hours. Liesel says she will try to put a telephone call through to the death house from England if the prison will allow it. During the last close call, they let her talk to Dobie, but this time the phone's been silent. It depends on who's on duty at the switchboard. Some are more flexible than others.

It's 4:30, and we step back as the guards put Dobie in his cell.

I take his hand through the bars. I know the greatest gift I can give him now is to shore up his strength, help him make it through the unfolding last hours and die with dignity in this crazy warp, where time stands still and where it zings forward.

"Dobie, Jesus is close to us here. Jesus is helping you. Every human being is scared at a time like this, Dobie, but look at you, you're handling this. You're doing it, Dobie. You're about to do the bravest thing you've ever done in your life."

I feel like his coach.

He nods. "I'm okay," he says, and he reads a letter from his friend Father Barry Moriarity, who had been his first spiritual adviser but had been moved by his religious order to Chicago. Dobie wrote to me then, asking if I knew of anyone who could visit him. I wasn't acting as an adviser to anyone on death row at the time, so I said, "What about me?" That was eight years ago. Now, here at the last, Father Barry is coming through. He has faithfully written Dobie over the years. He's been a good friend.

Warden Cain comes in. "How y'all doing? Need anything, Dobie? Drink plenty of fluids. It'll help you." I know why he's telling Dobie to drink fluids. A greater volume of fluids keeps the veins from collapsing and will make the insertion of the intravenous lines easier. "How about some ice cream, Dobie? Want some ice cream?"

Dobie says yeah, he'd like a little ice cream.

"What kind?" the warden asks. "Any kind you want—vanilla? chocolate? strawberry?"

Dobie looks at us. Paula says, "Whatever kind you want, Dobie, we're game. We'll all eat whatever you're eating."

"Chocolate," Dobie says.

The warden is enthusiastic. He turns to one of the guards. "Get four pints of Borden's chocolate and four plastic spoons."

In very short order, guards bring in four pints of ice cream. My senses don't work too well at a time like this, and I scarcely know what I'm eating. I remind Dobie of how Jesus ate his last supper with his most treasured friends, and here we are, all eating with him. Dobie eats slowly. "It's creamy, huh?"

A guard comes in to bring him to the phone in the captain's office. Dobie goes with the guard, and when he comes back, he says it was John Koneck, one of the lawyers up in Minnesota who had worked on his defense.[8] "He told me it was a privilege to work on my case." He repeats "privilege," and I can tell it amazes him that his lawyer used that word. Shortly after that call, Nick Trenticosta calls to thank Dobie and to say what a privilege it was for him, too. "He choked up," Dobie says. "He's real mad at what the courts did to me." I'm beginning to know this scene: lawyers calling to say good-bye to their clients about to be killed. They feel the failure of it, the biggest failure of all—they failed to save the life of their client. What do you say to tell your client good-bye?

I remind Dobie that he has a phone available to him if he wants to make any calls, and he says he'd like to call his aunt Ruby and his uncle Bobby. A guard hands him the receiver from a phone right next to his cell, and he tries to get his aunt Ruby first, but she's not home. So he tries his uncle Bobby. I wonder if his uncle is going to ask him one more time if he's saved. I hope they have a good conversation. Dobie thanks him for accepting his collect phone calls and for sending him a little money over his years of imprisonment. He doesn't seem to mind that his uncle never once came to visit him; he doesn't ever seem to expect much from other people, even his relatives. He's just grateful for loving attention when it comes his way, and now in the last hours of his life he mostly wants to thank people. I have noticed this same spirit of gratefulness in every person I have accompanied in this bizarre death process.

With the others, who were truly guilty of terrible crimes, I always experienced a wrenching tension—on the one hand, abhorring their crimes against innocent victims, and on the other, feeling compassion for them in their torturous ordeal. But Dobie? I feel only compassion for him and his family and a roaring anger at the injustice and cruelty done to him this night and over the past fourteen years. I reach through the bars and touch him on the arm. "Dobie, I do not know exactly where you'll be when you die. It's a big, big mystery—death. But I believe that you are going to be welcomed into the arms of God and that somehow you're going to be at the heart of all the loving energy that is at the heart of everything, and I'm going to call on you to help me in the struggle to end the death penalty. Will you help me, Dobie?"

I didn't know all this was going to pour from me. Dobie looks at me. "Yeah, Sister Helen, I'll help you."

Who knows what it means, stretching out like that in belief to a communion with Dobie beyond death? I used to think heaven was a far-off other world for souls that had been separated from bodies. Now I believe that life is a continuum, that dying and living are like knitting and purling, all woven together, that somehow love binds us beyond death, and God is the life force that brings life out of death and loves us through all the dying.

Paula, sorting through the mailbag, hands Dobie letters from three little girls—Rachel, Annie, and Erin—the children of a good friend of mine, Karen Charbonnet. The letters, in children's big-lettered scrawl and brightly decorated with suns and flowers from busy crayons, make Dobie smile. The children pour on him earnest love and prayers. Annie tells him he's lucky because he's going to be with God and she hopes he has a "good time." That's what makes him smile, and he reads it to us. "Listen, she hopes I have a good time." We all laugh, and I can see that he's holding together emotionally, taking his death one step at a time, and the fear that so paralyzed him when he was here in June is at bay. Maybe he's just too tired to be scared anymore. This is the third time he's undergoing this ordeal, and it feels like the other two times, except this time they're really going to kill him. But how do you get your mind around that? He says how tired he is, that he can't go through it again, and there's a part of him, I know, that just wants it to be over. Not just for him, but for his mama and family. "Look what this puts them through," he says. He hasn't been able to sleep well the past few weeks and certainly didn't sleep much last night. Who, unless they were locked into fierce denial, could climb into bed and go to sleep on the night before they are to be killed?

A guard has come to get me to sign the witness agreement. I'll be present at Dobie's execution. I've signed this form three other times, and I'm very clear about what I'm doing. I sign not as an official witness to the state's killing of Dobie, but because only if I sign will I be allowed to be with Dobie at the end. In no way do I give my consent to this killing.

Dobie and I talked about it. I told him that I'll stand where he can see me and to look at my face, to look at me, loving him, upholding his dignity, praying for him. "I'll be as close as they will let me come," I tell him.

The time is precious. I hate to leave him even for a minute. But Carol and Paula are with him. He's not alone. It's a comfort for me, too, to have them. When I return, we'll be in the last steps and things will be moving fast. Will they put a diaper on him? I know the diapering and cutting of the left pants leg were part of the electric chair ritual, but now that Louisiana has lethal injection, I'm not sure. I want to shore up Dobie's dignity all I can. I want to strengthen him against the dark, dehumanizing forces that will strap him onto the gurney and put needles into his arms.

"I'm scared of needles," he once told me. He'll be in there alone with his executioners when they insert not one, but two needles, one into each arm. For most other states that use lethal injection, one intravenous line is enough, but Louisiana has designed a fail-safe protocol so that if one line should happen to clog, there's a backup so the lethal fluids can flow unimpeded and there won't be any awkward, embarrassing hitches. It's all very medicinal, clinical, bloodless. The technicians will even rub alcohol on Dobie's arm before they inject the needle. A germ-free death.

The guard escorts me to the building next door, where I am asked to sign a form agreeing to comply with all prison regulations pertaining to the execution. Witnesses have all gathered in a nearby room. There's a buzz of voices, and I can see tables with refreshments and some people with plates in their hands, eating and drinking. I wonder if Mr. Knippers is in that room. I expect he'll be one of the witnesses, and I wonder if DA Burkett will be there, too. No doubt he'll say something proper and respectful to the press when the deed is done and Dobie has been killed. Something like "This has not been easy for me. Nobody relishes the death of a man, but I've done all I could possibly do to ensure that justice was served. I even intervened and ordered DNA testing to be absolutely sure of Dobie's guilt. It has taken fourteen years, but now at last justice has been done."

I sign the paper as soon as I can and hurry back to Dobie.

I draw on the strength of all the people I know are praying for Dobie now, including the cloistered Trappist monks of Gethsemani Monastery in Kentucky, where I go to make retreat every year. The monks promised to pray, and I know that just about this time they are assembled in their stalls in the cavernous old church, chanting compline. On retreat I join them for prayer, and in my mind now I can hear the drone of male voices rising and falling in the sacred prayers. Because it's Friday, the day of Christ's Crucifixion, the words that they are praying from Psalm 22 coincide with Dobie's agony: *They have pierced my hands and feet. They have numbered all my bones.*

Whenever I go for retreat, the abbot invites me to talk to the monks about my ministry to death row inmates and victims' families, and some of the monks write to death row inmates. They all know about Dobie and have sent comforting notes, assuring me that they will be praying for him and for his family, especially at the time of his execution.

Others are praying, too—the Community of Sant'Egidio in Rome, the sisters in my religious community and other religious communities across the United States, and many people in the United Kingdom who saw the BBC documentaries about Dobie. Thousands of people are caring about Dobie and praying for him this night. It is like an underground stream, unseen but real, and I feel the strength of the communion.

Things are busy when I reenter the death house. There's a swarm of people coming in and out of the door—associate wardens, staff, the Tac team that will surround Dobie and walk with him to the execution chamber. Inside the holding cell section, Sergeant Henry has turned off the TV and is standing at silent attention. Paula and Carol are as close to the bars of Dobie's cell as they can get, reaching through, holding his hand. I join them there and reach to touch Dobie for the last time. I know every word counts now, that these are my last words, and they come in a torrent, words that thank him for the gift of knowing him, that tell him he is one of the bravest people I ever met in my life, that say God is with him now and he will have all the strength he needs. "Look, Dobie, you're doing it. Look how strong you are. You have a dignity no one can take from you. Your death is so wrong, so unjust, and just know, Dobie, that I will tell your story, and the whole world will know the truth about what happened to you. I will be your voice, and I'll tell the truth, Dobie, I'll tell the truth."

He's ready, I can tell.

Carol, as his attorney, is also allowed to be present at his execution. Dobie, ever polite and anxious not to offend his women friends, had Carol and Paula work out between them which one would witness.

It's time.

Warden Cain comes in to tell us that we will have to leave the holding cell area now, and we all reach to Dobie for the last time. Carol will go in with the witnesses. Paula will be allowed to remain in the visiting room. I notice she is holding a rosary. I will walk just behind Dobie as he walks to the chamber. *Oh, God, they're doing it again, they're killing Dobie.*

Which scripture passage to read for Dobie? For Pat and Robert and Willie, I had selected a passage beforehand, but now I'm unprepared. Guards show me where I can stand and wait, just inside the door of the visiting room. I go there and open my Bible, and it falls to Jesus's farewell discourse to his disciples in the Gospel of John. What attracts me to the passage is the part where Jesus talks about surrendering his life to God and says the rulers of the world have no power over him. I'm thinking of the DA and the courts and the police investigators and the all-white jury—all the powers of the criminal justice system and the media arrayed against Dobie, bringing about his death tonight. At least this essential spiritual freedom is his, to walk to his death with dignity and to protest his innocence to the end. Then I realize that they will ask him if he has any last words. I know how, under pressure, it is difficult for him to express what he wants to say, and I panic because I didn't think to help him get his words. But it is all too late, because he's coming now, here he comes, walking ever so slowly, surrounded by all the guards, a mountain of blue around this slight black man with rheumatoid arthritis, chains on his ankles and wrists strapped to a belt around his waist, coming now through the doorway. I say, "Dobie," and look full into his face. He is just trying to make it, his face has no expression, he is putting one foot in front of the other, dragging the chain across the floor, and I walk behind the guards, too far to touch him. Only my words can touch him now, the words from Jesus about a peace he gives that the world cannot give and about the rulers of this world having no power over him.

We're there.

There's the chamber, the gurney waiting, the bright fluorescent lights making its black cushion gleam, the steps beside it, the large clock on the wall giving the time of 6:30, Warden Cain waiting near a podium and microphone where they are leading Dobie now.

"Any last words, Dobie?"

I'm seated with the witnesses now, and I freeze. *God, please help him. Help him get his words.*

Dobie nods, looks down to his left, concentrating. "I just want to say I got no hard feelings for anybody. God bless everybody, God bless," and as he's saying "God bless," he is already beginning to turn toward the cruciform-shaped gurney.

He forgave them. He forgave his persecutors. He forgave them all.

Guards have to assist him onto the gurney, where they stretch out his arms and buckle six or seven straps quickly. You can hear the *click, click, click* as the buckles snap across his chest, legs, arms, and trunk. Under his feet is a small cushion about two inches high, which elevates his feet somewhat so he can't dig in with his heels if he tries to resist. He looks over toward me. I'm standing so he can see me, but then they draw the curtains so we can't see anything while they insert the intravenous lines into his arms. Until recently, witnesses were kept in another building while the intravenous lines were inserted and brought in only when the last step remained. But lawyers for the condemned objected to being so removed from their clients. The insertion of needles into human veins is not always an easy and painless process, and lawyers wanted to be nearby.

As do I for Dobie.

The curtains are drawn, and it's silent on the other side except now and then for the drone of a voice. Silence. Waiting. Five minutes. Seven minutes. I have my head down, my soul force gathered around Dobie. *Oh, Jesus God, be with him now. He's scared of needles and in there strapped down and helpless and being killed. Oh God, be with him, be with him now, be with his mother.* Carol and I are sitting next to each other. We are holding hands tightly, and she is praying, too. Ten minutes. *It's taking too long. They can't find a vein. Oh no, poor little Dobie.* I look around. There, in the front row, is Herb Knippers. I can see the side of his face. He is looking at the curtain. His face is blank. He is here, husband of the victim, front row seat, privileged witness. Will Dobie's death be healing for him?

Over in Camp C, another family waits. Betty Williams, Jean,

Royce, and little Antonio. All they know is that the execution was to proceed at 6:30, but no one is informing them, step by step, of what is happening now. All they can do is imagine and pray. When I think of victims' families, I always think of two families—the family of the murdered one and the family of the executed one. I pray for Betty Williams and Dobie's brothers and sisters at home.

The curtain is being pulled back. Almost fifteen minutes. Later, outside the gates of the prison, a journalist will inform me that they had to insert one of the needles into Dobie's neck, but that was on his left side, which I couldn't see. When they open the curtain, I see only the intravenous line in his right arm. From the gurney he turns and lifts his head to look for me. I am on my feet, reaching my hand to him, holding the cross around my neck toward him for him to see. Warden Cain is holding his hand, talking to him. Later I find out that the warden asked him if there was anything he was sorry for.

Deathbed confession? Now's the time.

"Yeah," Dobie said, the trouble he put everybody through, his mama and his family. And there it was again at the very end—the remorse over his disobedience to his mama, drinking that night at Fred Harris's store when he had promised his mama that he wouldn't.

Warden Cain looks up to the executioner, behind the one-way glass, and nods his head, and I know that the killing process is beginning. Immediately Dobie's eyelids start closing, and now I just want it to be over for him. I entrust him into God's merciful arms, one more black man executed by the state of Louisiana for a crime against a white victim.

Dobie is dying.

His head lifts involuntarily from the gurney, and Warden Cain puts his hand on his forehead and pushes his head back down. It must be the potassium chloride causing his heart to go into cardiac arrest.

Dobie is being killed in front of my eyes.

I know he's not suffering anymore now. He handled his fear. He walked to his death maintaining his integrity. *Into your hands, O God, I commend Dobie Gillis Williams.*

All the witnesses file out silently into the visiting room to sign the witness form. I walk into the arms of Paula Montonye, tears running down her face. I tell her, "Paula, he died very bravely." I look past her to Elijah being swept up in a fiery chariot.

We sit in silence around a long table, about twelve of us, and sign four copies of the witness form. All you can hear is the sound of papers rustling and pens scratching. Herbert Knippers and his son are sitting on the opposite end of the table from me.

Carol, Paula, and I walk past the armed guards out into the mild January night. It is January 8, 1999, a date sealed forever now in my mind. We get into Carol's car and follow a prison vehicle that escorts us out of the prison. We drive past Camp C, where Betty and the family have been waiting. They must know now. When we are standing outside the prison gates, Betty tells me that a guard came in to tell them of Dobie's execution and she said, "Well, okay, then." Impossibly mild words to mark that she now knew God's will for Dobie, that God "called him home and ended all his suffering." Several sisters from my community are waiting for me outside the gates. They have been praying for Dobie and for his family and for me and for the Knippers family—they pray for everybody. Now, seeing me, they move in and hug me warmly, each one. This is the way it always is. Every time I come out of these gates after an execution, my sisters are waiting for me. Thank God for the sisterhood.

Later, Paula would tell me that when she got home, she received a call from Stuart James, the methodical man of science—not the type you would expect to be emotional. But he was devastated. After what he had discovered, he couldn't believe they went ahead with the execution.

Five days after Dobie is killed, Sister Margaret Maggio and I drive to Many for Dobie's wake. We walk inside Jenkins Funeral Home, in the black section of town, where Betty and all the family and friends have gathered, and I see Dobie for the first time in a suit.

"Look at the peace on his face," Betty says. "God called him home and, see, he's glowing, and look how handsome he is and how good he looks in that white suit. He's the most handsome of my boys, and look at how that gold shirt sets him off. I had wanted a white shirt, but the funeral home people knew that the gold would set him off."

Oh, Dobie, they killed you.

I try to take it in that he's dead, but I can't. The eight years of visits, of talking, of fighting for him to get the medication he needed for his arthritis, of all the suffering he endured, of the way other guys on the Row would tease him and call him "stiff," of how the women

DOBIE GILLIS WILLIAMS · 53

in his life were his biggest comfort and how glad I was that Paula and Carol and I could be with him at the end, the way that even in the last hour of his life he could taste the ice cream and say it was creamy, of the brave way he walked to his death and forgave those who wronged him and apologized for the trouble he caused his family— all of it is flooding through me now, and I'm grieving. Yes, I'm going to miss him, yes. But mostly what I feel is the outrageous wrong of his death. I'm a witness to it, and my mission is to keep getting on planes and crisscrossing this country to talk in cities and towns to awaken people's souls about the need to abolish the death penalty. Seeing Dobie dead here fires this resolve in me, and I know I will do this work until every gurney and electric chair and gas chamber sits behind velvet ropes in museums the way auction blocks and bills of sale and bullwhips and other memorabilia of slavery are on display in museums today.

Dobie's wake consists of prayers, hymns, and testimonies, and I'm asked to give a testimony. I follow Nick Trenticosta, Dobie's lead attorney in his postconviction appeal, who worked so hard to keep Dobie from execution over fourteen years. Many of the eleven stays of execution granted Dobie were due in no small part to Nick's good work.

When I get up to speak—Sister Margaret, the lawyers, and I are the only white people at the wake—I talk about Dobie's dignity, how bravely he died, how he loved his family, how wrong his killing by the state was, and how we all have to struggle for justice, that it's never just handed to us, as Frederick Douglass and Martin Luther King used to say. I say what a privilege it has been to know Dobie and to be his friend. I shore up his family, so dehumanized and voiceless with all the worldly powers arrayed against them, and I tell them that it is an honor for me to know them and to be welcomed into their family.

Afterward we go to the trailer where the family lives, stand in the kitchen, eat ham and potato salad, and talk about Dobie. I repeat to Betty the promise I made to Dobie that I would write his story, and that comforts her. "Nobody ever heard his voice," she says. "He never got to speak." And then my mission to write his story is sealed. The image flashes in my mind of Dobie's head rising from the gurney when they were killing him, of the warden putting his hand on Dobie's forehead and pushing his head back down again.

TWO · JOSEPH O'DELL

I

What I remember most in her voice is the urgency. *Please,* can you come to Richmond for a press conference. Maybe your being there, you know, with the notoriety of *Dead Man Walking* and Susan Sarandon portraying you, maybe your presence will help draw the press; *please,* because Virginia is hell-bent on executing Joseph O'Dell—but he's innocent—I know a lot of inmates claim that—but he's *really* innocent, he did not kill Helen Schartner. He's not an angel, he spent most of his life in prison since he was fifteen, but he didn't kill Helen Schartner, and it was all circumstantial evidence they put up against him and junk science, insinuating that the blood on Joe's clothes was the murder victim's blood.

I tried to stop her or at least to slow her down, but she went on. What really clinched it for Joe was the testimony of a jailhouse snitch, Steve Watson, who lied that Joe had confessed to him about murdering Helen Schartner. He lied, and everybody and their cat—

even law enforcement people—knows Steve Watson makes deals with prosecutors and judges—she continued without a pause—but we've been investigating and finding all kinds of facts that point to Joe's innocence, but the Virginia courts won't hear Joe's new evidence because Virginia has this unbelievable twenty-one-day rule, which means that any evidence of innocence has to be presented just twenty-one days after your trial—can you believe that?—just twenty-one days—and Joe has been on death row protesting his innocence for ten years, but they're closing in on him now, and if we could just have this press conference to present all these questions about Joe's innocence to the public, then what could happen—what we hope for—there needs to be a public outcry to the governor's office, asking him to use the power of his office to grant a new DNA test, which Joe is trying to get and which would definitively prove that Joe O'Dell did not rape and kill Helen Schartner. So, *please, please, please* will you come to Richmond?

A press conference to put pressure on the governor to get a new DNA test for a man on death row when every court he has appealed to has upheld his guilt and refuses to allow the test? How desperate can you be?

I know how desperate.

In 1984, three days before Louisiana executed a young man named Patrick Sonnier, whom I had visited in prison, I was making phone calls like this, waking up lawyers at 4:00 a.m. "What can we do? What are we going to do? Can we have a press conference and just tell the truth about this case?"

"I'll see if I can come," I say to the woman, who has identified herself as Lori Urs. She tells me how in September 1993, Joseph O'Dell came into her life. Her mother had died a few years before, and she had separated from her husband, who was kind and sweet to her and their little girl and had built her a million-dollar home, but it wasn't enough and she was tired of her social life and always having to dress in a coordinated outfit with matching shoes and getting her nails manicured. One day she was sitting in a café reading the *Princeton Packet* and saw an article about Centurion Ministries,[1] which works to free innocent persons from prison. She decided to volunteer. She asked herself, *What could be worse than being in prison for something you didn't do?* She began to spend her days in the middle of a room alongside other volunteers at a big square table, sifting through mountains of letters. One day she pulled out of the heap Joseph O'Dell's plea for help. She wrote to him very carefully, very cautiously, because he was a convict; maybe he happened to be innocent of this crime, but she knew from his record that he had spent most of his life in prison for other crimes. So she waded through the thirty-one volumes of trial transcript and couldn't believe what she read there. For two years she wrote him letters, at first formal, businesslike letters and then more personal, and she pored over the verbatim transcripts of his six-week trial and even took them with her to Cape Cod on vacation, and she scribbled notes, made lists and lists of questions, read and read and sensed that *something was outrageously wrong here,* and she was changed forever from a garden club socialite into a passionate activist. She set out with an investigator to get affidavits from witnesses, scrutinize autopsy and police reports, comb through investigators' notes, and she wondered "how on God's green earth, with all the evidence pointing to O'Dell's innocence, could any jury find him guilty?" She was amazed that such a huge amount of exculpatory evidence could be kept from a jury that was deciding life or death. "Imagine! In a country like the United States!"

I sense the innocence in her shock that such things could happen. I sense it because I was once that innocent myself and believed that a wrongful conviction could be only a rare fluke in the system, one that would immediately be set straight as soon as a higher court reviewed the case. Our innocence has been betrayed.

Lori Urs sounds young.

She hasn't even been to law school.

I know she's working against great odds in Virginia, which is right behind Texas in the number of people it has killed[2] and which even beats Texas in the speed at which it kills them. Its supreme court has reversed fewer death sentences than any other state supreme court in the country, and its Fourth Circuit Court of Appeals has turned down almost every death penalty petition presented to it since 1977. The harsh Fourth Circuit is especially bad news for death row petitioners like Joseph O'Dell. Second only to the U.S. Supreme Court, it is O'Dell's final arbiter of justice in the federal courts, and chances are that if O'Dell's going to get a fair review of his grievances, it's going to happen in federal court, not a state court. That's usually the way it runs in the pro–death penalty South, which carries out 80 percent of executions in this country and where the state court system is filled with indigent defendants, vulnerable to local prejudices and "good ol' boy" politics.

I feel torn about responding to Lori Urs's plea to go to Richmond because my dearest friend, Ann Barker, is undergoing chemotherapy and radiation for breast cancer and I am spending every minute I can with her. Already she's had both breasts removed, and the pathology report of the biopsy of her lymph nodes is very bad. Nothing seems to stop the malignancy. After each round of chemotherapy and fierce doses of radiation, which burn her terribly, the defiant tumors keep growing—in her back, in the fluid seeping into her lungs, even in the long scars across her chest where her breasts had been. It's a vicious cancer, and she knows it. She's a physician and she's scared, and I'm scared, and I can't believe she might die, and I want to be with her and can't bear to leave her side. She's my best friend in the world, my friend of over thirty years.

I tell Lori about my sick friend but promise to try to squeeze in some time for the press conference. "Maybe if I can fly in and out of Richmond the same day."

Which is what I do.

On July 24, 1996, on the plane to Richmond I read reams of letters, newspaper articles, and Lori's notes on her own investigation. For the first time, I start to look closely at the facts of the crime and what happened at O'Dell's trial.

Joseph Roger O'Dell III, a Caucasian male, was arrested for the murder, rape, and sodomy of Helen Schartner, a forty-four-year-old secretary, also Caucasian, who was bludgeoned and strangled to death after she left a nightclub in Virginia Beach on the night of February 5, 1985. Her bloodied body was found in a muddy field across the highway from the County Line Lounge, where she was last seen alive. Joseph O'Dell had also visited the County Line Lounge on the night of February 5.

On the day after the murder, O'Dell's clothes, with bloodstains on them, came to the attention of the police when O'Dell's landlord and girlfriend, Connie Craig, called them. She told them she had read about Helen Schartner's murder in the newspaper and an "intuition" had told her to look in the garage, where she had found the bloody clothes in a bag. The police responded to Craig's call, took the bloody clothes to the crime lab for ABO typing,[3] found a blood type similar to the victim's, and arrested O'Dell.

At trial, which lasted six weeks, commonwealth assistant district attorneys Stephen G. Test and Albert Alberi succeeded in persuading the twelve-person jury that O'Dell was guilty. In their version of the crime, they said that O'Dell had abducted Helen Schartner from the parking lot of the County Line Lounge and forced her into his car and there began raping and beating her with some sort of blunt object, then dragged her from his car into an empty field nearby, where he continued to beat her, holding her head between his knees, and then strangled her. They estimated that the crime happened sometime between midnight and 1:00 a.m.

O'Dell adamantly resisted the attorney appointed to defend him by the court and insisted on providing his own defense at trial, and I make a mental note to find out why. With his life at stake and with no training in the law, he took on prosecutors Alberi and Test and the Commonwealth of Virginia, and I'm amazed as I read this. However strenuous his objections were to the defense appointed to him, surely any legal counsel at trial would be better than none at all. During trial, O'Dell wouldn't know how to raise a formal objection or cross-examine a witness or put forward a properly phrased motion—it would be a kamikaze defense, if you could call it defense. Did O'Dell have a death wish? That was my first surprise, that he chose to defend himself. My second surprise was that the court let him do it, and then that the trial lasted for as long as six weeks. O'Dell had managed to muster pretty stiff resistance, but then I wonder if most of the court time was filled with the state's witnesses and experts. My final surprise, though I would come to this later, would be that every court in the land would fail to render a judgment of ineffectiveness of counsel. Or, to state it positively, that the courts would uphold they were satisfied that O'Dell's constitutional right to defense counsel had been met.

In their case against O'Dell, prosecutors Alberi and Test presented evidence of the bloodstains on his clothes, which their state lab expert had tested and found to be "consistent" with the victim's blood. The state then presented the expert testimony of five forensic scientists, who affirmed the accuracy and reliability of the method of serological testing the state crime lab had used to arrive at its conclusions. The state crime lab expert also testified that the semen, extracted from the victim's rape kit, proved to be "consistent" with O'Dell's semen. The blood evidence combined with the fact that

O'Dell had been present at the County Line where Helen Schartner was last seen alive was the prosecution's main line of evidence against O'Dell. But they also had in their corner a surprise witness, Steven Watson, whom they put on the stand to testify that O'Dell, while in the Virginia Beach County Jail, had confessed to him that he had killed Helen Schartner.

The prosecution introduced a second line of physical evidence against O'Dell: hairs found in O'Dell's car that their lab expert said were "consistent" with the hair of the victim; a cast print of a tire track from the crime scene, which had design elements similar to the treads on O'Dell's car; a Marlboro cigarette butt, found near the body of the victim, which they alleged matched the brand that O'Dell smoked; and the cast of a footprint found near the victim's body, which prosecution witness S. W. Dunn had to admit did not match the cowboy boots O'Dell wore on the night of the crime. They also put a minister on the stand to testify that a gray blue London Fog jacket found among O'Dell's clothes strongly resembled a jacket of his that had been stolen from his car two days before the crime, alleging that O'Dell had stolen the jacket to wear during the murder so that he could disguise his identity.

Prosecutors presented the testimony of coroner Faruk Presswalla, who testified that the autopsy showed the cause of death to be manual strangulation but also that the victim had sustained multiple blows to her head by some sort of blunt instrument, which had caused copious bleeding. The prosecution seemed keen on specifying just what blunt weapon might have been used.

"Such as the barrel of a gun?" prosecution asked.

"Yes, possibly a gun," the coroner said.

Then Connie Craig, O'Dell's fractious girlfriend, testified that O'Dell had owned a Crossman .357 pellet gun, a sample of which she had purchased at the local Kmart and presented in the courtroom. She presented the "sample" gun because the alleged gun used in the crime had not been found.

Prosecution also summoned witnesses to corroborate that O'Dell had been seen at the County Line Lounge on the night of February 5, the night of the murder.

It looked like a pretty tight case.

But it was the jailhouse informer, Steven Watson, who sealed O'Dell's guilty verdict. Since there were no witnesses who could testify that they had seen O'Dell with Helen Schartner, Watson's testimony was crucial for the prosecution's case. Watson testified that O'Dell had confided to him that after Helen Schartner left the County Line Lounge, he had "put his hand around" her throat and "strangled her." Before calling Watson to the stand, prosecutor Test stated unequivocally that no agreement or rewards had been offered in exchange for his testimony,[4] and in his closing statement Test conceded that their physical evidence against O'Dell was a bit tenuous except for the testimony of Steve Watson. He said that the case had "gone beyond circumstantial because Steve Watson has taken it out of the clouds. . . . Steve Watson puts the finger on the man. No doubt about it."

During the sentencing phase of the trial, prosecutor Test cross-examined O'Dell in exacting detail about his previous parole releases from prison and conveyed clearly to the jury that Joe would manage to get out of prison again should he be given any sentence less than death. Stephen Test told the jury: "No sentence ever meted out to this man has stopped him, and nothing ever will except the punishment that I now ask." He was well aware, of course, even as he said these words, that in Virginia the sentence for murder was a true life without parole—that O'Dell would never be free again. He knew it and Judge H. Calvin Spain knew it, and, of course, Joseph O'Dell knew it. Only the jury didn't know it.

Finally, prosecutors Test and Alberi read from the letter[5] of Dr. Stanley J. Kreider, who had conducted a psychiatric evaluation of O'Dell to determine his sanity at the time of the crime and mental competency to stand trial. O'Dell had fiercely resisted the psychiatric evaluation because he feared that Kreider, appointed by the state, would readily diagnose "future dangerousness" in a way that the prosecution desired—which, in fact, Dr. Kreider did, giving as his professional opinion that O'Dell would continue to be extremely dangerous to those around him. Kreider's prognosis satisfied the last statutory requirement for Alberi and Test to demand the death sentence for O'Dell. Only by killing someone so dangerous, Alberi and Test argued, could society's safety be assured.[6]

On September 10, 1986, the jury found O'Dell guilty of murder and on the next day voted unanimously for him to die. On November 13, 1986, Judge Spain formally sentenced him to death.

Joseph O'Dell is older than most prisoners on death row. A

newspaper article says he was forty-three years old at the time of his trial in 1986.[7]

On the way to Richmond, I read O'Dell's monograph, "I Was Wrongly Convicted of Murder," which Lori had published on the Internet to build grassroots support for Joe's case. I can't help but notice how cogently and clearly O'Dell has presented the issues of his case, and it makes me wonder if maybe that's why he attempted a pro se defense. Maybe he thought he didn't need a lawyer to defend him because he could walk into the courtroom and tell his version of events to the jury so compellingly that surely he could convince them he didn't kill Helen Schartner. A friend, Denise (Denny) LeBoeuf, a first-rate criminal defense attorney,[8] tells me that people who are actually innocent often feel that all they have to do is tell their story and the compelling nature of the facts will convince the jury to acquit them. "They seriously underestimate what the prosecution will be doing to block their version from being told," Denny says. "They don't realize that what you present at trial is not just fact after fact, but competing stories, competing versions of what happened, and the prosecution will use its full arsenal of resources to make sure its version prevails."

At the present time in the United States, with over a hundred wrongly convicted death row inmates vindicated in the last thirty years, we're hearing stories of just how many ways prosecutors make sure their "version" prevails—even when the accused is innocent. They are the first to get police reports, interviews with witnesses, crime photos, and forensic evidence, and they work hand in hand with the forensic experts and psychiatrists hired by the state. It is up to them to preserve and maintain the physical evidence, and they also must judge—especially when they are hard-pressed to convict an accused offender—whether or not to entertain the testimony of jail-house informers. When physical evidence is flimsy, it can be tantalizing indeed for a DA to get word from a sheriff's deputy that a certain inmate has heard "something of interest" (confession to a crime) to the prosecution and the inmate would be willing to share this information "in a way that will be mutually beneficial to both parties" (prosecution gets the confession, inmate gets pending charges reduced or suspended). And often the prosecution has ready access to the media to manage the facts of a case that fit their version of the crime.

Joseph O'Dell does not realize what he's up against when he steps into the courtroom to defend himself against this charge of felony murder. O'Dell can't imagine that he would be found guilty, much less sentenced to die.

Michael Graham, who was wrongly convicted of killing an elderly couple and spent thirteen years on Louisiana's death row, testified in 2001 before the Senate Judiciary Committee[9] that he was "stunned" by the jury's guilty verdict and sentence of death, which had been brought about mostly by the prosecution's use of a jailhouse informer, whose nickname, known even to law enforcement officials, was "Lyin' Wayne."[10]

I notice that in his version of events, O'Dell gives many details. My lawyer friends have taught me that one sure clue to truthfulness is that truth tellers give exact details; liars usually speak in generalities.

In his monograph, O'Dell recounts that he had been at the County Line Lounge on the night of February 5 and met two women there, Arlene Van Dyke and Joyce Sawyer.

> We sat at the bar drinking and talking for hours. At about 11:30 Joyce left and at 11:45 Arlene left. I stayed at the bar until midnight, then visited the men's room before I left. In the parking lot a Virginia Beach police car was blocking my car and I asked the officer to move his car so I could leave. I asked what was going on and was told that a Bronco had been robbed. I got in my car and left.

O'Dell says that he did not know Helen Schartner, nor did he ever meet her or talk to her, including on the night of February 5 at the County Line, and he challenged anyone to come forward who could say that he was in Helen Schartner's company that night or ever. He said that he had blood on his clothes because he had been in a fight. After leaving the County Line in Virginia Beach around midnight, he had stopped in a number of places and ended up at the Brass Rail in Ocean View, where he became embroiled in a fight in the parking lot. After leaving the County Line en route to the Brass Rail, he had stopped in Norfolk, about fifteen miles away from Ocean View, to get a hamburger and Coke either at Hardee's or Burger King—he couldn't remember which. Then he went to the pub on Bay Street in Ocean View and had a beer, talking to the bartender, whom he called "Bear." He left there around 1:00 a.m. and went down the street to Rappin' Ralph's, where he talked for a few minutes to Becky Davis, Sue Dye, and Anita Chappell, then went to the Brass Rail for a cup of coffee, arriving there about 1:15 a.m.

> As I entered the parking lot I saw two guys fighting. I told them to knock it off or the police would arrest them. They stopped until I started to walk off, then started again. I tried to break it up by bodily separating them, and one of them slugged me. At that point all three of us were wrestling and punching each other on the ground. I had the first one in a scissor lock with my legs and was punching the second one with my arm around his head. The first one began bleeding from the nose and the second one from a cut to the cheekbone, and I was bleeding, too.

That, he says, is how he got blood on his clothes. He also had sandy soil on his clothes from being on the ground in the parking lot, which he could show by soil analysis to be an entirely different kind of soil from that found in the muddy field where Helen Schartner's body was found.

> Whoever dumped the victim's body in that field would have picked up mud on their shoes and clothing, and assuming the killer had returned to his car after disposing of the body, the same mud would have been found in the car . . . and fuzzy spores from the cat-o-nine-tails growing in that field would have been on the clothing and in the car, just as they were found all over the victim's body and clothing . . . but not one scintilla of this material was ever found in my car or on my clothing.

O'Dell said that when two Norfolk police officers arrived at the Brass Rail to break up the fight, the two men tried to run away, but one of them, John Nutter, who was in the navy, was apprehended and taken away by the shore patrol. O'Dell then walked over to his car and threw in his bloody jacket, which he contended was how the bloodstain came to be on the passenger seat of his car:

> The blood spatter was consistent with the jacket being thrown in the car, but I was unable to get a blood spatter expert to testify in my defense, and the prosecution refused to get one because a blood spatter analysis would have proven to be consistent with my story. No fingerprints of the victim were found anywhere in my car, and one thing is, no rape could have occurred in my car because I had a small Camaro with a stick shift, bucket seats, and the back seat was too small to accommodate sexual intercourse. I am six feet, four inches tall and there is just NO WAY.

In O'Dell's version, after the fight at the Brass Rail, as he was on his way to his car, a police officer named Kangas offered to call the rescue squad, but he had told him, no, he didn't need it. Then he went inside the Brass Rail to clean up, talking to Timothy Bougades, the manager, as he went in. There were no towels or hot water in the men's room, so he left and drove to the 7-Eleven convenience store a block away, where the manager gave him a wet towel to wash his face. If he had just committed murder, he reasoned, and had the blood of his victim all over him, why would he go to a public place like a convenience store with such telltale marks of his crime so visibly on him?

He says he then went to Pete's Place, just down the street from the 7-Eleven, and ordered some coffee; he went to the bathroom and washed up, then chatted with a girl working there as he drank his coffee. She asked him what had happened, and he told her that he had been in a fight.

Then he says he arrived at Connie Craig's house "in the wee hours of Wednesday morning" but said that they had had an argument on the previous Sunday and he could see that she was still angry with him because he saw that his suitcases and belongings had been put on her porch and out in the yard in the rain.

I knocked on the door but she wouldn't answer, and so I changed my clothes in the car, then went to Hardee's for breakfast and cleaned up some more. After breakfast, around 7:00 a.m. I called Connie from a pay phone and we talked over our differences and she told me to come over. I told her I had blood on my clothes and asked her to take it out for me, and when she asked how the blood got there I told her I had vomited from my bleeding ulcer because when she had been mad at me before, she had called my parole officer, who had warned me not to go to Ocean View or he would send me back to prison.

He says that he then went to sleep, and that's when Connie Craig must have called the police, because they came running into the bedroom, guns pointed at him, and told him that he was under arrest for the murder of Helen Schartner. He says he later learned why his girlfriend turned him in: "She was mad at me in the first place because of our argument, and then some of her girlfriends told her that they had seen me at the County Line with two women. When Connie read in the papers on the morning of February 7 that a woman who had been there the same night had been killed, she saw her golden opportunity to get back at me once and for all." (On an earlier occasion when Craig was angry at O'Dell, she called the police to accuse him of killing a fourteen-year-old girl.)

O'Dell explains why he chose to defend himself at trial:

Three months after my arrest I was given a public defender and a preliminary hearing was held and evidence was presented that the blood on my clothes was the same blood type—Type O—as the murder victim's and that I had been in the same nightclub as the victim on the night of her murder. I was assigned William Burnside as a public defender, but he went into private practice. I was then assigned Peter Legler but he withdrew, citing a conflict of interest, because a lawyer in his same office had been assigned to defend David Mark Pruett, a serial killer, who, along

with other confessions, had admitted to killing Helen
Schartner. Then Paul Ray was assigned to me, who
was a military lawyer whose legal experience was
limited to domestic cases. His advice was for me to
plead guilty by reason of temporary insanity. He told
me the blood evidence proved I did it. I insisted the
blood was from the fistfight, but he refused to even
try to find the sailors to confirm my story. I fired Ray
and defended myself. The court appointed Ray to
serve as "standby counsel" . . . but he did nothing to
help.

Sorting through Lori Urs's notes on O'Dell's case, I see why O'Dell
wanted Paul Ray off the case. In one of our phone conversations,
Lori had said, "Paul Ray worked against Joe," and explained that she
had seen the trial notes Ray had written before the trial, which she
believed showed that he held back important exculpatory evidence
from O'Dell. Many of Ray's trial notes were apparently jotted down
straight from the mouth of Tommy Collins, an investigator appointed
to help O'Dell. Collins was interviewing witnesses and checking out
the physical evidence to get ready for trial, and he worked closely
with Ray before O'Dell fired him. Collins had gathered information
soon after the crime, when forensic evidence is fresh and witnesses
"uncoached," a critical time for the defense to uncover any exculpatory evidence that can help their clients.

But from the beginning, O'Dell did not trust Paul Ray. He suspected him of divulging defense strategy to the prosecution, so he set
up a test. He lied to Ray about the store where a pellet gun had been
bought, and "soon afterwards the prosecution checked out the very
store I had told Ray about." It was O'Dell's belief they could have
known about that store only through Ray.

Lori's excerpts from the pretrial hearings show how acrimonious
things were between O'Dell and Ray. Ray told the judge that O'Dell
was "crazy" and "paranoid" and dangerous and had made threats to
kill him. O'Dell accused Ray of betraying him to the prosecution
and fired him several times, only to have the judge reappoint him.
Finally, the judge insisted that O'Dell would have Ray or no defense
collaborator at all, so O'Dell had allowed Ray to assist him with some

of the most formal procedures, such as questioning the state's expert witnesses.

One crucial piece of potentially exculpatory evidence that Ray failed to share with O'Dell was the existence of the black umbrella that Helen Schartner was carrying on the night of her murder. The prosecution claimed that the umbrella was missing, but Collins, Ray's investigator, had photocopied several police photos of the umbrella, which showed that the handle of the umbrella was noticeably bent. Collins had made these copies, which revealed the umbrella's existence, before the trial. Yet during the trial, the prosecution claimed that the umbrella was missing, and on Detective Dunn's affidavit to search O'Dell's belongings was the following statement: "The victim's beige purse, car keys . . . and a black umbrella that the victim was last seen with is still missing." Paul Ray had seen the photos of the umbrella, and in his trial notes he wrote: "umbrella—need it." The fact that the handle of the umbrella was severely bent suggests that it may have been used as a weapon in the assault against the victim and could be tested for fingerprints.

But the prosecution insists that the umbrella is missing, a point that prosecutor Test emphasizes even in his closing argument.

How did the umbrella go missing? And why didn't Paul Ray go all out to find it so that it could be tested for fingerprints and entered into evidence? As O'Dell's attorney, Ray should have been sniffing out every piece of exonerating evidence for his client. Likewise, the duty of the prosecution is to disclose *all* the potentially exculpatory evidence, even if it casts doubt on its version of the crime.

I'm reading all this on the plane on my way to the press conference, and the horror that such crucial evidence did not come to light during Joe O'Dell's trial hits me in the pit of my stomach. But according to Joe and Lori, the umbrella is not the only piece of evidence that Paul Ray knew about before trial and failed to discuss with his client.

Ray also failed to tell O'Dell about the Marlboro cigarette—which he knew was not O'Dell's—found at the crime scene. At trial, the prosecution spent an entire day presenting the testimony of an expert witness from Philip Morris, in an attempt to link O'Dell to the Marlboro that had been found near the victim's body. Paul Ray's trial notes record Collins's interview with Joseph Moore, who discovered Schartner's body in the empty lot. Moore had told Collins that he didn't see a cigarette near the body but that he himself was smoking a Marlboro at the scene, and when the cops had told him to put out his cigarette he had. Paul Ray had written in his trial notes that Collins had said the cigarette was "excellent paper for finger-printing." But the prosecution did not test the cigarette for fingerprints. If they wanted to link O'Dell to the scene of the crime, why not test the cigarette for fingerprints to show that they matched O'Dell's?

Ray's notes also mention a saliva test, but no saliva test was done. Saliva is a body secretion, and O'Dell, like 85 percent of the population, was a "secretor," which means that his blood type could be determined not only from his blood, but also from other body fluids, such as saliva and semen. A saliva test on the cigarette could be a sure way to determine whether or not it was O'Dell's.

But Ray said nothing to O'Dell about the cigarette and failed to get testing done on both fingerprints and saliva, even as the prosecution itself "neglected" to test the cigarette or even to bring to trial Joseph Moore, the man who had discovered the victim's body in the first place. Moore would tell not only about the cigarette, but also about the man he saw hiding in the bushes nearby and that the body had no flies or other insects on it at 3:30 p.m. when he found it, some fourteen hours after it had been dumped there, if you believe the prosecution's timeline. He also could have reported that the body was in a different position when he found it from what the police photos showed. But at O'Dell's trial, Joseph Moore, like the umbrella, will be absent. Instead, a policeman who was called to the crime scene will describe what he saw, suggesting that he had found the body.

Some prosecutors, driven by personal ambition, are determined to win at all costs. Once they announce that they're going for murder one and the death penalty and they have a prime suspect, many of them refuse to backpedal if they run into troubling evidence or witnesses who might raise questions about their version of the crime. Worst of all, they don't want to admit that they have made a serious mistake. With defendants like Joseph O'Dell, prosecutors may sometimes justify their actions by rationalizing: *With his long criminal record, even if he didn't do this crime, he could have done it and probably did a lot of other crimes and never got caught, so we're doing a little catch-up justice; it's our job to protect people from such violent predators.*

Some prosecutors may have their eyes on a judgeship or a seat in the legislature, and it helps if they can cite among their achievements the incarceration of a goodly number of criminals and, for good measure, a death penalty or two. After the O'Dell case, common-wealth assistant district attorney Albert Alberi will go on to become a state judge on the General District Court for Virginia Beach.[11]

So goes the modus operandi of some prosecutors, but Paul Ray is a defense attorney. Isn't he supposed to move heaven and earth to uphold and defend the rights of his client? *Supposed to.*

No wonder O'Dell chose to strategize and conduct his own defense. No wonder he reluctantly allowed Ray's help at trial in such a restricted way.

It gets worse.

Paul Ray's notes from before O'Dell's trial also indicate that he knew from witness interviews that Helen Schartner's motel room at the Executive Inn on the night she was killed was near the County Line Lounge. The victim's name appeared on the registration list, as does the name of her boyfriend, Ike (Floyd Isaac) Wright. The victim had checked into her room on the night she was killed, and her car was found parked on the south side of the Executive Inn, the side on which her room was located. So Helen Schartner could easily have been in her motel room with Ike Wright before and after she was at the County Line Lounge. Though Collins's notes say that in the initial investigation police had checked out the motel room, the room is never mentioned again and is not brought up by the prosecution. At the trial, when O'Dell tried to elicit information about the motel room from a witness, his question was deemed irrelevant and overruled, though other witnesses had testified that Helen Schartner and her boyfriend had argued at the County Line on the night she was murdered. Lori Urs's investigative notes say that investigator Collins knew that the victim had room 203 at the Executive Inn, which meant that Paul Ray must have known it as well. In his interview with Collins, Joseph Moore, who found the victim's body, intimates that he, too, knew the victim had a room at the Executive Inn on the night of the murder. Paul Ray's trial notes show he also knew that a man named Jeff Elliot had walked past the crime scene at 7:30 a.m. and did not see the victim's body. Elliot also pointed out trailers located at the rear of the empty lot, which he said people sometimes used for quick sex or smoking dope.

But Jeff Elliot, like Joseph Moore, the umbrella, and the Marlboro, does not appear in the courtroom. The jury never hears his testimony.

In his trial notes, beside Elliot's observation that he didn't see the victim's body in the field at 7:30 a.m., Paul Ray writes: "controversy as to when body was dumped." Controversy indeed, because in the prosecution's version, O'Dell killed Helen Schartner around 1:00 a.m. in the field, and here is a witness saying he didn't see the victim's body as late as 7:30 that morning. But along with the time of the murder, a question arises about where the murder took place. The prosecution's version of the crime assumes O'Dell began to rape and beat his victim in his car, then brought her to that presumably quiet field, where he could finish killing her and escape undetected.

But as Jeff Elliot tells about the activities in the trailers behind that field and the locals drifting over from the After Midnite bar or maybe even the County Line, which was just across the highway, the field doesn't seem so quiet and secluded anymore.

If Jeff Elliot's description of the trailers is accurate—and police photos of the crime scene clearly showed several trailers there—there was considerable activity in that field that night, which hardly makes it a good place to kill somebody, especially if the victim is struggling. The autopsy report shows that Helen Schartner did struggle. Her hands are bruised, which indicates that she used them to protect herself from the blows of her assailant. And in such extremity, fighting for her life, she was probably not silent, she must have been crying out.

In his monograph, O'Dell writes:

> A vagrant named Joseph Moore found the victim's body when he took a shortcut across the field at 3:30 p.m. on February 6. He told Paul Ray that he saw a man crouching in the weeds and took off to call the police. He testified at the pretrial but could not be found to testify at the trial. Due to my lack of experience representing myself in court [at a pretrial hearing], I didn't know how to phrase the question in the correct way so he could tell about the man he saw hiding in the bushes. When he asked the judge if he could say something, the judge told him he could not. When he left the witness stand, he said to me as

he passed by, "They don't want to know the truth, O'Dell." After my conviction, I heard that Moore had been arrested for public drunkenness and told police how Virginia Beach police had supplied him with whiskey and put him up in a motel, keeping him out of sight until my trial was over. He also boasted that Virginia Beach police would have him released as soon as he was booked.

A man seen crouching in the bushes at 3:30 in the afternoon? Who might that be? What if it was the murderer of Helen Schartner? What if he had just dumped her body there and run into the bushes to hide when Joseph Moore happened to walk into the field? These questions feed an alternative version of the crime and put the time when the victim's body was dumped in the field much later than 1:00 a.m.

O'Dell's monograph states: "An aerial photograph was made which showed tire tracks circling into the field up to the body from a dirt road, but the prosecution tried to suppress it because it did not tie me to the crime."

As it turns out, it wasn't just Jeff Elliot who did not see a body in the field in the morning hours around 7:30. O'Dell writes in his monograph:

> Workers at the Rolling Door Company told investigators that they saw no body in that field when they came to work between 7:00 and 8:30 a.m. that morning, but their names were not taken and they were never called as witnesses. Although it had rained all night until at least 5:45 a.m., the body was absolutely dry when it was found, so it must have been placed there sometime after 5:45 a.m.

And Joseph Moore had said that when he found Helen Schartner's body around 3:30 p.m., he didn't see any flies or bugs or other insects on the body, which would be unusual had the body been there for fourteen hours or so.

So there was, indeed, "controversy about when the body was dumped," which a decent defense attorney would have pursued until the inconsistencies were plumbed and a reasonable explanation found. Nor did Ray call attention to evidence of the "residual meal" found in the victim's stomach. The autopsy report indicated about 100 grams of potato, tomato, and some greens, the residue of a meal that, it seems, the victim had eaten about two hours before she was murdered. I'm no detective, I don't read crime novels, I don't know much about investigating crimes, but this residual meal is like an elephant in the living room, and it seems to contradict the prosecution's version that O'Dell abducted the victim immediately after she left the County Line. The County Line is a bar, not a restaurant. From other witnesses, we know that Tuesday was ladies' night at the County Line, and they said that Helen Schartner had arrived there around 8:30 p.m. and left around 11:30. So how to account for food eaten by the victim two hours or so before she was killed? The County Line did not serve such food, and there is surely no evidence that O'Dell gallantly took the victim out to dinner before he murdered her.

If I'm asking questions as I read Lori Urs's investigative notes, why didn't Paul Ray? Even Dana Wade, the victim's cousin, was so disturbed by the proceedings that she expressed "serious concern" for O'Dell—and that's concern coming from a relative of the *victim*.

O'Dell writes:

> Dana Wade, Helen Schartner's cousin, was with her at the County Line Lounge on the night of the crime, and she told Paul Ray, while he was my lawyer, the following story. At 11:15 p.m. Ike Wright, a prison guard who was dating the victim, entered the County Line . . . and walked over to the table where Helen, Dana, and another woman were sitting. He danced with Helen and then with the other woman. This sparked an argument with Helen, and she got up and walked out. The time of her leaving the club was fixed by this incident at 11:25, give or take a few minutes . . . at least 35 minutes before I did . . . The doorman of the County Lounge, Bruce Cooper, adamantly fixed the time that I left as after midnight because he collected a cover charge up to midnight, and remembered that he was counting

the money when he saw me go into the men's room before leaving the lounge.

The victim's family filed a $6.5 million lawsuit against The Executive Inn for failing to have security in the parking lot to protect Helen Schartner, who was a patron, from abduction. Mr. William Hombarger, the investigator for Travelers Insurance, told me that witnesses at the motel had seen the victim arguing with a man in the parking lot outside the County Line, which was on the property of The Executive Inn. The victim was allegedly heard to say, "I'm not going anywhere with you." When I received the invoices for the guests staying at the motel that night, there were over sixty missing, and the invoice numbers were out of sequence. A settlement of the lawsuit was made and the investigation was stymied.

Why were the records at the County Line hidden so I could not locate the witnesses that witnessed the victim arguing with someone in the parking lot? Somebody there knew something, but have kept their mouths shut. The missing folios and invoices are from midnight on February 5 until 10:00 a.m., February 6, 1985 [the time the victim would have been arguing with someone in the parking lot]. I was provided all the records of all transactions on those dates but the ones I just named.

Lori Urs records in her notes:

Dana Wade, cousin of the victim, states in an interview that "Helen was upset that night about a break up with her boyfriend." Yet at trial she and Ike state he only had a date or two with Helen. This "date" was a 13 hour date to Richmond in HER car, which would account for any fingerprints of his in her car. It is felt [by investigators] that Ike Wright was never fully investigated and should certainly be considered a suspect. This would account for the hidden room that night and also the fact that in Richard Reynas' report[12] he believes that the evidence of food contents still in the victim's stomach shows that she ate within two hours of being killed. He quotes Michael Baden's theory: [given in his testimony at the O. J. Simpson trial] Ike and Helen could have gone for breakfast sometime early in the morning and he could have used his pickup truck, which he owned at the time, to dump her body in the field. This may also account for the disappeared umbrella, which may have had Wright's fingerprints on it [retrieved from the motel room at the Executive Inn?]. Also, the medical examiner, Paul Ferrera, said that the victim's body did not show anal or vaginal tears or rips, which argues for consensual sex, followed by some sort of argument which escalated into murderous violence. Ike Wright's alibi was that he slept at his sister's house. He worked 170 miles away in Powahattan [sic] Correctional Center. He was never interviewed as a possible suspect by police detectives.

Wright worked at the Powhatan Correctional Center and was part of the law enforcement circle. Not only was he not interviewed as a possible suspect, but all the evidence that pointed toward him as a suspect disappeared: evidence that he shared a motel room with Helen Schartner on the night she was murdered; Schartner's umbrella that may have had his fingerprints on it; residual food in the victim's stomach, which indicated that she ate a meal after she left the County Line; witnesses who could give evidence that the victim's body was placed in the field later than 8:30 a.m.; signs from the autopsy that the victim had had consensual sex, which would account for the presence of semen in her body; witnesses who knew Schartner was upset about her breakup with Wright and who witnessed her arguing with him outside the County Line on the night of the murder; a witness who saw someone hiding in the bushes near the victim's body at 3:30 p.m.; an aerial photograph that showed tire tracks circling into the field from a dirt road.

In his monograph, O'Dell tells how the prosecution was so fixed on him as the culprit that they not only glossed over the victim's boyfriend as a possible suspect, but refused to pursue an alternate scenario even when they heard of an outright confession from someone else that he had murdered Helen Schartner.

> When serial killer David Mark Pruett was arrested for a rape/murder on February 14, 1985, a week after Helen Schartner's body had been found, he confessed to killing Helen Schartner. This confession was hushed up, and, although the case did not match his established M.O. [modus operandi] of stabbing his victims, his confession still merits investigation.

O'Dell's experiences remind me of Dobie Williams's: The prosecutors wove a preposterous and convoluted scenario of the crime in which Dobie was the only possible culprit, while the victim's husband, who was alone in the house with his wife when she was murdered, was never investigated as a possible suspect. Moreover, Dobie's alleged confession was attested to by two policemen, who claimed to have "lost" the tape on which Dobie confessed. And both Dobie and Joe had previous records, making it easy to believe that they could have committed the crimes. They were easy targets.

O'Dell writes of his experience with interrogating police officers:

> When police officers William McLaughlin and Steven Dunn interrogated me the night of my arrest, I told them the truth: that the blood on my clothes was from the fistfight and that I left the club a little after midnight. They claimed that I told them the blood was from a bleeding ulcer, and that after I left the County Line I went to the After Midnite club. I admit that I had lied to Connie Craig so she would not call my parole officer about being in Ocean View, but I did not lie to the police. Although all Virginia Beach murder suspect interrogations are routinely videotaped, the tape of my interrogation was never produced at trial, and the police allegations that I lied to them were accepted at face value by the jury.

O'Dell tells of the challenge he faced trying to manage his defense from jail:

> I stayed in the Virginia Beach County Jail without bond for almost two years before my trial. . . . I was hampered in preparing my defense. Legal materials and books, pens, pencils, and paper were confiscated from me and put in the basement of the jail. I was limited to one law book, one pen, and one legal pad at a time. Each time I needed more, my requests to go to the property room took at least a week to be processed. I was only allowed 15 minutes per day to use the phone to call lawyers, investigators, and witnesses. Each time I used the phone, a deputy sheriff was standing right beside me listening so that he could relay the information to the prosecutor. My outgoing and incoming legal mail was stolen. My witnesses were threatened and disappeared. The Virginia Beach officers Kangas and Graham, who were there at the Brass Rail to break up the fistfight I was in, failed to materialize as witnesses for me, which would have helped me immensely since they could have backed up my alibi about how the blood got on my clothes and also the time sequence because it was around 1:15 in the morning when the fight occurred. I was really counting on these witnesses, but Officer Graham could not be located and Officer Kangas evaded questions about the fight and could not produce the report. Tim Bougades, the manager of the Brass Rail, told me he called the police to report the fight, but I was unable to obtain a record of that call. He testified that he saw me in the parking lot of the Brass Rail with a "dark substance" on my shirt (he wouldn't say blood) and that a fight had occurred, but he would not say that he saw me in the fight. A previous incident might explain his reluctance to back me up. In late 1984 he had run over Anita Chappell, who was pregnant with

my child. Both of her legs were broken and she mis-
carried. After Bougades fled the scene, I tracked him
down and had him arrested.

The trial lasted one month (with pretrial, six
weeks), during which I was in court all day every day
up until late at night. I lost over twenty pounds
because of the stress. Each night, I was only given a
bologna sandwich and Kool-Aid after my day in
court was over. Then I was allowed to shower and
shave and was placed in my cell. By this time it
would be nearly midnight, and only then I would be
able to go over my notes, prepare motions for the
next day, and study legal precedents. I was doing the
work of six lawyers by myself, while the prosecution
had two lawyers and a full staff of secretaries and
assistants. It was like the local high school varsity
team going up against the L.A. Rams.

At his trial, O'Dell had protested vigorously when he heard the prosecution announce their surprise witness, Steven Watson, and he had
yelled out in the courtroom, "It's lies, all lies! Lies!" adding that it
was interesting, wasn't it, how so many of prosecutor Stephen Test's
capital cases seemed to involve the use of jailhouse snitches. He
names other Virginia Beach capital murder cases—Whitehurst,
Townes, and Zanetti—in which prosecutors had used the "services"
of jailhouse informers.[13] That's why, O'Dell said, when he was in jail,
he had tried to be put in solitary confinement, just so he could avoid
this kind of situation.[14]

Before calling Watson to the stand, prosecutor Test stated
unequivocally that no agreement or rewards had been offered Watson
in exchange for his testimony, but each time O'Dell had sought to
obtain information about Watson's past criminal record and the current charges he might be facing, the prosecution objected and the
trial judge upheld the objection. The judge had chastised the prosecution when Test announced that he'd be calling Steven Watson to
testify. He called their surprise tactic "trial by ambush," but that was
all. Watson took the stand and gave his devastating testimony against
O'Dell unimpeded.

The prosecutors must have known about the unreliability of jail-house snitch testimony. So why use it? Presumably because they thought the rest of the evidence was weak.

If O'Dell had had a sharp defense attorney like Denny LeBoeuf at his side, the prosecution would never have been able to put Watson on the witness stand. Someone like Denny would know how to stop the proceeding in its tracks until her client could inquire into Watson's character, criminal background, and previous "deals" with prosecutors. She would cite the case precedent of *Giglio v. United States*,[15] which allows a defendant to obtain "impeachment evidence" against someone like Watson, evidence about his character that might give jurors good reasons to impeach or doubt his truthfulness.

It is easier for courts to maintain integrity when a true adversarial system between defense and prosecution is at play. But against a defendant like O'Dell, and a judge all too willing to sustain their objections, prosecutors Test and Alberi were free to play the ultimate game of hardball. O'Dell was right: It was like the L.A. Rams going up against a high school varsity team.

In their analysis of why so many innocent people end up on death row, criminologists, jurists, and attorneys point out that most wrongful convictions in capital trials result from prosecutors who overreach, taking unfair advantage of evidence and witnesses that are in their hands before the defense gets a chance to see them. Without aggressive and skilled defense attorneys to counter them, some prosecutors may abuse their power by "coaching" or intimidating witnesses, causing "unsympathetic" witnesses to disappear, suppressing or destroying evidence, enlisting testimony from "jailhouse snitches," using "junk science," and manipulating information they feed to the media.[16] This, of course, is by no means true of all or even most prosecutors. Most, I believe, act with integrity and fairness. But even a few bad prosecutors are too many, as we are now learning because of DNA testing and the testimonies of so many wrongfully convicted people. The need for strong, skilled defense attorneys at capital trials is self-evident, but here we come to an intractable problem. What state legislature, especially in "death belt" states, is going to allocate sufficient funds to provide capable attorneys for indigent defendants charged with murder? In pro–death penalty states such as Louisiana and Virginia, prosecutors rack up political points for death sentences and have at their disposal double or even triple the financial resources defense lawyers have. In general, the quality of defense for indigent defendants in southern states is miserable, and it's going to take much more than some judicial committee calling for "reforms" and "fairness" to change that in a realistic way. Also, in a political atmosphere that enthusiastically supports death sentences, some pro–death penalty judges are all too happy to appoint inadequate defense attorneys, thus assuring a guilty verdict and a death sentence. In capital cases, such judges may be all too prone to side with the prosecution: supporting their motions, sustaining their objections, and—no small thing in a public forum—addressing them politely and with respect, while belittling and berating the defense. Some defense attorneys have spent nights in jail for "contempt of court" when they stubbornly raised too many objections on behalf of their clients.[17]

O'Dell writes about the testimony of the jailhouse informer who caused him so much harm:

> Steven Watson, a professional jailhouse informant, whom I had never met, testified that I had confessed the crime to him. He was lying to save himself and his wife, who were up for numerous felonies. His testimony didn't even come close to the evidence in the case, but it provided the missing link needed to sustain the conviction. Since he testified against me, he has been arrested many more times, and he is still free. Each time he gets into trouble, I am told that he calls the prosecutors and threatens to expose what they did to me if they don't help him.

At trial, O'Dell was also powerless to stop the testimony of a secondary witness, a minister who took the stand to testify that a coat belonging to O'Dell looked like a coat that had been stolen from him. A good defense attorney would block a witness who could not positively identify an item of clothing as his. In his monograph, O'Dell says:

> The prosecution brought in a preacher whose clothing had been stolen from his car on February 3, 1985. He testified tearfully that the gray/blue London Fog jacket in evidence had been given to

him by his children. The prosecution alleged that I had stolen the jacket two nights before, specifically to wear it while I committed the murder. I showed that the jacket was mine, and its resemblance to the preacher's jacket was inconsequential. The judge stated that if the prosecution failed to connect the preacher's jacket to me, he would declare a mistrial. However, even though no connection was made, he did not declare a mistrial.

I also discover in Lori's documents a description of a prosecutorial stunt that the judge allowed during the trial:

The prosecution dressed two mannequins in the clothing of the victim and Joseph O'Dell. Although highly prejudicial and without probative value, the mannequins remained in front of the jury box for most of the day. Blood was evident on Joe's shirt, pants, and jacket. The victim's clothes were soaked with her own blood. The state's expert testified that all of the blood was the same and "consistent" with the victim's blood. The mannequins were effective in turning the stomachs of the courtroom spectators. No doubt, the prosecution won that round.

The only expert witness who testified on O'Dell's behalf was Dr. Diane Lavett. O'Dell describes what happened to her at the hands of the prosecution:

Dr. Diane Juricek Lavett, a renowned forensic scientist, criticized the lab procedures used by Jacqueline Emrich and stated it appeared I had been framed. Dr. Benjamin W. Grunbaum said the testing violated all scientific methodology and volunteered to work on my case pro bono. The judge would not allow him to do so, nor to testify at my trial, saying that his testimony would be cumulative to that of Dr. Lavett. However, the prosecution was allowed to present five scientists, whose testimony did not address the specific lab procedures used in my case but only the general reliability of electrophoresis in bloodstains. My lone expert witness, Dr. Lavett, was taunted, disrespected, and even threatened to the point of tears by the prosecution.

One of O'Dell's letters to Lori Urs addresses possible motives for the prosecutors' fierceness in pursuing the ultimate penalty in the Schartner case. O'Dell writes:

> My trial was a circus at the least . . . lawyers from all over the city, including District Attorneys, would come to the courtroom to see me in action. These attorneys would chide Test and Alberi, saying, "Yeah, O'Dell greased you today." This would make Test and Alberi mad. They weren't going to let a "jailhouse lawyer" make them look like monkeys. They'd show me! Test and Alberi were obsessed with putting me in the electric chair, and they didn't care about my being innocent. They figured even if I was innocent, that my past record would justify it. The truth of the matter was, I was fighting for my life, and I was no match for two highly experienced lawyers.

The trial transcripts show that the prosecution clearly prevailed on almost every front during the trial; so the days when O'Dell managed to "grease" Alberi and Test must have been few and far between. But if the prosecutors' fellow attorneys were there to witness those rare occasions and teased them about it, maybe that explains the passion that drove Alberi and Test to stop short of nothing less than a sentence of death. It takes passion to fuel the hard work needed to secure a conviction and death sentence. The legitimate and righteous passion that should motivate prosecutors is the passion for justice. But in O'Dell's case, I wonder. It seems hard for some prosecutors to stay pure of heart in pursuing a case to its final outcome. I think of what Dorothy Day, the Catholic advocate for poor people, once said: "We have to build a society in which it is easier for people to be good." If we ever do find a way to "fix" the application of the death penalty to make it fair, helping prosecutors to "be good" and fair-minded servants of justice by being made accountable will need to be a vital part of the "fixing."

In one of his letters to Lori, O'Dell mentioned intimidations and threats against women he was encouraging to speak up for him at his trial: "The prosecution told Paul Ray that any of the girls who testified for me, that he would eat alive on the stand by inferring that they were girls of low moral standards."

In another letter to Lori, O'Dell explained a significant piece of forensic evidence that was *not* tested:

> The forensic scientist found sperm every place but where it should have been, there was no sperm found on the inside of my trousers. (I've never worn underwear and Connie Craig knew it, and you can bet the prosecution knew it.) If I had raped the victim and anally sodomized her, there would have been sperm, vaginal fluid, and anal residue, even a minute trace, on the inside of my trousers. There was NONE!

O'Dell also had noticed from the autopsy photographs something about the victim's neck, which he tells about in his monograph:

> Photographs of the victim's neck showed cuts from long, sharp fingernails, and evidence indicated the strangulation was done by a left-handed person. I am right handed, and I have never had long fingernails. On the contrary, I have always been chided by friends for biting my nails to the quick. My nails were chewed off when the crime occurred and are still being chewed off to this day.

At the end of his monograph, O'Dell summarizes what happened to him:

> I was convicted and sentenced to die on the basis of inferences, innuendoes, theories, and blatant lies. I was defended by incompetent counsel, namely, myself. Judge Calvin Spain didn't like me because I

insisted on defending myself, and the jury was mes-
merized by the confusing technical testimony and
the lying witnesses produced by the prosecution.

On July 24, 1996, I arrive at Richmond International Airport at 9:30
a.m. and take a cab to the hotel where the press conference is being
held. As I get off the elevator, there is Lori Urs waiting to greet me.
She's petite, blond, and dressed in a snappy black-and-white-
checkered suit, and she's excited because half a dozen members of
the media have come. I walk into the conference room and see a
poster board at the front of the room, with "Areas of Innocence"
written at the top. On the list are the results of the DNA analysis of
the blood evidence that was done in 1990 after the trial. Lori introduces me to Richard Reyna, the investigator, and I go around the
room and meet the media. Reporters from television and radio sta-
tions are here, as are several newspaper reporters, including those
from the *Virginian Pilot* and the *Richmond Times-Dispatch*. I shake
hands and thank each of them for coming. I've met plenty of
reporters since I watched Patrick Sonnier die in the electric chair in
1984 and found myself in the midst of the debate on the death
penalty. Since my book came out in 1993, I have given many public
lectures before university audiences, churches, and civic groups, and
I meet media folks all along the way. They seem especially interested
in my personal experiences with death row inmates (*What's it like to
make that last walk with someone?*) and murder victims' families (*Aren't
they angry at you for showing compassion to the killer?*) and Susan
Sarandon and Tim Robbins (*What was it like having Susan Sarandon
play you in the movie?*).

Lori introduces me as the first speaker, and I say I'm glad the film
Dead Man Walking got out there to the American public because it
allows people to watch close up what it means for the government to
kill a human being. I worked right alongside Tim Robbins in shap-
ing the movie script and saw how hard he worked to be evenhanded
and show the suffering on both sides: the victims' families and the
prisoner and his family. In the film, Matthew Poncelet is guilty, he's
not innocent, because Tim Robbins wanted the film to probe what
he believes is the deepest moral question about the death penalty: not
what to do about innocent people—we *know* we shouldn't kill
them—but what to do about those truly guilty of horrible crimes.

Aren't we justified in killing them? Then I turn to the case of Joseph O'Dell and say that I'm here today to stand by him in his quest for justice, because even though I'm just learning the issues in his case, it seems to me that he truly might be an innocent man. I don't talk long so Lori and the others can have time to present the issues in O'Dell's case.

I just hope it's not too late for Joseph O'Dell.

The many exculpatory issues presented here today ought to be heard at an evidentiary hearing in a court of law, not at a press conference, but Virginia's stringent rule about admitting evidence of innocence no later than twenty-one days after trial makes a court hearing in Virginia impossible. And, if that's not bad enough, the Virginia Supreme Court, the highest court in the state, whose task is to make sure that a petitioner's constitutional rights are respected during trial—rights such as "due process," the right to effective assistance of counsel, the right to call witnesses, the right to "equal justice under the law"—refused outright to hear any of his grievances. They turned him down flat and did not read his petition.

And why?

Because his lawyers had typed "Notice of Appeal" on the title page of his petition instead of "Petition for Appeal," and the Virginia Supreme Court had refused a hearing on this issue.

They typed one wrong word.

Can this be possible?

Because of one ill-chosen word, the highest court in the state throws this man's appeal for justice back in his face.

To what level of moral bankruptcy has the judiciary system fallen that a court can do this to a man scheduled to be killed by the state?

A clerk of the Virginia Supreme Court explained to O'Dell's dismayed lawyers the basis of the court's action. In filing a *notice* of appeal, O'Dell's lawyers made it appear as if the court must automatically hear the appeal; but the appeal is not automatic. The court must be allowed ample discretion to decide whether or not it will hear the appeal, which is why *petition* is the proper word to use.

In my anger, I think of the words of Jesus to the spiritual ancestors of these justices: "You strain out gnats and swallow camels."

The blanket refusal of the Virginia Supreme Court to review any of O'Dell's claims had the disastrous result of barring him from a hearing in any federal court, which is the jurisdiction in which the vast majority of death row petitioners get relief.[18] Juridical protocol requires that federal courts hear petitions only after appeals in state courts have been exhausted, and the subject matter of federal review is the state court's arguments in response to the petitioner's constitutional claims. But since the Virginia Supreme Court had refused to review any of O'Dell's constitutional issues, it resulted in a juridical vacuum—a cruel twist for O'Dell. The federal courts would not grant him a hearing because they had no "subject matter" to review.

O'Dell was becoming alarmed that he might get killed without a federal court hearing his petition. After his trial, with no money and against great odds, he had managed to get DNA testing on the blood evidence, and all he needed was a court to allow him one evidentiary hearing—just one—so he could present the DNA results. He couldn't wait to get the DNA into court because it was the first hard-nosed evidence he had to contradict and unravel the "consistent with the victim's blood" testimony that Alberi and Test had presented over and over during his trial.

But what court would give him a hearing?

So in 1991, after six years of imprisonment, writ of habeas corpus in hand, Joseph O'Dell stands before the U.S. Supreme Court.[19]

The writ that O'Dell holds is every American citizen's greatest safeguard against the powers of government. Some call it the "great writ" because of the protection it gives, and it comes straight from the Magna Carta and common law. The Founders were keen to incorporate it into the Constitution—it's right there in Article I— because they knew all too well what kings and other government powers could do to a solitary individual.

It reads: "The Privilege of the Writ of Habeas Corpus shall not be suspended, unless when in Cases of Rebellion or Invasion the public Safety may require it."[20] The Founders called the writ a privilege and made special provision to preserve it, and in this country's history, the writ has been suspended only once, during the social upheaval of the Civil War.

The writ of habeas corpus guarantees Joseph O'Dell and all citizens that a higher court will review their trial proceedings to make sure that their constitutional rights are upheld. "Habeas corpus" means "We have reason to think that you are unjustly imprisoning this citizen, and we demand that you transfer him or her into our jurisdiction so we may review this citizen's case." Literally translated:

You have (*habeas*) the body (*corpus*), and we want it. At the state level, O'Dell has been unable to secure this promised habeas review, so he turns to the federal courts, though in earlier days of the Republic, citizens viewed the writ as protection only against the new federal government (they didn't trust "King George" Washington). They had no fear that the states themselves might abuse their power. But in 1867, after the Civil War, concerns arose when southern legislatures restricted the rights of African Americans. Then, for the first time, the reach of the writ began to extend to state prisoners. Until the 1960s, however, the U.S. Supreme Court considered every state supreme in the exercise of its "police power" and generally did not extend federal habeas corpus to state criminal courts. But during the 1960s, the U.S. Supreme Court, responding to concerns for the rights of indigent defendants, minors, and minorities, ruled that states must respect defendants' federal constitutional rights (right to counsel, a fair and impartial jury, and so forth) and thus opened the door for federal habeas review of state court proceedings.[21]

If anyone knows the saving power of the writ of habeas corpus, it is Ruben "Hurricane" Carter, an African American who became the number one contender for the middleweight boxing crown in 1966—until the police in New Jersey arrested him and a friend and tried them for the murder of three white people. The two were soon convicted, and for nineteen years their appeals were rejected by New Jersey courts until Carter heard about the writ of habeas corpus. Only in 1985 did federal district court judge H. Lee Sarokin grant Carter habeas review. In prison, Carter had written a book about his life; a college student bought it for a dollar at a used-book sale and with other friends began to work alongside a team of attorneys[22] who filed his habeas petition. The result was a miracle, a liberation story as powerful as the story of the Israelites escaping slavery in Egypt. Judge Sarokin, after hearing how the prosecution had withheld critical exculpatory evidence and improperly argued racial hatred as the motive for the crime, banged his gavel and told Carter that he was a free man.[23]

Once on a panel with Ruben Carter at Tufts University, I watched as he stood before a room full of students and held up a worn and creased copy of the writ of habeas corpus, issued by Judge Sarokin, which set him free. "This writ saved my life," he said.

O'Dell *dreamed* that he might share Hurricane Carter's good luck—that the Supreme Court would order a hearing in federal court of the evidence in his case that was withheld or distorted at trial. O'Dell was in treacherous waters, his boat so near the waterfall that he could feel the spray and see the flat line on the horizon where the water plunges downward. All his hopes were riding on his request to the U.S. Supreme Court.

On December 2, 1991, the U.S. Supreme Court refused to hear his constitutional claims on grounds that he had not yet re-petitioned the Virginia Supreme Court; juridical protocol demanded that only when that re-petition was completed could the Court consider his claims.

The Court's decision not to hear O'Dell's petition was unanimous.

All seemed lost.

Then O'Dell heard a heavy clunk, and he couldn't believe it. A lifeline had been thrown from the shore, a thin one, but strong enough to keep him from careening over the waterfall. Three Supreme Court justices—Harry A. Blackmun, John Paul Stevens, and Sandra Day O'Connor—while concurring with the Court's decision not to hear his case, issued a rare "statement" of concern.

Justice Blackmun wrote:

> There are serious questions as to whether O'Dell committed the crime or was capable of representing himself—questions rendered all the more serious by the fact that O'Dell's life depends upon their answers. Because of the gross injustice that would result if an innocent man were sentenced to death, O'Dell's substantial federal claims can, and should, receive careful consideration from the federal court with habeas corpus jurisdiction over the case.[24]

O'Dell must have leaped for joy. *Yes! Yes! Yes! This is what I've been saying all along. Now, at last, I'll get my hearing and all the truth can come out. Yes!*

What he hoped for was the kind of full evidentiary hearing in federal court that had freed Hurricane Carter so that everything— the false "match" of the blood with the victim's blood, the soil evidence withheld, witnesses hidden who could prove he had been in a fight, witnesses intimidated or made to disappear, the testimony of the jailhouse snitch Steven Watson—every shred of injustice done to him by prosecutors Alberi and Test would now be brought into the open. Surely any court with integrity would see through the state's flimsy, contrived evidence; and surely any court that was fair would see the pattern of withheld evidence that pointed to another killer— the umbrella, the witnesses who proved the victim's body had been put into the field later than 1:00 a.m., the witnesses who could verify that the victim had a room in the Executive Inn, the witnesses who had seen the victim arguing with her boyfriend—and all of this might now be brought out into the white light of truth. It was delicious to think about, and here he had not one, but three Supreme Court justices, the most astute legal minds in the land, who could see that he might be innocent. Those were strong words, "serious questions as to whether O'Dell committed the crime." The justices could see that the physical evidence against him was weak. They well knew that finding blood that was "consistent with" did not mean a "match." They knew a jailhouse informer's testimony was untrustworthy and that O'Dell was no match for impassioned prosecutors like Alberi and Test. They knew what prosecutors are capable of and their power to control evidence. O'Dell knew that the justices' statement on his behalf was very, very rare, so their concerns must have been great indeed.

What had Blackmun said? . . . *the gross injustice if an innocent man were sentenced to death.* . . .

At last, someone in the court system understood. At last, the truth of what had happened to him was beginning to be recognized. At last. He memorized the justices' words and said them slowly and reverently like prayers in his bunk at night. For six years he had been in this terrible place, watching in mute numbness as the guards in black uniforms came to lead prisoners away to the death house. Already he had watched twenty of them go, some his close friends, and whenever someone was killed, he fasted that day. Some of the guys treated an execution day like a regular day, with the TV on and talking and eating and carrying on, but he couldn't do that.

Through Lori's extensive notes and O'Dell's letters to her, I learn about his life.

O'Dell knew about prisons and detention centers. He had been in them most of his forty-three years. By the time he was thirteen, he had been arrested in Casa Grande, Arizona; Eloy, Tennessee; Maryland; North Carolina; and Virginia, mostly for store robberies. By the time he was twenty-five there were fourteen felonies on his record, most of them committed in his teens and most of them store robberies, until he was convicted of car theft at age nineteen. They sent him to the "brick yard," the place for incorrigibles, the Powhatan Correctional Center. He was the youngest man ever sent there; when a homosexual with a knife tried to assault him, he had fought back, seized the knife, and stabbed the attacker. He was indicted for second-degree murder, despite his claims of self-defense. Another convict had lied on the stand in order to make parole, saying that he saw O'Dell stab the man in the back, even though the autopsy recorded no stab wound in the back. The jury believed the convict, and twenty more years were added to O'Dell's twenty-four-year sentence. Before the "brick yard," there had been the juvenile centers, where O'Dell first saw raw and open sex and learned to be afraid and to defend himself, and for punishment, he had to stand for hours at the edge of his bed with his finger held to his nose or was made to run outside in a circle with unbelted trousers and untied shoelaces, a guard behind him slashing his buttocks with a belt when the pants fell down. But this place, death row in Mecklenburg Correctional Center, was the worst. His mother had died soon after he was sent here, and he told Lori in a letter, "My coming here killed her. She already had so much sorrow." His mother was petite, and he had always tried to protect her from his drunk, angry father, who stood six feet and weighed 240 pounds and beat her with his bare fists. On her way home from school when she was fourteen years old, his father, then eighteen years old, had raped her, which was how O'Dell had come into this world. He was born on September 20, 1941, in Florida. At the age of seven, he watched his father slam into his mother's face. Joe grabbed a butcher knife; his father took it from him and then beat him severely. At eleven he ran away from home, hitchhiking to nearby towns and stealing food. Sometimes the police arrested him and called his father, who came to pick him up and bring him home—and beat him.

O'Dell told Lori: "I'm not talking about spanking. He would hit me in the head with his fist. More than once I went to school with both eyes blackened and bumps on my head."

In her notes, Lori recorded that O'Dell always capitalized the word *mother* but never the word *father*.

When his mother died, they would not let him go to her funeral. He told Lori that he was full of hatred. And then one day he saw a broken typewriter in the trash can; he rebuilt it, named it "Lazarus," and used it to write a novel. For six months, he hammered away at his story about a man sentenced to die for a murder he did not commit but who was vindicated and teamed up with his girlfriend, Holly, who had been sexually molested by her father, and together they pulled off a masterful act of revenge. They kidnapped the judge, jury, prosecutors, police—everyone involved in the false conviction—and killed them one by one in a homemade electric chair.

"I got all my bitterness out," O'Dell told Lori Urs in a letter. "I have never gotten a single disciplinary write-up since I've been here."

As O'Dell's anger and bitterness drained away, righteous resistance took over and he became a poised and veteran warrior in his own defense, determined to reveal the truth. Sometimes he felt his mother's presence, he told Lori. One night shortly after she died, she came to him in a dream and whispered, "Fight for your life, Joe. You don't have to accept this injustice. Fight."

Now, at last, with the Supreme Court justices' intervention, he had his first chance to come before a fair and impartial federal judge who could overrule the Virginia courts and the prosecutors.

With Blackmun's words he imagined himself coming through the courthouse doors triumphant, telling the press, "At last I got justice in the courts. Thank God for the United States of America."

That he had managed to get DNA analysis on the blood evidence in the first place was a small miracle. Soon after his trial, he had proposed the idea to the lawyers handling his appeal, but they seemed uninterested, so he pursued it on his own. He presented a motion to the trial judge, Calvin Spain, asking for the testing, and, surprisingly, Spain supported his motion. It was the first time in the history of Virginia that a trial judge approved post-trial forensic testing. O'Dell had no money to pay for the expensive DNA analysis, but he had read about a millionaire philanthropist, Percy Ross, and wrote to him; Ross sent him $1,200, enough to pay for the testing. His lawyers then chose LifeCodes, a reputable laboratory, to perform the tests.

Armed with the precious mandate of the three Supreme Court justices, Joseph O'Dell finally got an evidentiary hearing in a federal court. On August 2, 1994, he appeared before Judge James Spencer in the Federal District Court of Virginia to present the results of the DNA blood analysis. Two forensic experts were present to argue the commonwealth's position, but thanks to Lori Urs's tireless efforts, for the first time O'Dell had skilled experts and lawyers at his side to argue for him. Clearly their expertise made a difference.

Judge Spencer's ruling on the evidence was favorable to O'Dell.[25] Now, at this press conference two years after the hearing (appeals courts in the South are notoriously slow), Lori Urs will present Spencer's conclusions. She had told me that one of the reasons the press conference was necessary was to make known the DNA results, because she had a "big fear" (which later proved to be well founded) that the Fourth Circuit might make "mincemeat" of Judge Spencer's favorable ruling and simply overturn it. They had the authority, she explained, and they had used it against death row petitioners in the past, to overturn federal court hearings they deemed too "lenient." So Lori figured getting information out to the public about the DNA results could help build support for O'Dell's cause.

And what was Judge Spencer's ruling about the DNA?

At the press conference, Lori points to the top of the "Areas of Innocence" on the poster board. The first item says: "DNA blood evidence: Shirt—exclusion; jacket—inconclusive." Although LifeCodes had originally judged the bloodstain on the jacket a "match," Judge Spencer, upon hearing the arguments, judged it to be "inconclusive" because LifeCodes had used a method of testing later found to be flawed by the scientific community.

The DNA results were good news for Joseph O'Dell. Two bloodstains had been tested, and neither of them confirmed the commonwealth's position that the blood on O'Dell's clothes was "consistent with" Helen Schartner's blood. It pointed in the direction of O'Dell's innocence, which was very good news indeed.

The "exclusion" on the shirt was the strongest. It showed that the blood was definitely *not* Helen Schartner's blood, which clearly contradicted the state's claim. The bloodstain on the jacket was judged "inconclusive" owing to the deteriorated state of the evidence. Then Lori explains that the form of blood analysis used at the time of O'Dell's trial in 1985 by the Virginia crime laboratory was a traditional serology test, so unreliable that the Virginia crime lab abandoned it soon after O'Dell's trial. The FBI had stopped using it in 1986 during the time of O'Dell's trial. The most this test could do was place an individual in a group of people whose blood happened to contain similar enzymes. Lori explains that the most Jacqueline Emrich, the Virginia lab expert, could say was that the blood on O'Dell's clothes was "consistent with" the victim's blood. "All that is really saying," she says, "is that you can't exclude the possibility that it *might* be the victim's blood; but equally true, it might *not* be the victim's blood, which is really not saying much at all." And she tells about the prosecution's stunt of putting mannequins in the courtroom, dressed like Joe and the victim, their clothes covered with blood, and saying that the blood on O'Dell's clothes was "all the same," so the jurors were sure to think that it was Helen Schartner's blood. These mannequins were in front of the jury box almost an entire day while the commonwealth's experts testified to the reliability of the serology testing. "And you know that every time the jurors heard 'consistent with' they heard 'match,' " Lori says, her voice jumping a decibel or two, trying to contain her outrage, "and just in case the jurors didn't get it, the prosecution said it for them in the closing argument when they flat out referred to the bloodstains on Joe's clothes as Helen Schartner's blood, and I have copies of the trial transcript if you want to see it."

That the trial judge, Calvin Spain, allowed DNA testing after the trial is telling, Lori says, because he had seen the contrived evidence that the prosecution presented and said frankly that he had "problems with the scientific evidence in this case all along." Judge Spain knew, as we know, she says, that the blood evidence was the only physical evidence the state had against O'Dell. Without that, Lori says, they have nothing, and that's what this DNA test shows.

Lori adds that the bloodstains for DNA testing were chosen very carefully. Mr. O'Dell's experts were careful to pick only those stains that the state had already tested, so that an exact comparison could be made. Because the state had failed in its duty to preserve the evidence, LifeCodes, the laboratory chosen to analyze the evidence, determined that DNA tests could be performed only on the shirt and the jacket. Two stains on the shirt and jacket already tested by the commonwealth were chosen for DNA testing. O'Dell's defense didn't want the commonwealth attorneys to object if the tests didn't go as they wished. They did not want them to say that the stains were selectively tested and so proved nothing. The swabs from the victim's rape kit had also not been properly preserved and were too deteriorated to be tested, according to LifeCodes.

Lori recapitulates for the press: The stain on the shirt was an exclusion, and the jacket was judged to be inconclusive, but the jacket test was more complicated. She gives the press a handout to help them follow the technical arguments. LifeCodes had judged that the bloodstain on the jacket was, in fact, a *match* with the victim's blood. And that's where the complication came in, because to arrive at that conclusion, LifeCodes had used a controversial method that many in the scientific community were coming to distrust. Lori explains that LifeCodes had used special kinds of probes to correct something known as "band shifting," which can happen when the sample tested was in a deteriorated state. Band shifting occurs when the DNA samples do not fall into clear bands or windows, and in this state it is difficult to see if, in fact, there is a *match*. When the special probes are used, they stabilize the moving bands or windows, a pattern emerges, and a judgment can be made. LifeCodes had used these probes to correct the shifting bands of DNA that had occurred when they tested the jacket, and that is what had led them to declare a match with the victim's blood. When LifeCodes did the testing for O'Dell back in 1990, Lori explains, DNA methods were still in something of a formative stage; a number of laboratories were using the probes, but the probes seemed to produce mixed results. In 1992, the National Research Council, which is the representative body of the scientific community, had issued a report criticizing the use of the probes to correct band shifting, since the probes tended to produce artificial or contrived results. After the NRC's critique, use of the probes began to fall into disfavor within the scientific community, and the method was eventually banned by the FBI and by the state of Virginia.

As Lori takes the press through the technicalities of these arguments, I am struck by their complexity and the close attention such arguments require.

After hearing experts from both sides, Judge Spencer came to the judgment that the DNA test on the jacket stain was inconclusive, not a "match." His judgment that the stain on the shirt was an "exclusion" of the victim's blood was easy, since O'Dell's experts and the commonwealth's experts readily accepted the LifeCodes conclusion.

No debate there. But the debate over the jacket and the use of the probes was fierce, Lori tells the press. She had read the transcripts and seen how the commonwealth had strongly argued to validate LifeCodes's original finding that the jacket was a "match" with the victim's blood. They needed that finding, Lori explains, to bolster their position, because the blood on the shirt had proved to be an exclusion. They had disputed the NRC's criticism of the probes by downplaying the authority of the NRC in the scientific community, saying that they were simply one group of scientists among many, but without any real authority. But O'Dell's experts had countered that the NRC is *the* representative body of scientists, so its judgments and critiques are authoritative.

And as Lori continues to explain what happened at the hearing, I realize how intelligent and attentive Judge Spencer would have to have been to follow the highly nuanced and technical arguments. He did more than follow the arguments—he managed to facilitate the arguments in such a fair and clear way that both sides reached a consensus, deciding to accept NRC's critique of the use of the probes, which nullified LifeCodes's judgment of a "match" on the jacket, thus rendering it "inconclusive."

Lori had told me how cheered O'Dell had been when Spencer ruled in his favor. It had taken him eight years to get this first "break" in the courts. He spent much of his time in his six-foot-by-eight-foot cell reading about legal arguments, but especially about DNA testing, which he realized was the only "truth buster" strong enough to dismantle the commonwealth's case against him. In one of his letters to Lori, he said that he kept his mind busy reading and writing strategies for his defense so that he could stay sane "in this place of incessant noise and ignorance and television sets blaring." He was reading about how DNA testing was "exonerating people all over the place" and getting them new trials.

O'Dell was hopeful. Barry Scheck, one of the foremost DNA experts in the United States, was joining his team, having been recruited by Lori Urs. Scheck was drawing up an amicus brief to present to the Virginia Supreme Court, explaining how the new PCR method of DNA testing could be conducted on the vaginal and anal swabs in the victim's rape kit, because the test required only microscopic amounts of DNA material and yielded incredibly accurate results. PCR testing had not been available at the time of O'Dell's trial, and O'Dell knew that such DNA testing on the swabs could prove that he did not rape Helen Schartner. Without rape as an aggravating factor in her murder, his death sentence would dissolve.

The press conference is moving on. Lori Urs now holds up an affidavit from Carol Kelly, one of the jurors at O'Dell's trial. Kelly states that if she had heard at trial the results of the DNA testing on the shirt and jacket, she would not have voted to convict O'Dell.

That statement from a juror points to the most profound problem O'Dell has: All the truth about evidence revealed today never reached the ears of the original jury.

One of the journalists interrupts with a question: In light of the DNA findings that pointed to O'Dell's possible innocence, why didn't Judge Spencer call for a new trial?

Lori answers that Judge Spencer wrote in his opinion that while the DNA evidence pointed toward O'Dell's possible innocence, which normally would provide grounds to call for a new trial, Steve Watson's testimony of O'Dell's confession blocked the way. When O'Dell's evidentiary hearing took place in Spencer's court, Watson's testimony remained unimpeached. Judge Spencer did, however, overturn O'Dell's death sentence and order a new sentencing trial on the grounds that the jury had been prevented from hearing the truth about his eligibility for parole.

As Lori talks, she cannot disguise her anger. "The so-called confession to the jailhouse snitch Steve Watson blocked Judge Spencer from mandating a new trial for Joe."

With that said, Richard Reyna, the investigator, says that Steve Watson has a long record of past felonies and a reputation for offering "deals," and he reads from a letter that Watson had once written to a judge, saying, "Let's make a deal, judge. . . . I want out of jail any kind of way I can get out. . . . I'm a dead man if I have to stay in Virginia. . . . I have been labeled as a snitch." At O'Dell's trial, the letter was excluded by Judge Spain, and when O'Dell sought to cross-examine Watson about the letter, Spain wouldn't let him.

In October, just three months after this press conference, Watson in an affidavit will admit that he had lied about O'Dell's confession:

> Since my testimony in Virginia Beach, I have been
> troubled about things that I said that are untrue but I
> have been afraid to come forward for fear of being

charged and prosecuted for perjury. I can no longer live with the fact that Mr. O'Dell may die because of . . . statements that I later changed and passed on to Virginia Beach prosecutors in hopes they would help me with charges that I had pending in West Virginia.

One of the reporters asks Lori about the semen evidence. Hadn't the state's expert found semen in the victim's body to be consistent with O'Dell's?

Lori explains that, to the contrary, the autopsy report indicated that the semen sample from the victim's rape kit contained a genetic marker that was clearly different from O'Dell's and so should have excluded him. At trial, the state's expert, Emrich, testified only that the samples were "consistent with" O'Dell's semen, and she had arrived at that conclusion through a theory, which she admitted was "conjecture," that *somehow* the body secretions of the victim and O'Dell had mysteriously *mixed*. Lori explains that Emrich's "conjecture" was so scientifically unfounded that even the state's expert, G. F. Sensabaugh, admitted at trial that the "mixture" theory was highly suspect. Emrich, who had analyzed all the forensic evidence for the state—blood, body secretions, hair, everything—had just completed her training in serology method testing, and O'Dell's was her first criminal trial. Lori says that a number of forensic experts who examined her procedural methods found them to be unprofessional: samples were contaminated, unlabeled, or undated; lab notes were an illegible scrawl with no initials or signature; photographs of test results were so blurred that independent testing was impossible. And there had been no supervisor to guide or check her work. Dr. Lavett, O'Dell's forensic expert, testified at trial that Emrich failed to obtain a single "replicated reliable result" on any piece of O'Dell's clothing and on Helen Schartner's clothing. "There was no item that was tested twice and gave the same result twice." Lori notes that almost 80 percent of state crime labs are overseen by the police. Most of these labs examine only evidence submitted by the prosecution, with no outside regulation or external review. During the trial, Lori continues, when O'Dell's lone forensic expert, Dr. Diane Lavett, dared to critique Emrich's methodology and procedures, she was taunted and ridiculed by the prosecution and later threatened with a libel lawsuit.

There's one other point about the blood evidence, Lori says, and brings Richard Reyna, the investigator, to the podium. Reyna says that the state's forensic team had found a bloodstain in O'Dell's car that proved to be neither O'Dell's nor the victim's. If this blood had been shown to come from one of the men O'Dell fought in Ocean View, it might have corroborated O'Dell's alibi. But the jury never heard about this blood. Joe couldn't pay for a forensic investigation and did not have the legal skills to introduce the blood analysis at trial. What the prosecution did to O'Dell, Reyna says, was withhold exculpatory evidence, and he adds that some prosecutors in Virginia assume they can get away with "playing fast and loose with physical evidence" because they're never censured for it or penalized.

Reyna says that the prosecutors also withheld other crucial evidence—the soil samples from the crime scene, which he believes they knew would not match the soil on O'Dell's pants; the victim's umbrella, which may have had fingerprints of the real murderer on it; an important witness, Joseph Moore, who had found the victim's body.

Then Reyna holds up a letter to the trial judge from Dr. Joseph H. Guth, a forensic scientist appointed to help the defense. The letter is dated May 6, just two weeks before O'Dell's trial. In it, Guth complains vehemently that the prosecutors are withholding crucial evidence from the defense. Reyna quotes from the letter:

> Extremely important physical evidence collected by the state was either never evaluated or analyzed or was analyzed and would not be introduced at trial. I was deceived by the Commonwealth as to its existence. At the time I picked up the evidence, I was assured by Sergeant Wray Boswell that what I was in receipt of was all the physical evidence in the case. . . . It must be made available. . . . In this case I believe the sin of omission is just as serious as the sin of commission since it can lead to a miscarriage of justice. . . . Soil and debris [from the crime scene] could either put Mr. O'Dell at the scene of the crime

> or vindicate him! The state crime lab has not men-
> tioned this evidence in any of their reports and did
> not even acknowledge or proffer its exis-
> tence! . . . [This is] tantamount to the concealment
> of evidence.

The press conference is over. Lori hugs me and can't thank me enough for coming. She and her team did well today. The turnout was good. Cameras were whirring, pens scribbling, questions sharp. I'm glad I came. When I tell her good-bye, I assume I will never see her again, that this press conference in Richmond will be my only involvement with Joseph O'Dell. I get on the plane, and my thoughts turn toward my sick friend waiting for me in New Orleans.

II

"You'll never believe it. The pope spoke out for Joe!" It's Lori Urs on the phone, telling me that Pope John Paul II spoke out against the death penalty and mentioned Joseph O'Dell. "Imagine! The pope saying Joe's name to the whole world! It gives me goose bumps. I've been trying to get powerful people to speak for Joe because that's the only language the governor and other politicians understand. They have to know that they're not killing a nobody if they kill Joseph O'Dell. They have to know that very important people care about this man. Who knows? With the pope speaking out, maybe even the courts will take Joe's case more seriously. Aren't there some Catholics on the Supreme Court? Like Scalia? Isn't he Catholic? Isn't he sup-posed to listen to the pope? And guess what? I hear that some peo-ple have told Mother Teresa of Calcutta about Joe and are asking her to intercede with Governor Allen. Sugar! Can you picture that? Mother Teresa, a living saint, giving a piece of her mind to Governor George Allen? I hear that Mother Teresa doesn't kowtow to gover-nors or presidents or anybody. Did you hear that when she visited death row at San Quentin, she poked her finger into the chest of a guard and said, 'Remember, what you do to these men, you do to Christ'? Can you imagine her with Governor Allen?" (Laughter.) "He'll never know what hit him!"

The call from Lori a week later is not happy.

Please, Lori is asking, please, will I come to be with Joe if they kill him, because the date is set for December 22, just a week away, and she's "out-of-her-mind worried" because his case is before the U.S. Supreme Court and "you *know* how fickle they are, you *know* how they let people die if their lawyers file one day late or write one wrong word." But she says that Joe's petition contains a "clear-cut" constitutional issue, which had opened up for Joe because of the Supreme Court's decision in *Simmons v. South Carolina*,[26] in which the Court had found that Simmons's constitutional rights had been violated because his jury was not allowed to know about the life-without-parole sentence that he faced for his crime. The Supreme Court had determined that withholding this information from the jury violated Simmons's constitutional right to "due process."

"You can see the Simmons issue clear as day in the transcripts of Joe's trial," she says. "Prosecutors Test and Alberi not only blocked Joe's jury from knowing about Virginia's life-without-parole sentence, they also deliberately misled them into thinking that Joe would be walking the streets again if they didn't vote to kill him."

When I hear this, I'm glad for Joe O'Dell because now his petition can be based on precedent, which greatly increases the likelihood that the Supreme Court will hear it. In the grisly business of warding off state killing, that's how to save a life: If the Court gives O'Dell a hearing, his killing will be delayed, which means at least six more months of life, maybe a year; and if they rule in his favor, his death sentence will be overturned and he'll get a new sentencing trial.

I was appalled when I found out that district attorneys on a regular basis try to keep juries from knowing about life-without-parole sentences. District attorneys know that juries tend to choose life over death if they know the offender will be locked away and not eligible for parole for a long time, if ever. Public safety is, naturally, of great concern, and life-without-parole sentences for felony murder, which most states now have in place,[27] save jurors from the terrible task of condemning a fellow human being to death. I have always thought that fairness to jurors demands, at the very least, that they know the truth about the sentence the defendant will receive if they choose not to impose death. I have heard horror stories of juries begging to know if the defendant might be let out on parole and judges refusing to answer their question. For the rest of their lives, such jurors bear the burden of their decision—no small weight for a human soul to carry.

I was just one juror among many. We all decided unanimously that the defendant deserved death. The judge told us to brace up to our hard task for the sake of society. I know what I did was legal. But was it right? Was it right before God?

Prosecutors like Albert Alberi and Stephen Test who seek the death penalty tend to see any lesser sentence as failure, which gives rise to their impassioned closing arguments to jurors in which they portray death as the only reasonable choice for a God-fearing juror who wishes to protect society from dangerous criminals. Several studies show that when jurors know that the defendant will get a true life-without-parole sentence, the number of death sentences drops dramatically.[28]

Arguing fiercely for the death of a human being hardly brings out in prosecutors the "angels of their better nature." My friend Denny LeBoeuf told me of once watching an assistant district attorney who had worked assiduously to secure a death sentence crumple at the prosecution's table and weep when she heard that the jury had not decided on death. "It's not going to happen for me," Denny heard her say through her tears.[29]

"She felt defeated," Denny said. "When prosecutors go for death, they are so driven to 'win' that they forget what 'winning' means. They're so geared for death that even a sentence of life without parole seems unsatisfying. Take this kind of behavior out of the courtroom and it sounds a lot like blood revenge: Only death will do."

Denny, who has faced such prosecutors in Louisiana courts for thirteen years, adds, "That's one reason why the death penalty is not good for our society. It tends to corrupt the sensibilities of prosecutors, especially if they feel that getting death sentences enhances their careers." The decision to go for the death penalty or not, which is at the discretion of district attorneys, also points to an intractable problem. "How can such decisions ever be anything but arbitrary," Denny asks, "when it's left to individual district attorneys to decide to go for death or not?" She can tick off on her fingers which prosecutors in Louisiana are enthusiastic proponents of the death penalty: Harry Connick Sr. in New Orleans, Doug Moreau in Baton Rouge,

Paul Connick (nephew of Harry Connick Sr.) in Jefferson Parish, and Jerry Jones in Monroe. Most inmates on death row in Louisiana come from the districts of these prosecutors. But in a neighboring parish (county) where equally terrible murders occur, Denny says, you may have a district attorney who hardly ever goes for the death penalty, maybe because a DA doesn't have the heart for it, or maybe because there's just not enough money in the coffers for a capital trial, which is more costly than a regular trial. "You can see this pattern of unevenness all across the United States," Denny says, and names death pockets across the nation. In North Carolina, there's DA Joe Freeman Britt; in Texas, there's DA Johnny Holmes; in Philadelphia, there's DA Lynne Abraham. And Denny goes on to explain that the application of the federal death penalty is no less hit-or-miss, with a small percentage of the districts accounting for the majority of death sentences.

I know what Denny means about prosecutors losing perspective. I recently saw an article in the Baton Rouge *Advocate* that the local district attorney, Doug Moreau, took the entire prosecution team out for drinks and dinner at an expensive restaurant when they "won" a death sentence. The dinners happened fairly often because Moreau's office is a top contender in Louisiana for most death sentences attained, setting a record of sixteen straight death sentences in a row a couple of years ago. From 1996 to 2000, Louisiana's death row population doubled, owing in no small part to Moreau's string of "victories."[30] A journalist for the *Advocate* discovered that taxpayers were footing the bill for Moreau's "celebration" dinners, and when he asked Moreau to justify such expenditures, Moreau explained that capital cases were "stressful" and demanded far more work and longer hours than other cases. The dinners, he said, helped team spirit.

"So if the defendant happens to get a life sentence instead of death," the journalist asked, "hasn't the prosecution team worked just as hard and doesn't that call for a special meal?"

No, not then, said DA Moreau.

On the phone, Lori tells me about Joe's latest devastating blow from the Fourth Circuit Court of Appeals.

"This court always sides with the prosecution," she says. "They not only overturned Joe's new sentencing trial granted by Judge Spencer, but in one fell swoop dismissed the results of the DNA blood tests and said that Joe's claim of innocence wasn't even 'colorable.' They said that it was *irrelevant* that the blood on Joe's shirt proved not to be Helen Schartner's blood. Can you imagine? Irrelevant! The blood on Joe's clothes was the main physical evidence that the state had used against Joe, and their constant theme all during the trial was that the blood on Joe's clothes was consistent with the victim's blood. And the DNA tests for the first time gave hard scientific evidence to the contrary, especially the shirt results, which clearly proved to be not the victim's blood. For that matter, it proved not to be Joe's blood, either, and so pointed to the presence of a third party, which Joe had claimed all along, saying the blood had come from a fight. To call this scientific evidence irrelevant? It directly contradicted the state's claim, but the Fourth Circuit, voicing the prosecution's argument, claimed that the blood spots for testing had been randomly selected and so were inconsequential.

"But remember how carefully the blood spots for testing had been selected? Remember how Joe's lawyers made sure that only those spots were chosen for testing that the state had already tested so an exact comparison could be made? Far from being irrelevant, the exclusion of the victim's blood on the shirt clearly warranted further testing to see if, perhaps, other spots of blood might also contradict the state's findings.

"And wait until you hear what the Fourth Circuit did with the jacket results; it's even worse than the shirt," Lori says. "The Fourth Circuit said the blood on the jacket matched the victim's blood. Matched? Judge Spencer, after painstakingly listening to the scientific arguments, had declared the bloodstain on the jacket inconclusive, certainly not a match.[31] The court well knew that by declaring a 'match,' they were shutting down all further discussion of the DNA evidence. And, of course, to declare this 'match' on the jacket, the court had to debunk the authority of the National Research Council, whose critique had led to a different conclusion from theirs. The NRC, after all, is *the* representative body of scientists, and their critique is authoritative in the scientific community."

Lori is white-hot mad; her words come in a torrent, and I'm thinking of the levels and levels of complexity in this debate. It takes smarts and careful attention to follow the arguments about monomorphic probes and "match windows," so it was easy enough for the Fourth Circuit to dismiss the authority of the NRC when it disagreed with its conclusions. Who would care enough to follow the intricacies of such arguments? Lori Urs cared, of course, and Joseph O'Dell's appellate lawyers cared enough to file a seven-page rebuttal of the factual errors in the Fourth Circuit's decision.

"The Fourth Circuit plays with scientific evidence like putty," Lori is saying, "and do you know what I have come to realize? They used the exact right word when they said the DNA results on the shirt were 'irrelevant.' That's exactly right, because for them the scientific evidence truly is irrelevant. Only innocent Joe O'Dell, who still believes in the integrity of the system, thought the courts would be fair-minded and really look at the DNA results. Forget it. Joe's innocent, and all this Fourth Circuit has done is rubber-stamp his guilty verdict and push him along to his death. They make me sick."

I feel her frustration. After fourteen years of involvement in these death penalty cases, I should have learned to steel myself not to expect fairness from the Fourth Circuit Court of Appeals or any such court in the southern death penalty belt. I remember Nick Trenticosta, Dobie Williams's attorney, telling me that when he delivers his clients' petitions of appeal to certain judges in Louisiana, he keeps the car running because he knows that a few minutes after delivery the judge's clerk will come running out with the petition stamped "Denied."

"You work for hours and hours on these petitions," Nick says, "and you know the judge could not even have read the petition, much less thought about it."

In Virginia, as well as in other death penalty states, judges are infected with the same pro–death penalty bias that infects legislators, governors, and other political figures, especially now that so many judges are elected to office. Judges are all too aware of what happened to Rose Bird in California and Penny White in Tennessee,[32] both voted off the state supreme courts because they were judged too lenient to death row petitioners. I've heard criminal defense attorney Millard Farmer[33] say many times that death penalty cases are 95 percent about politics and 5 percent about criminal justice.

The social pressures that affect judges on death penalty cases are not unlike pressures judges faced in Jim Crow days when African American defendants accused of crimes against white persons were brought to trial. Both judges and defense attorneys then needed courage and a gritty sense of integrity to assure African American defendants a fair trial.

Lori has a lot more to say about what the Fourth Circuit Court of Appeals did to Joseph O'Dell.

Point by point, she tells me, the Fourth Circuit parroted the commonwealth's arguments. "They said the physical evidence against Joe was 'overwhelming,' that Joe and Helen Schartner were *together* at the lounge, that the wounds on the victim's head matched Joe's gun. Gun? What gun? The stock model the prosecution purchased from Kmart while keeping hidden what may have been the real weapon, Helen Schartner's umbrella with the bent handle? It's as if, verbatim, Alberi and Test wrote this opinion for the Fourth Circuit. The court agrees with them on every single point, even that the semen found inside the victim was found to be 'consistent with' Joe's semen, which meant they bought the cockeyed 'mixture' theory of the state's expert, which even one of the state's own experts had to admit was unscientific."

Lori has told me that she's applying to law school. No doubt she'll be a good lawyer, another Denny LeBoeuf, a strong advocate for poor people. Even as a law student she could probably help teach the criminal law section on capital punishment.

"You should *read* this decision," Lori continues. The Fourth Circuit says that Joe failed to explain why his investigator did not interview the jailhouse informer Steve Watson *before* trial. Interview him? It's clear as day in the trial transcript that Steve Watson was a surprise witness. The Fourth Circuit does not even mention one piece of exculpatory evidence in Joe's case: the sandy soil on his pants and boots that could prove he was not in the muddy field; the footprint that didn't match his; the witness Joseph Moore, who found the body but then disappeared at the time of trial. Why didn't the Fourth Circuit question the fact that the victim's umbrella was missing and the fact that not one fingerprint of the victim could be found in Joe's car? Why doesn't the Fourth Circuit question that not one hair of Joe's, including pubic hair, could be found on the victim's body, though he was supposed to have raped her and struggled with her? Why did they ignore the abundant information about the jailhouse snitch's readiness to "make a deal" with prosecutors and judges? How, Lori asks, can Joe ever get justice when the prosecution has the highest federal appeals court in its back pocket? And if you check into the track record of the Fourth Circuit on death penalty cases, you'll see that they hold the national record for upholding more death sentences than any other appeals court in the entire country.

"How can we hold this court accountable for their actions?" Lori asks. "I want history to know their names and what they did to Joseph O'Dell.[34] You just watch. One day I'll write a book—I hope a book with a happy ending—and I'll expose what these judges did to Joe and to so many others. I'll demonstrate how, plank by plank, they constructed the juridical scaffolding of Joseph O'Dell's gallows. They're like those kangaroo courts in some countries, where the accused walk into court already knowing they're going to be found guilty and killed. I told Joe to stop putting those little stickers on his letters that say 'Thank God for America.' The courts of America are corrupt. The courts are doing their best to get Joe O'Dell killed."

Corrupt is a tough word. For me, judicial corruption has always been associated with bribery. But Denny LeBoeuf told me that prosecutors who withhold exculpatory evidence are also corrupt, because corruption occurs whenever judges or prosecutors or police have an interest in a certain outcome and manipulate the law and evidence at the expense of justice. All the courts so far in O'Dell's case—the trial court, which let him defend himself and allowed the prosecutors to manipulate evidence and witnesses; the Virginia Supreme Court, which summarily refused to hear any of his constitutional issues because of a wrong word on the title page; and the Fourth Circuit Court of Appeals, which without scrutiny endorsed what the lower courts had done and, worse, overturned a federal district judge's decision on the results of DNA testing—each of these courts has denied justice to Joseph O'Dell.

What happened to O'Dell in the Fourth Circuit reminds me of what happened to Dobie Williams in the Fifth Circuit. Dobie had gotten his first glimmer of hope from a federal judge who had mandated a new sentencing trial for him. During the sentencing phase, Dobie's lawyer had been so inept, the federal judge contended, that it was as if Dobie had no lawyer at all. How Dobie's hopes had soared then, and how his mama and family had cheered. But the Fifth Circuit Court of Appeals summarily overturned the federal judge's decision and sent Dobie to his death. The Fifth Circuit ranks right behind the Fourth Circuit in upholding almost every death sentence it considers. It is rare indeed that they ever uphold that the constitutional rights of death row petitioners have been violated, especially the claim of ineffectiveness of defense counsel—even when defense lawyers have been shown to sleep during trial.[35] Explaining why it had ruled that a sleeping defense lawyer should not be considered ineffective, the Fifth Circuit majority argued the point that the court did not know *exactly when during the trial* the defense attorney had fallen asleep; maybe it had been during one of the "non-critical" stretches.[36]

Lori's voice catches and she swallows hard and is silent for a little while, but then her voice gets strong again as she talks about how the Simmons issue might get a new sentencing trial for Joe from the U.S. Supreme Court. "If it's against Simmons's constitutional rights for the jury not to hear about the life-without-parole sentence, then it's surely against Joe O'Dell's constitutional rights."

I can hear the hope rising in her voice, and I'm hopeful, too. "True, it's not the totally new trial Joe deserves, which could acquit him once and for all," she says, "but at least a new sentencing trial could get him out from under the death sentence and keep him alive so we can prove his innocence."

I'm hopeful, but I buy an airline ticket to Richmond just in case they decide to kill Joe. He had telephoned me a few days ago and asked me to accompany him to the death chamber. In Virginia, he tells me, spiritual advisers are allowed into the chamber itself, and I will be allowed to touch him after he's strapped to the gurney and can say a final prayer for him. The killing is only a week away.

On December 17, Lori telephones—jubilant.

The U.S. Supreme Court agreed to hear Joe's petition, the warrant for his death has been lifted, and Joe has been taken out of the death watch cell and returned to his cell on death row.

"Sugar!" she shouts. "I heard that applause broke out in the Italian parliament over the Supreme Court's decision. And the Vatican expressed 'satisfaction' at the news. And—get this—the mayor of Palermo, Italy, has made Joe an honorary citizen.[37] Joe O'Dell's name is getting to be a household word in Italy and in the Vatican—isn't that unbelievable? Joe told me that with all these Catholics coming to his aid, maybe he ought to think about becoming a Catholic." And she laughs.

The jubilation fades as Lori tells about Joe's near death experience.

"What this human being is going through," Lori says, and her voice quivers.

Joe had called her in tears: "Lori, I'm next." It unnerved her to hear him crying. He was usually the one to calm her. She appreciated his intelligence and the way he handled himself with dignity through all this terrible, unjust, outrageous . . . and she can't find the words.

"How could he not be upset?" she says. "They'd have to wrap me in one of those white coats and haul me off to the loony bin if they had me sitting in a cell right next to the place where they were about to kill me. Can you believe this is the United States of America?"

She's scared.

Of course she's scared. I remember the cold fear when I waited with Pat Sonnier, Robert Willie, and Willie Celestine for the "strap down" team to come for them. Normally I am warm and humming inside but in that surreal house of death, I was cold and paralyzed in the presence of such a calculated protocol of death. When the state kills a human being, it is forced to write the truth of its deed on the death certificate. In the space after "Cause of Death," officials must write, "Homicide." The word *execution* is a euphemism. It's a general word that means the carrying out of a plan or order. "Homicide" tells the truth, even though they insert the word *legal* in front of it.

This situation in which human beings are forced to sit in a cage while they wait to be taken to their deaths has a name, even if the courts of the United States refuse to use it. The Supreme Court justices well know the noble words of the Eighth Amendment of the Constitution, which states that our society will not practice cruelty. But—with the exception in recent times of Justices Thurgood Marshall and William Brennan—the Court has ruled that killing human beings for their crimes is not cruelty. It has even gone so far as to state in *Furman v. Georgia* that state killings are "not inconsistent with our respect for the dignity of men." Nor has the Court considered it cruel to kill those who are as young as sixteen years of age at the time of their crime and, until very recently, the mentally handicapped.[38] Neither the courts, the prosecutors, nor the legislatures can bring themselves to call it cruelty. They hide behind euphemisms: carrying out justice, being tough on crime, getting closure for victims' families, practicing "an eye for an eye," which they claim God tells us to do in the Bible.

But the family of Dobie Williams and the nine hundred[39] other families whose loved ones have been electrocuted, lethally injected, hung, or gassed to death in the United States during the past twenty-seven years know the real name. The Human Rights Commission of the United Nations calls it by its real name. The countries in the world that now outlaw the death penalty know its name. And Eleanor Roosevelt and the committee that drafted the text of the United Nations Universal Declaration of Human Rights in 1948 also knew its name.

Joseph O'Dell is being tortured.

He is not flogged or stretched on the rack or burned with hot pincers. He will appear to crawl painlessly onto the gurney to be injected with the sodium pentothal that will put him to sleep while the state of Virginia kills him. But for human beings who are mindful and conscious, and who anticipate over and over again the death that is forced on them, what word other than *torture* seems appropriate? The best definition of torture that I know has been given by Amnesty International, which defines it as "an extreme mental or physical assault on someone who has been rendered defenseless."

I think of Dobie Williams brought to the death chamber once, twice, three times; and once, twice getting a reprieve and returning to his cell to wait for death once again; and then, on the third try, finally being killed.

What blinds us to the reality of torture that state killing entails? Is it the same blindness that allowed our forebears to practice slavery without flinching? How else could they walk through the town square and watch as African slaves were auctioned to the highest bidder and not be horrified?

Do you see that mother weeping as her children are taken from her?

Do you see that girl in chains, and do you know what will happen to her when her white master lusts for her?

Do you see?

Yes, but you must understand, they're not human like us. They don't have feelings as we do. Our whole agricultural system would collapse without slavery. And haven't you read in the book of Genesis that it's part of God's plan for these dark-skinned people to serve us? Is not this their role and destiny in life?

It is usually only in hindsight that societies recognize that they have engaged in torture. Until then, torture is normal and justified and even sanctioned by religious beliefs. I remember reading about a member of the military in Algeria whose task it had been to extract information from the "enemies of the government" and then to "dispose" of them. He told how he would gag and tie these persons hand and foot and fly them over the sea in a helicopter, split open their abdomens with a machete, and push them into the sea. It's what "everybody was doing," he said, and at the end of the day he'd go home to his family and not think any more about it. In the future, when we look back on this practice of the death penalty, won't the "strap down" teams and death row guards and wardens have their own stories to tell about how they participated in the torturous deaths of fellow human beings?

They are already telling the stories.

Recently, Warden Jim Willett, who participated in the execution of eighty-nine prisoners in Texas, spoke at length with a journalist from *The New York Times,* telling of his burdened soul;[40] and Warden Don Cabana candidly tells of his anguish in officiating at executions at Parchman Penitentiary in Mississippi. The title of his book says it all: *Death at Midnight: The Confession of an Executioner.* He did not pull the switch himself, but he knew he was an active participant in the killings. At the time, he justified his actions, he says, telling himself that he was "just doing my job," but deep in his soul he knew he was doing something terribly wrong. After killing two men, he couldn't do it anymore and quit his job as warden.[41]

Lori and I are talking on the phone several times a week, but one day the phone rings and it's Joe O'Dell. "I wrote a letter to the pope," he says, and gives a little laugh. "I asked him to come and see me in Mecklenburg. I know he's real busy and all, but, look, I'm the kind of person he really cares about." And he says that the prison and governor and everybody are "mad as hell" about all the thousands of faxes (ten thousand) the Italians are sending on his behalf. "Those Italians are something else," he says, and he's glad that Lori's hard work is paying off.

Joe's voice is deep and resonant, and his intelligence comes through. He's easy to talk to, and he speaks of Lori with affection. I can tell by the gentle way he talks about her that his feelings for her go deep. I've noticed how often relationships between women and death row inmates flare into romantic love. In such an intense crucible of life against death, the dross of trivial interactions burns off quickly and passionate love flares. In the exchange of letters between Lori and Joe, I can trace the growth of trust and openness. Lori the legal advocate, at first cautious and wary, demanding answers from O'Dell about his past and his crimes and insisting on the truth and telling him that he'd better not lie, that she'd find out if he tried to hide things, that he must come clean with her. And Joe the prisoner, with his miserable history of crimes and bungled relationships, trying hard to be scrupulously honest. Joseph O'Dell loved women, and on his last night of freedom at the County Line Lounge, he was talking to two women at the bar, and even in Mecklenburg Correctional Center he nurtured relationships with women through letters and phone calls. He had been on death row for seven years when Lori Urs, the new volunteer at Centurion Ministries, arrived unannounced in his life. That was in the fall of 1993, and he could never forget the exact date when she came into his life because she was the first to bring hope that he would be vindicated. She could summon allies he never dreamed of. She sparked life into everybody. His appellate attorneys had kept him alive—no small thing—but Lori had spurred them to new initiatives, such as the press conference in Richmond.

At first in his letters he was careful to answer all her questions truthfully and took polite pains to thank her for the "enormous" amounts of time she devoted to reading his thirty-one volumes of trial transcripts. She had even purchased a dictionary of legal terms so she could look up words she didn't understand. In his early letters to Lori, he calls her "little lady," then "friend," then "best friend," and then he can't tell her enough how much he appreciates her coming into his life and how he could trust her more than anybody else in his whole life, ever. But it took her longer to trust, and it took time for her to confide that she had been recently divorced and then, after many months, to send him her photograph. When I do finally meet Joe, he will tell me that when he first saw Lori's picture, he couldn't believe his good luck, that someone so devoted to saving his life was also so beautiful; from the beginning he could see the little girl in her, naïve about the evil in the world, and he saw himself as her protector. When other inmates tried to get her address, he never gave it to them. He knew that she admired him for the way he managed to eke out a life of dignity on death row, and he was dumbfounded by her loyalty to him and the energy of her sheer, relentless will. She simply refused to accept that he would be killed by the state of Virginia. "Look, just look at all that has happened because of her," he said to me. "Even the pope is on my side and the Italian parliament, and who next?"

Once during a visit, he showed Lori a certificate of Indian marriage he had designed, which declared them husband and wife. It wasn't a real certificate, but Joe submitted it to the prison officials in hopes that he and Lori, as spouses, would be allowed a contact visit. But the fake certificate introduced great complications. As a paralegal, Lori was allowed to visit Joe frequently and privately, which meant no correctional officer could overhear conversations, and letters stamped "Legal Mail—Confidential" would arrive unopened and uncensored. Privacy in communication was hard to come by in Mecklenburg Correctional Center, and when prison officials got wind of the marriage certificate, they were quick to call into question the legal status of Lori's relationship to Joe. Lori explained to me that from the beginning, her relationship with the officials at Mecklenburg had been strained. "They wanted me out of there as a legal advocate because I was uncovering evidence in Joe's case and raising a lot of questions." The officials used the Indian marriage certificate to claim that Lori Urs and O'Dell were sweethearts and so should be reclassified, which meant the end of private correspondence and visits. "Which was pure disaster for Joe from a legal point of view," Lori says, "because prison guards would be able to hear everything we said and feed to commonwealth prosecutors every piece of evidence we turned up, every strategy we planned." She says that the prison officials knew the certificate was fake but were using it to get rid of her as a legal advocate, so she had to file suit in federal court to safeguard her legal status. It was one more obstacle and complication—"as if we didn't have enough obstacles already"—and she was upset with Joe for showing the certificate to prison officials without consulting her. She won the suit and kept her legal status, but clearly prison officials were now her adversaries. "Of course," she says, "I'm sure they're upset as all get-out with all the international attention we're getting for Joe, and they'll do anything to get rid of me."

She roars with laughter. The power of the state had been so intractable against Joe that the interventions by the pope and the Italian parliament—such a sheer reversal of power—she found to be . . . what?

"Delicious."

December passes by, and I spend most of my days and nights with my sick friend, Ann. On Christmas Day and the last few days of the year, I cleanse and salve her fierce radiation burns. I'm a teacher, not a nurse, but I am learning to move efficiently to help her open the sterile gauze and gently apply the Silvadene on her raw burned chest three, four times a day. I speak quietly to her and sometimes sing to her, and each night we sit side by side on her bed and pray for healing. She's praying for a miracle, to be cured of this cancer, which began with a cell or two that went astray and incited other cells to mutiny. These enemy cells are silent and can be seen only in the fluid that collects in her lungs and in the lab reports, which she scrutinizes with her practiced doctor's eye. She knows about electrolytes and red and white blood cell counts and what the numbers mean. And she knows what cancer does to human beings, because during her twelve years as a nurse (before she became a doctor), she helped her patients who were dying of cancer; she knows the importance of controlling the pain, she knows how pain can sap strength and consciousness and poise. She instructs me that at the end the morphine will help her and tells me to work with the hospice nurse who will be there, and she tells me all this as the tears run down my cheeks and I can't stop them. Ever so gradually, I know but can't realize that the way things are going, she, my best friend in all the world, is going to die; but when I say *die,* my mind goes blank. Of course, I know that we all must die and I, too, will die one day. I watched my mama die; I was there and watched everything, and I learned from her about dying because she turned herself over to God, and I could tell she was surrendering to the next part of the adventure. But she was eighty-one years old and sick and couldn't travel or cook up gumbo or shrimp étouffée anymore, and she couldn't keep a room full of people captivated by her stories and jokes as she once could. And she, too, was a nurse like Ann and knew the medical prognosis long before Mary Ann, Louie, and I, her children, did. Her dying seemed like an unfolding that was natural and had to be. But Ann is not yet sixty years old and wants to live, and I can't comprehend how the cells got out of control and can resist her strong will, and the power of her imagination, and the force of her spiritual strength, so that no matter what she thinks or says or does, she can't stop the rampaging cells; and that's how she knows and then I know, too, that her dying must be God's will. Once I know that, I turn the energy of my prayer to align with God's love calling her home, and then all of my prayer is focused on letting her go and helping her to let go gracefully and not to hold back. An oxygen tank has made its way into the house, and friends are stopping by, looking stricken and bringing flowers. But soon she can't bear many visits, and I talk to friends on the phone and tell them to pray for her but not to come over. And when I go with her to the hospital for bone and liver scans and we wait together for the report, I think of Joe O'Dell, who reads his life-or-death scans in Fourth Circuit and Supreme Court verdicts. Only Joe O'Dell is not sick. If he dies, he will not simply die, he will be killed—which is not, I believe, God's will and must be resisted fiercely and actively every step of the way.

In the last days of December, the phone rings.

"Can you come with me to Italy?" It's Lori again, pulsing with energy. "Because Luciano Neri, a member of the Italian parliament, is inviting me to talk in various cities about Joe's case."

Neri, a member of the Italian Human Rights Commission, had read a tiny article in an Italian newspaper about O'Dell, traveled to the United States to gather information about the case, and met Lori Urs; he has been the prime mover in Italy of O'Dell's cause.

Lori says, "These Italians are wonderful. They're paying my way and everything—and guess what? The Italian parliament has issued a formal resolution on behalf of Joe, and Luciano's telling me the European Parliament is also planning to speak out for him to Governor Allen. Helen, the European Parliament! Isn't it amazing that there are all these European leaders who see the injustice Virginia is doing to Joe O'Dell, while here in the United States, politicians and the courts don't blink an eye about killing him? I was a babe in the woods about the criminal justice system until I got involved with Joe's case. Look, Helen, you just have to come with me to Italy! You'd be a good draw card for the press because *Dead Man Walking* was a huge success in Italy, huge! And the members of the Italian parliament are going to arrange for us to visit the Vatican and maybe even have an audience with the pope. Just think! You'll have a chance to talk to the pope face-to-face about the death penalty. I mean, of course he'll see you, because isn't the pope the number one head honcho Catholic in the world and you're a Catholic nun, and aren't popes and nuns, well, you know, tight?"

I have to laugh.

Lori continues.

"Maybe that's one good thing that can come out of Joe's terrible situation—bringing you and the pope together. Sugar! Imagine after we get to all those cities in Italy to rouse support for Joe's cause. You know, these Italians are strong on human rights. I heard that some priest in Italy got over a million signatures for Paula Cooper, the sixteen-year-old girl in Indiana who got the death penalty for killing her Sunday school teacher.[42] The Italians got her off death row, isn't that fantastic? So, you just have to come to Italy with me. We'll be an unbeatable team. We'll be Thelma and Louise!"

"I can't go," I say to Lori, and explain how sick Ann is, though I'd jump at the chance to talk to the pope about the death penalty. So she suggests I write a letter to the pope and when she goes to Italy she'll get the letter delivered "right into the pope's lap."

Which is exactly what happens.

I write my letter to the pope on January 1, 1997, and Lori Urs gets it delivered to John Paul II on January 22. Later, a Vatican official who was present told me, "The pope read every word of your letter."

Since I first walked out of Louisiana's execution chamber in 1984, I had been looking for a chance to talk to the pope about Catholic teaching on the death penalty, because everywhere I could see the disastrous results of the Catholic Church's support for capital punishment. Legislators freely used church teaching to legitimate their pro–death penalty stance, as did district attorneys, judges, and professors, and even priests solidly upheld the state's right to kill criminals for "grave" crimes in order to protect society—exactly the argument made by politicians and district attorneys, who claim that the death penalty is "tough on crime."

As I began to give talks around the country to raise consciousness about the death penalty, I came to expect that support for capital punishment from Catholic groups would be every bit as strong as support from those who never set foot in church.

So when Lori Urs gives me an invitation to write to the pope, I know I have to do it. I knew that to shift the foundational principles of church teaching on the death penalty would take nothing less than a clear mandate from the church's top leader. It takes a big push to bend a river that has been going in a certain direction for 1,600 years. I would have to find the words to persuade the pope to reformulate the criteria that had been used to uphold the death penalty in the church since the fifth century. We needed a paradigm shift.

Many times in his visits around the world, Pope John Paul II had spoken out on behalf of the "inviolable dignity" of human persons made "in God's image" and against the "culture of death" with its penchant for violence. On numerous occasions he had personally intervened with governors, begging to spare the lives of individuals facing death; but he had never uttered one word publicly against the death penalty. In the pope's past four visits to the United States, whenever he spoke of "pro-life issues"—abortion, euthanasia, and physician-assisted suicide—he never included the death penalty. In his 1995 encyclical, *Evangelium Vitae* (*Gospel of Life*), Pope John Paul II had challenged the use of the death penalty more than any other pope, saying that its practice in modern society should be "rare, if not non-existent." And he had spoken eloquently about the "sacred and inviolable character" of all human life and encouraged societies to use incarceration in place of state killing, because such "bloodless means" were more in accord with the dignity of the human person. When I read the words of his encyclical, I felt hope rise in my heart that here, at last, the Catholic Church was going to take a principled stand against state killing. But my hopes crumbled when I saw the words of the pope in paragraph 56, in which he stated that in cases of "absolute necessity" governments were justified in killing their citizens. Such words, I knew, would give death penalty proponents all the support they needed to legitimate their use of the death penalty. *Of course,* they would argue, the death penalty they were seeking for a particularly heinous crime was an "absolute necessity" for the safety of society. Harry Connick Sr., former district attorney in New Orleans and a practicing Catholic who went for the death penalty every chance he got, has said often and publicly that in his opinion, death penalties are all too few and hard to come by, so every death sentence sought is an "absolute necessity."

And Connick has had New Orleans archbishop Philip M. Hannan back up his quest for death sentences. At Connick's invitation, Archbishop Hannan drafted a letter citing traditional church teaching and assuring Catholic jurors that they could vote for a death sentence "in good conscience." During every capital trial, Connick or one of his assistants would read the archbishop's letter.

Archbishop Hannan had served as chaplain to paratroopers in World War II, and whenever I discussed the death penalty with him, he would explain to me that our society needed the death penalty to protect ourselves against terrorists. "You've never seen war, but I have, and I know how these terrorists think. Death is the only language they understand."

I had to wonder at this, because terrorists seem perfectly willing to impose the death penalty on themselves. I pointed out to Archbishop Hannan that he would be hard-pressed to find even one terrorist on Louisiana's death row, but he wouldn't budge. His moral reasoning, it seems to me, derived more from a military manual than from a book of theology.

So here I was, beginning to make my first public efforts to educate the people of Louisiana about the death penalty, only to square off against my own archbishop as a formidable opponent. For over ten years, Archbishop Hannan's support for the death penalty blocked other Louisiana bishops from issuing any substantive statement against the death penalty. Their statement, issued in the late 1980s, which accommodated the archbishop's views, was so weak and riddled with moral loopholes that any pro-death supporter in the Louisiana Legislature could quote it with enthusiasm—and many often did.

Beginning in 1974 and then in 1980, the U.S. Conference of Catholic Bishops had begun to express "pastoral concerns" about the death penalty, but in their statements they emphasized the "unfair and discriminatory" way state killing was practiced more than the moral principles that shored it up. In their opening paragraph, they upheld the state's right to kill—right in line with traditional teaching—even as they lamented that state-sanctioned killing prolonged the "cycle of violence" in society. Of course, as "shepherds and chief teachers" of the Catholic flock, the bishops felt an obligation to uphold traditional Catholic teaching, but they were beginning to raise questions and to express their concerns publicly about the death penalty, which was hopeful. They were not alone. More and more, Catholic bishops in countries around the world were expressing concerns about the death penalty, and some individual bishops in the United States—Walter Sullivan in Virginia, Tom Gumbleton in Michigan, Joseph Fiorenza in Texas—visited death rows, attended anti–death penalty vigils, and spoke up forcefully in opposition to the death penalty as a matter of principle. I welcomed their voices. But in such settings, bishops' voices were few. Most Catholic support for my work came from my fellow nuns and Catholic peace and justice groups such as Pax Christi. At our first death penalty protests in Louisiana, I came to expect, for the most part, not churchgoers, Catholic or otherwise, but members of the American Civil Liberties Union and Amnesty International. My main tutor on the subject of human rights was Magdaleno Rose-Avila, then Amnesty International's southern regional director, who taught me Amnesty's principled opposition to the death penalty and why governments can never be trusted to kill their citizens. I also joined the board of the National Coalition to Abolish the Death Penalty, and there I learned how to hone good, solid arguments for abolition.[43]

Archbishop Hannan had weighed in so heavily in dissent with the U.S. Conference of Catholic Bishops' 1980 statement on capital punishment that he was featured on national television. But the archbishop's support for the death penalty went far beyond public statements. He sent to the trial of Willie Watson, an indigent black man, two priests to persuade the jury not to listen to Jesuit priests who were urging them to vote for life. The archbishops' priests prevailed. The jury sentenced Willie Watson to die, and he was killed by the state in the electric chair on July 24, 1987. But before he was killed, Willie Watson wrote a letter to Archbishop Hannan saying that he thought it was "wrong" for him to have sent the "two old priests" to argue for his death, and he asked the archbishop to send a letter to the pardons board to urge them to grant clemency, which Archbishop Hannan promptly did. Evidently, despite his strong pro–death penalty rhetoric, the archbishop didn't want *real* people to be killed. After Watson was condemned to death at his trial, his mother, referring to the priests' testimony, told the press: "Ain't nobody who's of God want to see anybody killed."

With the Catholic Church I settle into a long, patient, and unrelenting dialogue to help my church realign its teaching with the non-violent Gospel of Jesus. I recognize that from the roots up, the very principles of church teaching on the death penalty will have to be changed, so I jump at the chance to have a direct dialogue with the pope.

The long tradition of Catholic support for the death penalty can be traced directly to the fourth century, when Emperor Constantine legitimized Christianity and Christianity all too quickly embraced the "ways of Empire." Once Christians were no longer the victims of Rome's death penalty and had assumed imperial power, they wielded the sword against their "enemies" as ferociously as the Romans had ever done. Augustine, bishop of Hippo (354–430), was one of the first church leaders to legitimate the use of violence by declaring that the wicked might be "coerced by the sword." And as quick as a brushfire, "enemies" who deserved to be "coerced" began to spring up everywhere. The church immediately added to the list of traditional enemies (thieves, marauders, traitors, and murderers) new kinds of enemies: blasphemers, heretics, pagans, infidels, and "witches." This right and duty to "coerce" by the use of violence soon became normal in the Crusades, the Inquisition, the "conversion to the faith" of indigenous people—and the hanging, gassing, shooting, electrocution, and lethal injection of criminals—a path that led straight to the death row cell of Joseph O'Dell.

The nonviolent Gospel of Jesus, with its emphasis on forgiveness and love of one's enemies and the "least of these," barely had a chance to spark and take hold before it was snuffed out by the church's embrace of the "ways of Empire." In the United States in the beginning of the twentieth century, only a handful of Quakers and Anabaptists refused to use violence in any form; and in the Catholic Church, only Dorothy Day and a few of her colleagues adhered unconditionally to Jesus's command never to demean, hurt, or to kill one's enemy. In Catholic circles, Dorothy Day was almost a solitary voice speaking out against the killing of Sacco and Vanzetti, Julius and Ethel Rosenberg, Richard Bruno Hauptmann, and Nazi war criminals.[44]

Dorothy Day was not a hero of the Catholic Church in the 1950s when I was a student at St. Joseph Academy in Baton Rouge. The traditional Catholic teaching about the death penalty, which I learned, came directly from St. Thomas Aquinas (1225–1274). In *Summa Contra Gentiles,* Aquinas had written: "The civil rulers execute, justly and sinlessly, pestiferous men in order to protect the state."

I wrote into my notebook and my conscience that the death penalty was not murder because it was a form of self-defense for society, an exception permitted under the Fifth Commandment (Augustinian version: "Thou shalt not kill"), which condoned what it termed "just wars," also considered a form of self-defense. Thomas Aquinas taught that the killing of "evildoers" was lawful when "directed to the welfare of the whole community." He also said that when a lawful authority kills an evil person, Christ's command to love is not broken, because "by sinning man departs from the order of reason, and therefore falls away from human dignity . . . and falls somehow into the slavery of the beasts, so that he may be disposed of according to what is useful to others. . . . Therefore, although it be evil in itself to kill a man who preserves his human dignity, nevertheless to kill a man who is a sinner can be good, just as it can be good to kill a beast."[45]

Belief in eternal life and saving one's soul were paramount in church teaching in those days, and I had written more pages in my religion notebook about what I had to do to "get to heaven" than any other subject. Like every other good Catholic, I well knew the requirements. I knew that one mortal sin could throw me into hell, where I would be barred forever from the beatific vision of God and the wonderful fun and happiness everyone in heaven would be having for all eternity—without me. That was negative motivation, but somehow the positive motivation never seemed quite as strong. "Love your neighbor" was taught as being important, but other than family, church community, and friends, the "neighbor" remained blurry. Certainly "pestiferous" criminals did not qualify as "neighbors."

Augustine had spoken of the death penalty as a form of charity: "Inflicting capital punishment . . . protects those who are undergoing it from the harm they may suffer . . . through increased sinning, which might continue if their life went on."

I never questioned the church's teaching about the death penalty.

Nobody in those days questioned Catholic teaching about *anything*. It was the 1950s, and criminals in Louisiana—mostly African Americans convicted of crimes against white people—were being electrocuted in Louisiana's portable electric chair, which traveled from parish to parish around the state. I don't remember anybody—Mama, Daddy, teachers, priests—ever mentioning these executions.

But then, before Vatican II (1962–1965) opened up the Catholic Church to social issues, no one was discussing issues of social justice—even the Jim Crow segregation laws in place everywhere. The official church never questioned that African Americans were forced to sit in the balconies of theaters (the "crow's nest") and the backseats of buses, even the backseats of churches. Blacks, it seemed, sat in the back of *everywhere* whites were present.

Sixteen hundred years is a long, long time for a religious body to uphold state killing, and the principles on which Catholic teaching has endured for so many centuries are clearly enunciated: *For the protection of society, the state has the right to kill those who have committed "grave" crimes.* Catholic teaching always stressed self-defense of society more than revenge or divine retribution as the reason for capital punishment, though in popular piety, God's "just punishments" was always writ large, with God pictured as Divine Judge so intent on "justice" that "He" (always imaged as male) was willing to accept the death of his own son as atonement for human sinfulness. The theological reasoning went that because a Divine Being had been offended, the offense was infinite, so only a divine being could offer fitting infinite reparation—no mere "creature" sacrifice would do. So surely such an expiation-seeking God would not quibble about throwing a guilty mortal into hell for all eternity—a theme stressed by DA Harry Connick Sr. when he debated me on the issue of the death penalty on a New Orleans television program. He reasoned that if a just God could punish wayward souls by condemning them to an eternity of hellfire, surely as DA he was justified in seeking the death penalty for criminals. He explained that the punishment he sought was a lesser punishment than burning in "unquenchable" fire for all eternity. Besides, Connick reasoned (as judges of the Inquisition once reasoned), imposing the death penalty could have the salutary effect of giving murderers time to repent and save their souls from hell.

When I first heard Connick express this idea, I was so appalled that I hardly knew how to respond. On reflection, however, I have found his argument helpful because it so transparently reveals the image of God that hovers behind many religious believers' support for the death penalty.

Is God vengeful, demanding a death for a death? Or is God compassionate, luring souls into love so great that no one can be considered "enemy"?

Since I had discovered that the Gospel of Jesus inaugurated a radically new community that included everybody and where no person was considered to be "outside the pale" of humanness, my soul expanded and I felt more compassion toward all sorts of people, even criminals, and even toward the ravaged earth itself and species threatened daily with extinction.[46] With such compassion growing in me, how could I worship a God less compassionate than I? This compassion had lured me in 1981 into the lives of indigent, struggling African Americans in a housing project in New Orleans and from there onto death row, a journey I recounted in *Dead Man Walking* and a journey I continue today. On this path I have learned that love, far from being passive in the face of injustice, is a vibrant force that resists and takes bold action to "build a new society within the shell of the old," as Dorothy Day used to say.

The Catholic Church has not been the only Christian denomination to teach support for the death penalty. Until the last quarter of the twentieth century, most mainstream Christian denominations in the United States blessed the state's right to kill criminals.

For Catholics, a wave of new consciousness about the death penalty began to build in the 1960s. At first, the wave was a mere trickle of insight, but it ran clear and pure and gathered force until it led to principled opposition to the death penalty. The clear stream of insight was this: Human persons have "inviolable" dignity and human rights simply because they are persons—no matter what acts they commit. This fundamental principle had first been spelled out in 1948 in the United Nations Universal Declaration of Human Rights, and Pope John XXIII was the first pope to grasp its importance. In his 1963 encyclical, *Pacem in Terris*, he wrote: "Any human society . . . must lay down as a foundation this principle: every human being is a person . . . and has rights . . . which are universal, inviolable, and inalienable. . . ."

But the problem I kept encountering among Catholics was the thinking that "inviolable" dignity and human rights belonged rightly to the innocent, but not to the guilty. Murderers had certainly not respected the human rights of their victims, the thinking went; so why should society respect their rights?

But Pope John XXIII made no such distinction between rights of the innocent and rights of the guilty. In *Pacem in Terris*, he stated that human persons, simply because they are human beings, have rights that can never be wrested from them, and he looked to the United Nations Universal Declaration of Human Rights to spell out those rights:

> Article 3: Everyone has the right to life . . .
> Article 5: No one shall be subjected to torture or to cruel, inhuman or degrading treatment or punishment.

Pope John XXIII called the Universal Declaration of Human Rights "one of the most important acts accomplished by the United Nations Organization."

It was to be expected when Article 3 of the Universal Declaration was debated back in the 1940s that such a declaration, which granted *everyone* the right to life without qualification, would provoke debate, and one of the first proposed amendments was that an exception ought to be made in the case of criminals lawfully sentenced to death. Eleanor Roosevelt urged the committee to resist this amendment, arguing that their task was to draw up a truly universal charter of human rights toward which societies could strive. She foresaw a day when no government would kill its citizens for any reason. The UN in its founding charter had proclaimed its "faith in . . . the dignity and worth of the human person," the foundational belief that made all the other rights possible. The rights were articulated under the guidance of French lawyer René Cassin, who insisted that the inalienable human rights that all persons have must be *protected from governments,* which are all too prone for various political reasons to punish citizens with death. By stating that the right to life is inalienable, the UN Declaration said, in effect, that there are some rights, such as the right to life, that are so intrinsic to human beings that state governments do not have the right to *alienate* or pry away those rights for certain kinds of behavior. No society, therefore, has power or jurisdiction either to *invest* citizens with these rights for good behavior or to *take away* these rights for bad behavior.

Thus far, this has certainly not been the position of the Catholic Church, which has begun every doctrinal pronouncement about the death penalty by asserting that the "state has the right to take life" for crimes it deems "grave" or "grievous." Until Pope John XXIII and the Second Vatican Council ushered in new consciousness, the Catholic Church had a history of making short shrift of human rights and did not recognize people's right to religious freedom until the last half of the twentieth century. In 1791, Pope Pius VI condemned the French declaration of human rights, in part because it advocated religious freedom; and in the nineteenth century, Pope Gregory XVI rejected freedom of conscience as a "mad" idea. Like human rights, the idea of democracy did not gain legitimacy in the Catholic Church until very modern times. In 1864, Pius IX had drawn up a *Syllabus of Errors,* which listed "democracy" as one of the "principal errors" of the time.

But Vatican II cut across such retrograde thinking and plunged the church as an active participant into global efforts for social justice and peace. In such an atmosphere, where questions about human rights were always at the fore, the church could not help but be affected by dramatically changing attitudes about the death penalty. Over the past sixty years, the number of countries that have abolished the death penalty in law or in practice has risen exponentially. In 1957, about a decade after the Universal Declaration of Human Rights was given to the world, only six countries in the world did not impose the death penalty, but by the year 2000 the number of abolitionist countries had risen to seventy-two; now, in 2004, that number is eighty.[47] Leadership in the abolition movement has come from Europe, which in 1950 gave birth to the European Convention on Human Rights, which prohibited not only the practice of the death penalty, but also the extradition of prisoners to countries where they faced death as a punishment.[48] In 1997, the Council of Europe made abolition of the death penalty a requirement of membership, and this sparked a dramatic shutting down of death chambers among former members of the Soviet Union.[49] Russia, when it applied for membership in the Council of Europe in 1996, immediately put in place a moratorium on all executions; and in 1999, President Boris Yeltsin commuted the death sentences of over seven hundred death row prisoners.

Such dramatic evolution in global attitudes toward the death penalty has, of course, impacted the consciousness of the Catholic Church, and in his encyclical *Evangelium Vitae* Pope John Paul II signaled the increase of worldwide opposition to the death penalty as a "sign of hope."

On January 1, 1997, I wrote the following letter to Pope John Paul II:

Dear Holy Father,

The very first words I write in this new year are to you. May the Spirit of Christ continue to strengthen you and give you joy in your awesome vocation and responsibilities.

Thank you for raising your voice on behalf of Virginia death row inmate, Joseph O'Dell. Though it is hard to point to exact causality, there is no doubt in my mind that your intervention helped to save his life. He was not executed on December 22. On December 17 the U.S. Supreme Court, which as a matter of course these days refuses to hear death penalty cases, unanimously granted a stay of execution and voted 8 to 1 to review Mr. O'Dell's case. Joseph O'Dell is alive, though still in grievous trauma from his ordeal. He cannot control his tears. "They tried to kill me," he keeps saying. While awaiting his turn to die, he watched two others, one a close friend, be taken to their deaths. Just across from his cell was the shower stall, and he watched in mute horror as his fellow inmates were forced to shower and put on "execution clothes" shortly before being led to their deaths. Joseph had asked me as spiritual advisor to accompany him to his death, and I kept looking at my airline ticket to Richmond as the days and hours ticked by bringing him to the brink of death. Thank God I did not have to use that ticket. I have already accompanied three men to their deaths in Louisiana's electric chair, and I have "seen with my eyes and touched with my hands" the suffering face of Christ in the "least of these" as they went to their deaths. I have seen the practice of the death penalty close up and have no doubt that it is the practice of torture. What all of the men I have accompanied have said when at last they died was, "I am so tired." Conscious human beings anticipate death and die a thousand times before they die, no matter what the "humane" method of death may be, even lethal injection, which is supposed to just "put you to sleep."

Interestingly, the lone dissent in the Supreme Court decision to hear the O'Dell case came from Catholic Justice Antonin Scalia, who is relentless in his pursuit of legalizing executions, even of juveniles and the mentally retarded, and who expedites the death process in the courts in every way he can. He seems to have no trouble squaring executions with his Catholic faith, and in this he is no exception. For 14 years I have been speaking to groups all across the United States about the death penalty, and, for the most part, find Catholics, including many priests, religious educators, and teachers supportive of government-sanctioned executions. Rarely is the death penalty questioned from pulpits at Mass, and "pro life," as it turns out, most often means pro innocent life, not guilty life. The death penalty is very much a poor person's issue (99% of the 3,100 souls on death row in the U.S. are poor), and I have found that as a general rule those involved with justice for poor people readily oppose the death penalty, whereas those separated from poor people and their struggles readily support it. They are more prone to see poor people as the "enemy" and to be willing to inflict harsh punishments to "control" them.

Your words on the death penalty in *Evangelium Vitae* have come as a fresh breeze. Your strong words on behalf of life even of violent offenders encourage church leaders to be more courageous in voicing gospel values in opposition to the death penalty and hopefully these words will make their way into classrooms and pulpits. Especially welcome were your words upholding the dignity of human life, the "sacred and inviolable character" that each human life possesses. In contrast, the U.S. Supreme Court in *Furman v. Georgia* upheld that retribution, even in its most extreme form, execution, is not "inconsistent with our respect for the dignity of men." How can one possibly subject human beings to torture and to death and yet respect their dignity?

Unfortunately, however, when in *Evangelium Vitae,* paragraph 56, you uphold the state's right to execute in cases of "absolute necessity," some pro–death penalty advocates such as Catholic District Attorney of New Orleans, Harry Connick, Sr., use those words to justify their vigorous pursuit of the death penalty. As the death penalty is practiced now, Mr. Connick has stated, the death penalty is "all too rare," so he feels that every death penalty that he succeeds in getting is an "absolute necessity." As Amnesty International has amply documented, whenever governments around the world punish criminals by killing them, they claim to act out of "absolute necessity." By way of contrast, one of the first acts of the Constitutional Court of South Africa was to unconditionally forbid state executions. The leaders of South Africa understand all too well that when governments are given the right to execute their citizens, invariably the deepest prejudices of the society exert full sway in the punishment of those considered the "dangerous criminal element." The United Nations Universal Declaration of Human Rights states in clear, unequivocal terms every human being's inalienable right not to be killed (Article 3) nor "subjected to torture" (Article 5). From the time of St. Augustine of Hippo, one of the first to argue that the "wicked" might be "coerced with the sword," we Catholics have upheld the right of governments to take life in defense of the common good. But, as you point out in *Evangelium Vitae,* the development in societies of penal institutions now offers a way for societies to protect themselves from violent offenders without imitating the very violence they claim to abhor. How can any government, vulnerable to undue influence of the rich and powerful and subject to every kind of prejudice, have the purity and integrity to select certain of its citizens for punishment by death? Even in a so-called developed country such as the U.S., for example, we are discovering how much the status of the victim plays a part in the decision to seek death as a punishment. The vast majority of people on death row in the U.S.—85%—are chosen for death because they killed white people; whereas, when people of color are killed (fully 50% of all homicides) not only is the death penalty seldom sought, but often there is not even vigorous prosecution of such cases. A society and its government would have to care equally about the life of all of its members to be entrusted with the death penalty, and we know that on this earth no society can make that claim.

I pray for the day when Catholic opposition to government executions will be unequivocal. I say this because I know that words of the law and words in church teachings can be used to justify and pursue the death penalty, and I have watched as these words become flesh in front of my eyes as I have watched human beings die at the hands of the state. "I just pray that God holds up my legs," each of the condemned said to me as they were about to walk to their deaths, and from the depths of my soul, from Christ burning within me, I found myself saying to them, "Look at me. Look at my face. I will be the face of Christ for you." In such an instance the gospel of Jesus is very distilled: life, not death; mercy and compassion, not vengeance. Surely, Holy Father, it is not the will of Christ for us to ever sanction governments to torture and kill in such fashion, even those guilty of terrible crimes. . . .

In the United States there is presently an initiative to gather and motivate Christian communities, Catholic and Protestant, across the country to become active in abolition of the death penalty. In the first Abolition Movement to abolish slavery in the U.S., Christian churches played a key role. Now the time has come to summon Christian churches to participate in the Second Abolitionist Movement to abolish state-sanctioned death. As I mentioned earlier about widespread Catholic support for the death penalty, surely there is much work to be done to enlighten hearts and awaken consciences. But I am full of hope. Over these past fourteen years of talking to groups I have found that when people are brought to a deeper level of reflection on the gospel of Jesus and can get real information about the death penalty, not just rhetoric from politicians or sound bites from media, overwhelmingly they reject the death penalty and choose life. A steering committee, of which I am a part, is planning national conference[s] for Christian churches. It would be wonderful if we could get vigorous and wholehearted participation of the Catholic community in this effort. Whatever you can do to encourage the Catholic Bishops to participate in this new initiative will be warmly welcomed. . . .

In closing, Holy Father, again, thank you for helping to save the life of Joseph O'Dell. I so appreciate your willingness to stand with the "least of these" as Jesus did. I so appreciate your close identification with the poor and struggling ones of earth. What a large heart and what strong faith in Christ you must have not to be overwhelmed by the sufferings of so many that you constantly encounter. May Mary, who brought Jesus to the world, comfort and sustain you as you continue her holy birthing task, bringing Jesus to our hungry, suffering world. My earnest prayers are with you.

In Christ,

Lori delivered my letter to the pope on January 22, 1997. Luciano Neri and other members of the Italian parliament had evidently been talking about my forthcoming letter and the press had mentioned it, so by the time Lori walked into the secretary of state's office in the Vatican, Monsignor Gabriele Caccia met her, saying, "I understand that you have a letter," which she promptly handed him. Later, Monsignor Caccia told me, "The Holy Father read your letter. He read every word."

At last.

One week after my letter was delivered, I wrote in my journal: "Big news. On Jan. 29 Cardinal Joseph Ratzinger, Prefect of the Congregation of the Doctrine of the Faith, announced that a change would be made in the Catechism to reflect recent 'progress in doctrine' about the death penalty."

The pope received my letter on January 22. Cardinal Ratzinger's announcement came on January 29. The change in the Catechism was officially promulgated September 8, 1997, on the occasion of the Latin edition. By this change in official teaching, bolstered by strong, unequivocal pronouncements against the death penalty by the pope, the Catholic Church at last takes its place among the many institutions and nations that stand in principled opposition to the death penalty and work to bring about its abolition.

My letter to the pope was only one small part of the dialogue about the death penalty taking place across the church. Increasingly, bishops' conferences across the world voiced concerns about government killings. From 1972 to 1998, the U.S. Catholic bishops, either individually or in conferences, issued over 130 statements against the death penalty. Other national Catholic conferences—Canadian, Irish, Filipino, and others—have gone on record in opposition. Perhaps my unique contribution to the dialogue was fourteen years of personal experience with perpetrators and victims' families, which enabled me to bring the pope close to the suffering and the contradictions inherent in the death penalty. I laid this suffering in the pope's lap, and his compassionate heart responded. Personal experience has a way of turning absolute-sounding moral formulas on their heads.

The change in the Catholic Catechism was effected by removing just a few words from the 1992 version—but the deletion of these words created the most substantive change in church teaching about the death penalty in 1,600 years. Following traditional teaching, the 1992 version of the Catechism had reiterated Thomas Aquinas's defense-of-society argument: "Preserving the common good of society requires rendering the aggressor unable to inflict harm. For this reason the traditional teaching of the Church has acknowledged as well-founded the right and duty of legitimate public authority to punish malefactors by means of penalties commensurate with the gravity of the crime, **not excluding, in cases of extreme gravity,**

the death penalty." Section 2266 of the revised Catechism now reads: "Legitimate public authority has the right and the duty to inflict punishment proportionate to the gravity of the offense." The words in bold print have been removed.

The omission changes everything, because Catholic teaching now says that no matter how grave (terrible, outrageous, heinous, cruel) the crime, the death penalty is not to be imposed. With that qualifying criterion taken away, whom then might governments kill? Killers of police officers? Or of children? Or of a room full of people? Or of a building full of people? Or . . . terrorists such as Osama bin Laden?

No one. Because in the church's view, the "extreme gravity" of the crime no longer serves as a qualifying criterion for governments to invoke when they wish to execute their citizens. The removal of this criterion represents a huge shift of moral perspective. It cuts the moral ground out from under Catholic politicians who advocate "restricted" use of the death penalty. It also undercuts the U.S. Supreme Court's claim that some crimes are so morally abhorrent, only the death of the perpetrator will satisfy society's need for retributive justice. Retributive justice, as the Catholic Church has always taught, has as its core purpose the restoration of moral order, but now the church envisions the restoration of social order in a holistic, life-giving way that eschews violence.

As Pope John Paul II pointed out in *Evangelium Vitae,* governments of modern societies must refrain from killing criminals because incarceration gives them a way to incapacitate violent offenders. The heart of Catholic teaching about capital punishment has always been about self-defense.

And its traditional teaching about self-defense has been governed by the moral principle of double effect, which states that the killing of another is justified only when violent force is the only way to prevent an immediate violent assault on others. If such preventive action brings about the death of the assailant, the killing is seen as a secondary effect, not the primary intent. The entire argument for self-defense changes, however, when violent offenders are incarcerated and thereby rendered defenseless. Where, then, is the threat of an immediate violent assault on citizens? Absent that threat, the act of deliberately killing a prisoner who has been rendered defenseless seems unnecessary and cruel. And I think this recognition of the true nature of government killing has been the catalyst that has led the church to its stance of principled opposition to capital punishment.

When my eyes first see the words of the revised text of the Catechism, my heart leaps. At last the river bends. With this seismic change, church teaching on the death penalty forever flows in another direction. At the end of the twentieth century, the official Catholic teaching about the death penalty has become aligned with the core value of the "inviolable dignity of the human person" that Pope John XXIII first illumined in *Pacem in Terris* forty years ago. At last my church upholds a moral position on the death penalty I can embrace. As stated in the 1997 Catechism:

LIMITS AND AIMS OF PUNISHMENT

2266 The efforts of the state to curb the spread of behavior harmful to people's rights and to the basic rules of civil society correspond to the requirement of safeguarding the common good. Legitimate public authority has the right and the duty to inflict punishment proportionate to the gravity of the offense. Punishment has the primary aim of redressing the disorder introduced by the offense. When it is willingly accepted by the guilty party, it assumes the value of expiation. Punishment then, in addition to defending public order and protecting people's safety, has a medicinal purpose: as far as possible, it must contribute to the correction of the guilty party.*

1897–1898

2308

DEATH PENALTY

2267 Assuming that the guilty party's identity and responsibility have been fully determined, the traditional teaching of the Church does not exclude recourse to the death penalty, if this is the only possible way of effectively defending human lives against the unjust aggressor.

2306

If, however, non-lethal means are sufficient to defend and protect people's safety from the aggressor,

*Cf. Lk 23:4–43.

authority will limit itself to such means, as these are more in keeping with the concrete conditions of the common good and more in conformity with the dignity of the human person.

Today, in fact, as a consequence of the possibilities which the state has for effectively preventing crime, by rendering one who has committed an offense incapable of doing harm—without definitively taking away from him the possibility of redeeming himself—the cases in which the execution of the offender is an absolute necessity "are very rare, if not practically nonexistent."*

Some theologians, in an effort to assure Catholics that traditional teaching on the death penalty remains unchanged, go to great lengths to explain that the Catechism revision has not changed the church's "core doctrine" on the death penalty, only its practical or "prudential" application. In other words, they argue that the church now teaches that the death penalty, while still justifiable in principle, is inappropriate in practice—most of the time. Nothing's really changed in church teaching, they argue; there may still be circumstances, albeit rarely, when state-approved capital punishment is acceptable. And if reading that kind of split-level thinking makes your soul weary, it's because it's confusing, and it arises from a desire to hold on, no matter what, to Catholic traditional teaching on the death penalty. But if in principle the church still holds that in some instances governments are allowed to execute their citizens, we can be sure that government officials will be quick to summon that principle to justify seeking the death penalty for crimes they consider particularly heinous. But you won't catch Pope John Paul II using such obfuscating language. Every chance the pope gets, he comes out foursquare against the death penalty and asks Catholics to work toward its abolition—such as when he came to St. Louis in 1999.

The pope had visited the United States four other times, yet never once did he mention the death penalty. But that was before 1997, when the quantum change in the Catechism took place, a change I believe the pope initiated personally. In his bold declaration in St. Louis, Pope John Paul's opposition to government executions

*John Paul II, *Evangelium vitae,* 56.

could not have been more uncompromising: "A sign of hope is the increasing recognition that the dignity of human life must never be taken away, even in the case of someone who has done great evil. Modern society has the means of protecting itself without definitively denying criminals the chance to reform. I renew the appeal I made most recently at Christmas for a consensus to end the death penalty, which is both cruel and unnecessary."[50] I see a wave of fresh moral energy pulsing through the Catholic Church.

Of course, I know that simply quoting church authority does not change hearts and minds. The message of liberation and compassion of the Gospel of Jesus sprouts and grows only through moral persuasion and good example; and persuasion includes presentation of facts and information, reasoned arguments, solid theology, and compelling stories, especially about murder victims' families who find a way to transcend vengeance as they search for reconciliation and peace.

In the highest echelons of the Catholic hierarchy, the effects of the change in the Catechism have been instantaneous. On June 18, 2001, Pope John Paul II publicly congratulated the government of Chile, the latest nation at that time to abolish capital punishment: "I am pleased at the recent decision taken by the government and the legislative authorities—with the faithful collaboration of the Church—which abolished the death penalty, and it is to be hoped that this move will continue to promote a most zealous and unyielding respect for the life of every human being from conception to natural end."

Cardinals and bishops, once conspicuously absent from public debate on the death penalty, now appear regularly at press conferences and state legislative hearings to present moral arguments against the death penalty. And as these members of the hierarchy bring new energy and resolve to the issue, they also bring resources: lobbyists, pollsters, public relations experts, editors—enlisted to assist them in becoming persuasive voices in the death penalty debate. Diocesan Catholic newspapers, under close supervision of local bishops, now regularly run editorials and articles to inform Catholic readers about the development in church teaching on the death penalty; and some Catholic organizations, once staunch supporters of the death penalty, have begun to issue formal resolutions in opposition to the death penalty "in accordance with the teachings of the Church and in obedience to the Holy Father." The doctrinal change has also made an impact on the church's educational institutions from elementary schools up through colleges and universities.

On the international scene, the repercussions of the September 8 revision of the Catechism have made a noticeable impact. At the First World Congress on the Death Penalty in Strasbourg, France, June 2001, the Vatican delegation, headed by Monsignor Paul Gallagher, issued a no-holds-barred call for abolition of the death penalty: "The universal abolition of the death penalty would be a courageous reaffirmation of the belief that humankind can be successful in dealing with criminality and of our refusal to succumb to despair before such forces, and as such it would regenerate new hope in our very humanity."

Before the change in the Catechism, statements by church officials usually emphasized that the deliberate taking of *innocent* life was forbidden, but not the killing of the *guilty*. Happily, that has changed, and the long, hard work of changing hearts and minds of "people in the pews" can now be undertaken.

At last.

It makes me wonder what the impact might have been if current Catholic Supreme Court justices had been educated in the church's evolved understanding of the death penalty instead of their schooling in the traditional pro–death penalty teaching.

A troublesome question arises: What if the Catholic Church opposes the death penalty on moral grounds? What's that got to do with the juridical role of a Supreme Court justice who happens to be Catholic? Isn't it the role of the Court to decide death penalty cases—or any case—not according to the religious beliefs of the justices, but according to their interpretation of the Constitution? Justices, after all, are supposed to make *legal* judgments, not *religious* pronouncements. And the question of juridical propriety becomes even more complicated if authorities in a religious body try to pressure judges to follow certain moral doctrines. *Mr. Catholic Supreme Court Justice, the pope opposes the death penalty and so must you.*

In jurisprudence, this is a nightmare. It would make us into a theocracy, not a democracy.

But is there no interplay between judges' moral values, nurtured by the religious community to which they belong, and the moral perspective they bring to their interpretation of the Constitution? Is it possible to hermetically seal off jurisprudence from religious morals? If Supreme Court justices are practicing members of a religious community—currently several members are practicing Catholics—is it at all surprising that their moral views on any issue might be challenged and deepened when they participate in worship? Every Sunday at Mass, Catholics hear a reading of the sacred scriptures, which include some very challenging teachings of Jesus, such as "You have heard it said 'an eye for an eye,' but I say to you . . . forgive your enemies, pray for your persecutors. . . ." And on a regular basis at Mass, pastors give homilies or sermons the intent of which is to make connections between faith and life situations, and this sometimes means calling into question cultural values. Not infrequently during Sunday homilies, pastors read letters from the local hierarchy or quote statements of the pope, such as "My dear people, the Holy Father has once again spoken out against the death penalty, and I want to ask you to consider. . . ." Who would say that exposure to such moral considerations week after week has no influence whatsoever on the conscience of a jurist? Aren't legal decisions influenced by moral considerations?

One such moral consideration embedded in the Constitution is its prohibition against cruel and unusual punishment. The Supreme Court has said that what makes a punishment "cruel and unusual" is determined by an "evolving standard of decency." "Evolving" standard means that what may be considered cruel *is not fixed in standards that existed two hundred years ago.* Ideas about cruelty change as a society matures. And what better way for Supreme Court justices to encounter "evolving standards of decency" than to witness this evolution happening in the teachings of their own church?

The Catholic Church has evolved to a position of principled opposition to the death penalty in no small part because the church is a worldwide body whose members are influenced by changing currents of consciousness across the globe, especially once Pope John XXIII freed the church to see "signs of the times" in a positive way. In the 1960s, this new position opened the Latin American bishops to the devastating suffering of peasants in Latin America, victims of "structural injustice." So moved were the bishops by the suffering poor that they drew up the Medellín Document, in which they declared that the church's rightful place should be "on the side of the poor." Afterward, this newly recovered Jesus ideal of identifying with the marginalized and oppressed began to be voiced in classrooms and church pulpits. Twelve years after its first utterance, it made its way into my life through Sister Marie Augusta Neal, whose talk to my religious community in 1980 changed forever the spiritual trajectory of my life. I found my way to poor and struggling African Americans in New Orleans and from there to the poorest and most despised community of all—death row prisoners.

In the 1980s, a dramatic shift in world consciousness occurred around the concept of human rights, which as we have seen again through the impetus of Pope John XXIII had a resounding impact on Catholic teaching about the death penalty. Perhaps the clearest embodiment of the world's "evolving standards of human decency" is evidenced in the decision of the International Criminal Court to outlaw the use of the death penalty even for "war crimes," genocide, and "crimes against humanity."

Shaped by such consciousness, Russian president Vladimir Putin, when responding to the bombing of an apartment building in 1999 by "international terrorists" that killed three hundred Russians, did not call for a reinstatement of the death penalty in Russia.[51] On national television, Putin said, "Sometimes it seems I would have strangled them [the terrorists] with my own hands. But these are only emotions. As a man with a basic legal education, I am well aware that the toughening of punishment does not reduce crime. . . . Only the Almighty has the right to take life."

III

On March 22, 1997, my friend Ann died. All the pieces of color in the kaleidoscope of my life shifted, but now with a jagged empty space in the center. During the last year, I curtailed my activities so I could hover close to her, and now a lonely new freedom opened up. Several months after Ann's death, when Lori Urs called to talk, I was able to give her all the time she needed. She had bad news: The U.S. Supreme Court had ruled against O'Dell on the *Simmons* issue.[52]

Why? I ask. Hadn't the prosecutors blocked Joe's jury from knowing that he would get a life-without-parole sentence? Hadn't the Supreme Court ruled in *Simmons* that withholding that kind of information is against a person's constitutional right of "due process"?

Lori explains that in its decision, the Court was forced to admit that Joe's constitutional rights had indeed been violated at his trial, but they engineered a legalism of "retroactivity" to deprive Joe of a new sentencing trial. The Court reasoned that since *Simmons* was decided in 1994 but Joe's trial was held in 1986, the constitutional right would extend forward in time, but not backward. "They just flat-out drew an arbitrary timeline, and Joe fell on the wrong side of the line," Lori says. She explains that the Rehnquist Court has not disguised its eagerness to speed up executions. The legal process of appeals, they claim, is bogging down the courts and taking far too long. "They claim that the need for 'finality' on death cases takes precedence," Lori says.

I'm appalled. I always thought that if a constitutional right of a citizen is clearly established in a ruling, the timing of when the issue gets raised would be considered irrelevant. Lori says the Court's decision was heartbreakingly close—5–4. One more vote and Joe would have been granted a new sentencing trial.

But I can see she's not dwelling on the latest court debacle. She's pressing ahead to another issue she and O'Dell's lawyers are pursuing: getting the new, sophisticated DNA test, the PCR, on the semen sample. If the DNA test confirms that the sperm found in the victim's body is not O'Dell's, it would prove he had not raped Helen Schartner; the aggravating factor would evaporate, and so would his death sentence. In 1990, when DNA testing had been done on the blood on O'Dell's clothes, an attempt had also been made to test the semen, but results were inconclusive because the technology of the time required a fair amount of DNA matter, which the deteriorated samples failed to provide. But now, Lori tells me, she and the lawyers have enlisted the pro bono services of Barry Scheck, arguably one of the nation's foremost DNA experts, and he is drawing up an amicus curiae brief to persuade the courts to mandate the new test. He says that the new PCR test can be done on the sperm evidence in Joe's case even in its deteriorated state because the test requires such a microscopic amount of DNA material.

But it's the same old struggle: O'Dell trying to get DNA testing done and the prosecutors, backed by the Virginia courts, refusing to turn over the evidence. Lori says that the prosecutors simply claim that Joe is "disentitled" to the DNA test, and they also say that they doubt such old and deteriorated samples could produce accurate results. This, Lori explains, is "pure speculation," and she questions what credentials they have to evaluate the accuracy of the new DNA test.

I can feel the waters rising around Joseph O'Dell.

"If the courts don't allow the DNA testing," I ask, "what recourse does Joe have?"

"The governor," Lori says.

Bad news.

Governor George Allen supports the death penalty.

"If the governor denies, how much time does Joe have?"

"Not much. Maybe only a month or two. It's June now, so they could set a death date as early as July or maybe August. It all depends on how long the courts take. If the state courts refuse to grant the test, we're going to the federal courts. Hopefully Barry Scheck's amicus brief will generate serious attention in federal courts or even with Governor Allen. Scheck is also writing a letter to Governor Allen, and we're hoping he'll do something for Joe. He has the power, and recently in at least two cases he's approved postconviction DNA testing for death row inmates who had strong innocence issues. Maybe if we can pitch it to him in the right way, and with the eyes of the international community looking on, maybe he'll do the right thing for Joe."

Lori sounds matter-of-fact. She obviously has more on her mind than Joe's legal issues.

Joe has proposed marriage to her, she says, and that's the real reason she wants to talk to me. What is she to do? She knows it's not the wisest thing in the world for a woman to marry a man in prison.

She likes Joe; she even loves Joe, she tells me. But she knows him only in a limited way. She has never been with him for longer than several hours, and she has visited him only on the other side of a plate of glass. They have never even touched, so how can she say yes to marrying him? she wonders.

I suggest that she try to discern the deepest emotions of her heart. Would she be inclined to marry him if he weren't facing death? Obviously she cares passionately about his life, but is she perhaps feeling that she should marry him so he can experience joy in his life before he is killed? Is it compassion or love? Or maybe it's both.

It must be confusing. I know it is strong inside her to want to give him happiness at such a horrible time, but they have had no way to test out their relationship as man and woman. He has shown his love for her in numerous ways, but does he love her mainly because she is such a faithful advocate for his cause? Is it like somebody dying of a disease who falls in love with his nurse?

She wants clarity. I suggest that she wait to see what happens with Joe. If he gets a new trial and freedom and the two of them have the possibility of life together, that would inform one kind of decision. But if he faces certain death, that would inform another kind of decision. I can tell Lori has a good head on her shoulders. She's clearly trying to consider all the angles, and she has a strong sense of self and passionate purpose. She's concerned about the impact such a marriage would have on her credibility in the legal profession. She has definite plans to go to law school and become a public defender, and she shudders to think what the tabloids would do with the story of a legal advocate who marries her death row client.

She ends the conversation by saying that if the courts turn down the request for DNA testing, then the governor is their only recourse and they'll do another press conference in Richmond. Will I come? She's hoping against hope that Governor Allen will mandate the DNA test. If a man's innocence is in question, she asks, why deprive him—and the state itself, for that matter—of the opportunity to definitively prove or disprove his guilt? The test won't even cost the state of Virginia anything, because Joe is offering to pay for the test himself at a laboratory approved by state prosecutors, Lori says.

On July 1, Lori calls. A death date has been set for Joe on July 23. His request for DNA testing has been turned down in state district court and is now before the Virginia Supreme Court, which is almost sure to deny. Will I come on July 10 to the press conference in Richmond? Barry Scheck can't come to Richmond, but he'll make a statement and answer the media's questions over a speakerphone. Joe's lawyers will give the legal history and read Joe's own statement if the prison won't allow him to phone in, and she'll talk about the international attention Joe's case has aroused. She gives a little laugh. "And you just get yourself there. You can talk about anything you want to."

Has it come to this? Another desperate press conference in Richmond?

On July 10, I catch a 5:00 a.m. plane to Richmond, and there's Lori as I come off the elevator in the hotel where the press conference is being held. She greets me with the news that yesterday the Virginia Supreme Court denied Joe's request for DNA testing, so it looks as though the bouncing ball of Joe's fate is pretty squarely in the governor's court. They'll file in federal courts straight up till the end, even to the Supreme Court again, though that's a long shot.

At the press conference, Joe's lawyers lay out the history of his futile twelve-year quest for a full evidentiary hearing on the evidence brought against him at trial and say that given the Virginia Supreme Court's recent refusal to grant Joe's request for DNA testing, they have no choice but to file in federal court a lawsuit to grant Joe entitlement to the evidence.

Joe's statement is simple and short. In it he implores Governor Allen to allow DNA testing on the sperm evidence and says, "When I was first arrested I begged to have a polygraph test to prove I was telling the truth, and this was denied me. All I have ever wanted in my case was for the truth to be told and for the true facts and evidence to be presented. This has never happened in twelve and a half years."

Barry Scheck's statement quotes from his letter to Governor Allen: "It would certainly be tragic and a travesty of justice if these tests offered exculpatory evidence for O'Dell after his death." The phrase *after his death* lets the governor know that should Joe be killed by the state without the chance to conduct DNA testing on the sperm, Joe's advocates will pursue a lawsuit to demand postmortem testing. Is the governor willing to run the political risk of refusing to allow a DNA test before O'Dell is killed—a denial that might come back to haunt him should a postmortem test reveal O'Dell's innocence? Why not just go ahead and get the DNA test done? It could all be over in two weeks, and these deeply troublesome questions could be settled.

Scheck spends most of his time with the press explaining how the new PCR testing works, its amazing track record of accuracy in past cases, and how O'Dell's case clearly warrants its use. A few short years after this press conference, Barry Scheck and Peter Neufeld's book, *Actual Innocence,*[53] will rock the consciousness of the American public by its compelling stories of 64 wrongly convicted people set free through DNA testing. As of October 1, 2004, that number has risen to more than 150.[54]

I'm not very hopeful for Joe when I leave the press conference and head to a Trappist monastery in Kentucky for a week of prayer. I give Lori the monastery telephone number in case she needs me. If the state of Virginia kills Joe, I have promised him and Lori that I'll be there. Some months ago, Joe had asked me to be with him at the end, but mostly he wanted me there so I could console and strengthen Lori. She has been so wholehearted and generous in trying to save his life that he worried about the emotional toll it would take on her if he was killed. While he was amazed at her fierce and relentless pursuit of justice for him—he had never seen anything like it—he sensed a fragility in her, an "innocence" that he feared would be devastated should all her efforts fail.

At the monastery, I descend into the silence and the prayer. Ann's death is still fresh, and much of my time at prayer is filled with grieving and aligning my soul to her loss. But Joe O'Dell is in my prayers, too, and as I chant the psalms with the monks, I'm struck by Psalm 56, which Joseph O'Dell must be praying mightily these days in sentiment, if not in words:

> Have pity on me, O God, for strong forces trample
>   upon me;
> all the day they press their attack against me . . . yes,
>   many fight against me.
> My wanderings you have counted; my tears are
>   stored in your flask. . . .
> rescue me from death, my feet, too, from stumbling;
> that I may walk before God in the light of the living.

On Monday, July 14, Lori calls the monastery. She reports that on the preceding Friday, Governor Allen denied Joe's request for DNA testing and issued a five-page statement explaining his denial.[55] Now only a very uncertain appeal to the federal courts stands between Joseph O'Dell and the black gurney waiting for him with its cruciform arms. Barry Scheck has filed his amicus brief, but it's a long shot. Everything now is a long shot. I pray for Joe's courage and for his peace in facing the death that will almost certainly be imposed on him. Even though I have accompanied four people into state killing chambers, it never gets easier. I am shocked each time it happens. Now I can't believe that it is happening to Joseph O'Dell, especially with all the haunting questions of his innocence.

I talk to Lori on July 21. She has decided to marry Joe. At least, she says, she can give him "one solid piece of joy" before he dies. Prison officials have become increasingly hostile to her, watching her every move, blocking her on every front, and allowing her to visit Joe only one hour a day. She says they haven't taken him yet to the waiting cells near the killing chamber where less than two years ago he came within a few days of being killed. All his clothes have been taken from him except his underwear, and he covers himself with his state-issued blanket. I suggest that perhaps his blanket might become his prayer shawl and that when he puts it around him, he can enter into a holy, protected space, shielded from the hateful forces all around him. Lori says that he'll like the symbolism. "He's a deeply spiritual man," she says. I'm thinking that she could use some protected space herself and, for that matter, so can I. I learned to go into that holy space when, alone and terrified, I first went into Louisiana's death house to accompany Patrick Sonnier to the electric chair; and in that cold house of legalized death, I managed to enter a circle of light where I felt calm and poised and strengthened. Love was in that space and protection, and I could abide in it, and I'm praying that Joe and Lori can enter that holy space, too. Some call it the presence of God. Some call it grace.

On July 22, I arrive at the airport around noon and go straight to Lori, who is waiting for me at the Hampton Inn in Emporia, a small town near Mecklenburg Correctional Center. As we get into Lori's red Cherokee to drive twenty or so miles to the prison, she fills me in on unfurling events. She hopes to pick up the marriage license from the courthouse later today, though the prison officials are keeping them dangling, thus far refusing to give permission for the wedding to take place. She's brought a pretty flowered dress to wear during the wedding ceremony. "Joe will like it," she says.

Joe is scheduled to die at 9:00 p.m. tomorrow night.

Lori is clinging to the hope that Governor Allen will still come through. He met with Joe's lawyers a couple of days ago and remarked publicly afterward that he was "impressed" with their arguments about "truth in sentencing." This was a new tack that the lawyers were taking. Governor Allen had made "truth in sentencing" a centerpiece of his gubernatorial campaign promises in 1993. Allen had actually used those words to support longer sentencing and abolishing parole. But Joe's lawyers ingeniously turned his tough-on-crime stance on its head. They showed him how the prosecutors at Joe's trial had misled the jury, disguising the truth that Joe would face a sure sentence of life imprisonment without any possibility of parole.

Had not Governor Allen promised to return "honesty and integrity" to the criminal justice system during his campaign, and wasn't this an opportunity to do just that? And think of the jurors, who now bore the burden of having sentenced O'Dell to death, the lawyers had argued. Wasn't it also clear that they had not been given the "truth" about the sentence he was to receive and so had been manipulated into choosing a death sentence?

I'm glad when Lori tells me that O'Dell's lawyers have found new grounds to keep a dialogue going with the governor, but I can't help wondering about the effect of the recent U.S. Supreme Court decision against Joe on the *Simmons* issue, in which the Court had thrown "truth in sentencing" to the winds. Lori's trying to be upbeat, and I realize that Governor Allen's public statement about being "impressed" with the arguments of Joe's lawyers is all she's got to hang on to. It's a mighty thin thread. Governors are notorious for standing behind court rulings to legitimize their actions. They never want to be accused of second-guessing the courts, especially the Supreme Court.

"Joe's attorneys explained to the governor," Lori says, "that the Supreme Court's decision against Joe on the *Simmons* issue was made on a 'legal technicality'—retroactivity—but that did not exempt Virginia from adhering to 'truth in sentencing' in state courts or the governor himself from adhering to the principle of his campaign promise."

It's early afternoon and we drive on 95 North through gray sheets of rain on our way to Mecklenburg prison. We talk about big things and trivial things: what the governor might do, why Lori chose the bright floral dress, Barry Scheck and the DNA, and how tomorrow morning we have to go to the courthouse to get the marriage license. She apologizes for the inside of her car, littered with papers, pop cans, and fast-food wrappers. I say that cars are like desks: They show how busy people are. "If they're too neat, I'm suspicious," I say. "I hardly ever have a neat car, and see this hard rain? I love it. It's the only way my car gets washed. Lucky for me it rains a lot in Louisiana."

Lori is stressed—how could she not be?—but she seems to be navigating her way well through this emotional firestorm. She's focused on the immediate future: the governor's forthcoming decision and her marriage tomorrow.

When we turn onto the road to the prison, I notice orange cones along either side of the road about five hundred yards out from the prison parking lot. Lori lets out a whoop. "Look at all these cones. They didn't have these here yesterday. Security alert!" And she bangs her hands on the steering wheel and laughs. "Prison officials have been soooo freaked out ever since the mayor of Palermo visited Joe."

Lori explains that Leoluca Orlando, the mayor of Palermo, was not content with merely speaking out in support of Joe. He personally called on him at the prison a few months before and even made Joe an honorary citizen of Palermo. Orlando is a no-nonsense guy who took on the Mafia a few years ago—and won. But maybe when the prison administrators heard his name and "Mafia" in the same sentence, it didn't register that he is *against* the Mafia and they pictured commando squads descending in helicopters to rescue Joe.

"Isn't this a hoot?" says Lori, and she has to laugh. But then she quickly turns serious. "Poor Joe, defenseless against the powers of the state of Virginia."

Armed guards approach the car and ask us to identify ourselves and state the purpose of our visit. Lori points to me and shows the official approval papers for my visit to Joe. The guard looks, then waves us on, but in the huge parking lot we're quite a distance away from the building. We locate a small umbrella among the items in Lori's car; the rain has slackened some, but we both know we're going to be two wet puppies when we enter the front gate.

Once inside, I follow Lori's lead through the security check. We show our driver's licenses, walk through the metal detector, and get patted down. In this place, *everybody* gets frisked, even the guards and the warden. I never saw a warden get frisked before. Maybe he's trying to set a good example, and I wonder if this frisking of the guards is effective in stemming the flow of drugs into the prison, a perennial problem in U.S. correctional facilities.

I make friendly small talk with prison personnel, looking them straight in the eye and asking how they're doing, and, hey, what about all this rain? From the time I first stepped into Louisiana's prison in 1982, I began to relate in a personal way with prison personnel, always showing them respect, even the unsmiling, glinty-eyed ones. But I don't see any unfriendly folks here, at least not to me. For Lori, I know it's a different story, not from the guards who process visitors into the prison, but from the big guys where the power dwells. Now that they have reclassified her status from legal advocate to girlfriend, there will be no more private visits. This is a big loss, since everything they say to each other can be overheard by a guard. She's still waiting to see if they have approved of her marriage ceremony tomorrow with Joseph. "If it happens, you can be sure it's going to be the tightest security wedding that ever took place in the world," she whispers after we've left the front building and are escorted to a white prison van that will take us back to the L-unit, where they are keeping Joe. The rain is now a soft drizzle, and everything has a gray look. Guards wear dark blue uniforms—just as in Louisiana. Lori whispers that at least by having this visit, Joe will get to dress in more than his undershorts.

Inside the building, we sign in and a guard behind a grated window takes our driver's licenses and puts them in a box. Accompanied by a guard, we walk down a short hallway and turn into a room, and there, behind glass, stands Joseph O'Dell. He's tall, has curly gray hair, and is older looking than I thought he'd be. His face is large, and so are his hands. He thanks me for making the trip, but his attention quickly locks on to Lori. He speaks through a phone on his side of the glass, and Lori speaks on the other. She says, "Look, Joe, no guard today."

Joe says, nodding toward me, "It must be the nun. They figure she won't try to break me out of here."

We laugh, but it's a tight laugh and short. Today is July 22, and tomorrow, if the state of Virginia has its way, Joseph O'Dell will be dead. Lori is not sure if this visit today will be her last one. I step back from the conversation and let them have time together. They pour out their love over the phones. Joe calls Lori "li'l darlin'." "I love you, my li'l squirt," he says, and she says that she loves him so much that she's going to marry him, and she tells him about the pretty flowered dress she's chosen to wear. His eyes well with tears. He puts a hand up to the glass.

"I so want to hold you close," Lori says. "Look into my eyes, Joe. My soul is in my eyes."

Lori looks around the room and says that this is one of the rooms where witnesses wait until they're called to the death chamber, and suddenly what was just a visiting room feels ominous. Joe's voice is strong. He has a deep vibrancy in him. I'm glad he has Lori in his life; she gives him a focus outside himself.

"I don't know if they'll let me come back tomorrow," she says.

"Over this nun's dead body you won't come back," I pipe up, which makes them both laugh.

"The fighting nun," Joe quips, and says that he's not Catholic and that I'm the first nun he ever met. Lori mentions Mother Teresa, that she's "the most famous nun in the whole world," and he knows about her.

We visit for an hour or so, and I wish the room were big enough so I could disappear to give Lori and Joe privacy. I'll have the privacy with Joe that Lori can't have. As his spiritual adviser, I'm allowed a private visit with him tonight from 6:00 to 9:00 p.m. Tonight, after we have talked awhile, I'm going to give Joe the freedom to cut our meeting short so that he can talk to Lori on the phone from his cell. Every minute of time is precious now. A guard sticks his head in the door and tells us visiting time is up.

It is still raining as they drive us away from the L-unit to the front gate. Lori may have seen Joe's face for the last time. We don't say much in the van. Back at the motel, Lori makes calls to the attorneys for updates. She's focused entirely on two big pieces of news: Is the marriage ceremony approved for tomorrow? (Yes, the lawyers say, it's approved.) Is there any word from the governor? (No word yet.) She's talking on the phone to Joe when I walk across the parking lot to Shoney's to get us something to eat. I take my time. Lori says she doesn't want anything to eat, but I get her soup and crackers anyway. "You have to eat, Lori," I say, and tell her about my experience of fainting in the Louisiana death house because I couldn't get food. She has to laugh when I tell her how good it felt to faint, to get a short little nap—no matter that I was out cold on a cement floor with a circle of blue-uniformed guards peering down on me. There's nothing stoic about Lori Urs. Whatever she feels—anger, indignation, amusement, joy—finds its way quickly to her mouth and eyes and voice. I'm glad I can make her laugh.

We're in a very small motel room with wall-to-wall double beds. I put my suitcase on the floor by my bed and leave room for her in the hanging closet space, which is just a bar near the sink and counter. Her wedding dress is hanging there, and beneath it sit her polished dress shoes.

Around 5:30, I drive to Mecklenburg to see Joe. It's summer, so there's plenty of daylight, but I make a wrong turn and don't arrive at the prison until 6:30. I'm bringing a Bible with me, a Gideon Bible borrowed from the motel room, and in the back on the last page I have written a message to Joe from Mother Teresa of Calcutta. A friend of Mother Teresa's had telephoned Lori to dictate it, and I get to be the bearer of this comforting message.

At the prison—the rain has stopped at last—they drive me back to the L-unit. I thought I'd see Joe in the same visiting room as before, but guards bring me back to the cells next to the lethal injection chamber. When I get there Joe is on the phone with Lori, and I signal to him to talk as long as he wants.

I sit in a chair nearby and thumb through the Bible and look again at Mother Teresa's words to him, words about his dignity and God's compassionate love for him and the assurance of prayers for him in his final hour. Her message will mean all the more to Joe because she was willing to go to bat for him with Governor Allen. Mother Teresa had not minced words in her phone call to the governor, so Lori had understood. Killing was wrong, period. It was against God's command no matter who was doing it and whether or not it was legalized. Joe had been cheered, Lori told me, when he heard that the saintly nun had cared enough about his life to make such a call. Now, when the time is appropriate he'll get to read these precious words from her. Perhaps they can be his night prayer before he goes to sleep on what may be the last full day and night of his life.

Now off the phone, he signals me to come near, and I pull my chair close to the bars of his cell. Four guards stand nearby, watching. Two are standing near Joe's cell and two are behind a counter desk a few feet away. As we visit, when it looks as though the guards aren't watching, I quietly tear out the last page of the Bible where I've written Mother Teresa's message and slip it to Joe. "I'll savor her blessing before I go to sleep tonight," he says. "It's kind of hard to sleep in a situation like this." He still has hope, he says, and he's even drafted an argument that the lawyers hadn't thought of. He knows it's a good argument, and he knows that Supreme Court justices are intelligent and know the Constitution, and surely they will see the wisdom of his argument. But mostly he wants to talk about Lori and the amazing fighter she is and that he's glad I'm here to help her. He says he's not eating much food these days and he's smoking a lot, but deep down he's not afraid to die. If it comes down to it, he'll go to his death with dignity, and in his last words he'll say just what he has on his mind to the governor and the courts and everybody. I believe him. He's not nervous and hyped and saying distorted and impossible things. I sense strength in him and integrity of purpose that has been honed over twelve years of struggle.

"From the beginning, all I've ever wanted is for the truth to be told," he says, and something in him is still flabbergasted that in the United States of America he has not once been granted the full evidentiary hearing on the evidence he requested. Maybe one factor that contributes to his sense of integrity is that he hasn't had to deal with remorse eating away at him for a terrible, irrevocable deed. He has a clean conscience, not about his whole life, but at least in the knowledge that he did not murder Helen Schartner. He quotes St. Paul: "I've fought the good fight." He keeps talking about Lori's innocence, the little girl in her he wants to protect.

I look at my watch: It's 8:00. I have until 9:00 to visit, but I know that the dwindling hours of this day are precious, and I want him to have time with Lori. I suggest that we pray together and then I'll leave and he can call Lori, and that is what we do. I hold his hands through the bars, a touch Lori has never been allowed, and I say to him that Lori asked me to be her proxy and to hold his hands for her, and he asks if I've ever noticed how tiny her hands are. His hands are large, and they hide mine almost completely as we pray. He prays in thankfulness for Lori and the wondrous miracle that she wants to marry him, and he prays for strength during the next twenty-four hours so that he can be strong for her. He prays that he'll be able to sleep a little tonight, because sleep has been so hard to come by, and he thanks God for the comforting message of Mother Teresa and all the Italian people. He breaks the prayer then to point to a plastic bulging bag. "See that? Letters from Italy, a whole bunch from children. If my life is spared, I'm going to learn Italian—I've already started, got a book—and Lori and I are going to visit those good Italian people and express our appreciation for all they've done."

When it is my turn to pray, I give thanks for the providence of God that has brought me into his life and Lori's, and I pray that God gives him the strength he needs, moment by moment. Because the one thing I know about making it through these last days and hours is that grace never comes ahead of time, it unfurls under you as you need it.

I rise to leave, and already Joe is asking one of the guards to bring him the phone so he can talk to Lori, who is waiting for his call in the motel room in Emporia. As I approach the security desk to retrieve my driver's license, a guard tells me not to give Joe any more written notes, and I realize that he must have been watching me through a videocamera. But they make no move to take Mother Teresa's note away from Joe, and I'm glad about that. No doubt it's because of her stature. How could anyone classify as "contraband" a message of blessing from Mother Teresa?

I get back to the motel around 9:00, and Lori is talking to Joe on the phone when I walk in. She gives me a slight wave of greeting, and I hear her talking about their wedding day tomorrow, that finally approval has been given and she's supposed to be there at noon. I take a long time in the shower to give them time to talk and then sit on my bed and read about Joe's case. In the court system, the only thing left is an appeal to the U.S. Supreme Court, and this is still pending. I know the feel of this: Defense attorneys, trying desperately to save their clients' lives, file one petition after another in the courts, hoping for pay dirt, hoping for a miracle.

Finally, Lori has to end the conversation because Joe's phone time is up. Her last words are "Tomorrow, Joe, I will become your wife." A pause, and she holds the phone, listening, and then it clicks and Joe is gone. She buries her face in the pillow and sobs. "How am I going to do this? How am I ever going to do this?" I hold her and let her cry, and gradually she calms. I am amazed that she's not stressed out of her mind, but I've noticed astonishing resilience in people during times like this, when death is at the door and life hangs in the balance. It's July 22 and Joe is still alive, and there is still hope with the governor and the Supreme Court. In my cosmetic case, I see four light sleeping pills I keep on hand for long international flights. I had forgotten I had them, and I persuade Lori to take one of the pills, telling her how important it is to get some sleep because she's going to need every bit of her energy and resourcefulness tomorrow. I sit close by her, and in a short time she's out like a light. I turn off the lamp on the table between our beds and lie there a while in the dark, wondering how on God's green earth I keep getting drawn into bizarre situations like this. When I packed my clothes to come here, I packed enough to last a week. Lori has told me that if Virginia kills Joe, members of the Italian parliament will fly to the United States to accompany his body to Palermo, where he will be buried. I've brought my passport in case Lori needs me to go with her, but I'm thinking that probably her Italian friends will be enough comfort and strength for her and she won't need me.

We are not allowed in the prison before noon on July 23, so we use the morning to do errands and pick up the marriage license. When she comes back to the car, she is laughing. "Look at my priceless wedding gifts," she says, and flings a bottle of Mr. Clean and two small boxes of detergent into the backseat. "They seem to be pushing cleanliness for newly marrieds these days." Driving around in the Cherokee and doing errands like this before the wedding makes the day feel normal.

We go back to the motel, and Lori showers, puts on her bright dress, and fixes her hair and makeup, and we head to the prison. Sometimes she slips and says "funeral" when she refers to the wedding. It's hard to take in the reality of this day. Is it possible that Lori is about to marry a man who will be killed nine hours later?

Around 11:45, we drive through the orange cones and are stopped by the guards. Radios are crackling. "Did you hear that?" Lori says to me. "On the radio they're saying that the wedding party has arrived. I guess that's you and me. We're it, the whole wedding party." This strikes her as very funny.

Nearby, in a grassy section near the road, members of the media have already gathered. Lori laments, "Oh, no, they're already here. The prison must have told them about the marriage because I sure didn't. It's the prison's way of trying to discredit me." A few flashbulbs go off. "I am not talking to them," Lori says. "I am not about to degrade the sacredness of my marriage to Joe by answering their prurient, sensational questions. I am not."

Russ Ford, the minister Lori asked to officiate at the wedding, waits for us inside the lobby. Lori and I meet with him to plan who will do what during the ceremony. Incredibly, Lori and Joe will not be allowed to touch. Lori must stand a few feet away from his cell, so we talk about how we can enable them to touch, at least through us. Lori has the rings. Russ has the Bible. Lori's wearing her bright-colored dress and around her neck the rosary from the pope.

We approach the security check, and Lori is told to step into a room with a woman guard to be strip-searched. The prison isn't taking any chances. During the final "death watch," prison officials want to make sure that Lori is not concealing some sort of weapon or perhaps a cyanide pill, which she might slip to the prisoner, allowing him to be the agent of his own death. Prison officials are especially wary of someone like Lori, about to marry a prisoner on the very day of his scheduled execution; it's a pretty desperate act by their standards. For all they know, Lori Urs and Joe O'Dell have planned a Romeo and Juliet double suicide. So no doubt the strip search is about security, but it is also about power. Lori had told me that not long ago the warden said to her accusingly that she imagined herself wielding a lot of power. This had stunned her. "Me having power?" she had said to him.

After the announcement of the strip search, Lori and I have been brought into a small room where we have a few moments alone, and Lori whispers, "They're showing me who has the power." She's upset. "They're not even allowing me to get close to Joe, so why are they doing this?" I tell Lori that no one can take away her dignity and not to let them upset her on her wedding day.

Lori gets it. "That's right. They can't take away my dignity," she says, and she disappears behind the bathroom door with the female guard.

When we arrive at the L-unit, Joe is standing, peering out, as close to the bars of his cell as he can get, waiting for the first sight of Lori coming around the corner. "You're beautiful, li'l darlin'," he says when he sees her. His eyes are shining.

Lori stands directly across from Joe, who smiles at her, and everyone gets quiet. I stand to Lori's right and Russ to her left, with Russ holding one of Joe's hands and one of Lori's, and I'm doing the same on the other side. We form a small circle with three guards standing very close, two near the bars and one behind Lori. Russ says an opening prayer, and I read a short passage from the First Letter to the Corinthians that love is patient and kind and that love endures. Then Lori and Joe exchange their marriage vows. Lori states her vows, kisses the ring for Joe, and hands it to Russ, who slips it on Joe's finger. Then Joe makes his vows and kisses the ring for Lori and hands it to me, and I slip it on Lori's finger. Russ suggests that since Lori and Joe are not permitted to kiss, they each breathe in deeply and exhale and so exchange the breath of their bodies as communion. A female guard laughs when she hears this, but everyone else is serious and silent, and for a short while all you can hear is the sound of their breathing. I say a prayer for them, asking God's blessing on this union forged in such a crucible, and then Russ and I congratulate them and leave. We don't want to linger. Lori and Joe are being given only an hour's visit. If the execution takes place as planned, they will never see each other again.

One of the guards places a plastic chair about twelve feet away from Joe's cell for Lori to sit in while she visits, and two or three guards stand nearby. To Lori's immediate left, just a few feet away, sits the death gurney behind a locked door.

A little over an hour later, when Lori comes into the lobby, Russ and I are waiting. We hug her warmly as the guards look on. Lori would never cry in front of them. We walk out the door and stand in the parking lot, taking stock. The media, by now a sizable swarm, await Lori out by the orange cones. Despite her reluctance, Lori knows that she needs to deal with them. Better, she figures, to give them real information about the ceremony than to be the victim of sensational fictions they might get from rumors or prison officials. I suggest that she begin by telling them about the wedding ceremony, allow a few questions, then move them on to the issues in Joe's case. She does just that, with great poise. She begins by saying, "I just married Joseph O'Dell," and she holds up her hand to show her wedding ring. Flashbulbs pop and cameras whir, and it's all over in about half an hour.

We head back to the motel in Emporia, where Lori changes clothes and collects a last-minute appeal that Joe asked her to file. We deliver it to the courthouse and leave at about 4:00 p.m. Lori puts in a call on her cell phone to Doug Curtis, one of Joe's attorneys, to see if there have been any breakthroughs from the Supreme Court or from Governor Allen. As she listens, her face seems to break apart. "No! No! No!" she screams into the phone. The governor. He has just announced that he won't grant a commutation to Joe or even a reprieve so that Joe can get DNA testing on the rape evidence. We pull off the road into a parking lot and Lori curls up to cry. After a while, I get her over into the passenger seat. My heart goes out to her. I don't know her well, don't know her breaking point. I wait and pray.

The governor was Joe's last hope. Almost certainly now Joe will be killed tonight at 9:00. Almost certainly, but you never absolutely know for sure, because it's a human process, and anything can happen when humans are involved. I rest my hand on Lori's shoulder and pray that God will give her courage for Joe's sake. I'm counting on her fighting spirit to see her through. I get in the driver's seat and distractedly drive straight through Emporia. After some time going down the highway, I say to Lori, "Are we supposed to be in all these pine trees?" And it makes her snap back, and she's calmer and is thinking of getting to a phone so she can talk to Joe. We switch seats again and head back to the motel in Emporia.

My path becomes clear: Tonight I accompany Joe when he is put to death, and afterward I accompany Lori. I take the Bible and head out to the prison around 6:30. Two of Joe's lawyers, Bob Smith and Andy Sebok, are also going to be there. As I leave the motel, Lori is talking to Joe. I kiss her lightly on the forehead and whisper that I'll see Joe through. She mouths, "Thank you," and quickly turns back into the magnetic pull of Joe's voice.

When I walk into the death cell unit around 6:45 p.m., Bob and Andy are already there, sitting over in the corner right near the door leading to the chamber. Joe is on the phone with Lori, and I sit with the lawyers, who have never had one of their clients killed. As lawyers—they're both young—they have been stunned by what has happened to Joseph O'Dell. They can't quite believe that a man with so many questions of innocence could be going to his death without ever getting one full evidentiary hearing from either a federal or a state court. This has shaken every principle of fairness and justice they learned in law school. Now they wait helplessly. They're not naïve anymore; they're no longer innocents about the criminal justice system in America. Shortly before I walked in, they learned they would not be allowed to witness Joe's death. They had assumed that as Joe's lawyers they would be admitted. They didn't know there was a rule requiring them to submit such a request several days ahead of time. It's just one more surprise in Joe O'Dell's case.

The phone barely reaches into Joe's cell, so he sits in a chair near the bars, and I look over at him talking to Lori, and once I see him wipe away a tear. This is the fourth time I am waiting with a human being about to be killed. Bob and Andy want to know what will happen when I go with Joe into the chamber, and I tell them all that I know about the process of lethal injection, even that they will swab Joe's arm with alcohol before they insert the needle. In Louisiana the spiritual adviser is kept at a strict distance from the killing chamber, but here in Virginia I'll be able to go in with him and touch him and say a prayer with him before they kill him.

Everything is unreal.

I can't believe it any more than the lawyers can.

At 7:30, they escort the three of us to the front of the building while they do the final prep. Joe will be made to take a shower and put on jeans and a short-sleeved blue shirt. This was the horrifying process Joe was forced to watch in December as two prisoners were led to their deaths. Now he must take the shower and don the "death clothes."

At 8:00 p.m., Bob, Andy, and I come back to Joe's cell. The shade has been taken off the window of the door leading into the killing chamber, and the gurney is clearly visible, right there just a few feet away. There it is, cross-shaped, with arms angled downward—Joe O'Dell's modern, high-tech crucifix. It has a lot of straps, folded neatly across the top of the gurney.

When we walk in, Joe is still on the phone with Lori, now saying good-bye and telling her to stay strong and thanking her and saying that he will love her through all eternity. At 8:40 he hangs up, and Bob and Andy go up to his cell, take his hand, and say good-bye, telling him it has been a privilege for them to have been part of his team. I move right over to Joe and take his hands in mine.

"They gave me a shot of Valium," he says. "It's a new part of the prep now. I had no choice. They say it helps keep the veins open so they can insert the needle easier." He's already moving past the tangible horizon. "I'm going to be with my mama. My poor mama suffered so much." He asks me to call his sister, Sheila, whose relationship with him had been somewhat problematic and who hadn't visited much, though recently she came to see him and they reconciled.

But mostly there is only one message: "Take care of Lori. Y'all look like you belong together. She made me so happy today, Sister Helen. She married me."

He turns to flip his last cigarette into the toilet. Instinctively I say, "Let's see if you can hit it." The cigarette falls short. He is talking now in a stream about how Lori was the best thing that ever happened to him and that he's okay, and he and God can do this, that he's not afraid, and he's got his last words ready, and I'm trying to hold all his words so I can tell Lori when he's gone.

Time is picking up momentum. I think of Lori in the motel. A friend of hers had come to stay with her, so she's not alone.

"What's the name again of that Catholic book that I helped to change?" Joe asks.

"Joe," I say, "you helped change a very big Catholic book, the Catholic Catechism. I personally think that when the pope heard of the suffering you went through when they almost killed you, maybe it helped him see the torture in the death penalty and that it can never be justified."

"I did that, huh?" he says.

Last night when Joe and I visited, he told me that when they came to take him into the chamber, I was to watch his eyebrows, that when he lifted them high I was to step back, because he was going to fight them all the way. He would not go quietly. He wanted them to know they were killing a man who was alive and who was innocent. Now I say to him that if he chooses to fight, he'll have my support all the way, but if he decides not to fight, that had dignity, too. "Just don't feel bound to fight because that's what you said you'd do. I surely don't know what I would do if a group of people were hauling me off to kill me."

He nods.

He had also told me that when the warden, as part of the final ritual, stood before his cell to read the warrant of execution and asked him if he understood, he was going to say, "No, I don't understand. I don't understand how you can be killing an innocent man." Last night he also said that he would say to the warden that he knew he was just doing his job, and I replied that maybe he didn't want to let the warden off the hook so easily, because "doing their job" is what everybody involved in these killings uses to legitimize their actions—the warden, the prosecutors, the governor—everybody. I see the graciousness in him, trying to reach out to the warden, trying to ease his burden in having to kill a man. I have found this graciousness in others who were led to their deaths. That conversation had happened last night, and it sits inside Joe now along with the teeming, tumultuous things in the mind of a person who is alive and conscious and about to be led out and killed.

"I can't believe what the courts did to me," he says. "How could they rubber-stamp all those wrong things that happened at my trial? How can they let an innocent man go to his death without the truth ever being told—even that last DNA test on the sperm?" And I can tell that he really doesn't understand and that he has hope that the appeal he had Lori file yesterday might still come through for him. Even now in the last minutes of his life, there is in Joe O'Dell an innocent trust that the courts will see the rightness of his claims and grant him justice.

It's 8:55. As the warden approaches, I take hold of Joe's hands. "I'll be with you, Joe. May Christ's love and strength be with you," I tell him.

Joe says, "Look. I'm about to get Allenized [killed by Governor Allen]."

As the warden stands in front of Joe's cell to read the warrant, I stand by very close. When the warden finishes reading, he says, "Okay?" Joe says nothing. Then they put handcuffs on him and lead him into the chamber. The warden says to me, "You can walk right behind him, and it's okay after we get him strapped to touch him while you say the prayer. Just don't make it a real, real long prayer, all right? Some of them go on for five, ten minutes."

It's a short walk for Joe. The chamber is just a few feet away. Inside, guards lift under Joe's arms to help position him onto the gurney. He lies down there and stretches out his arms on the inverted crossbars. Guards are moving quickly, strapping Joe's arms and legs, trunk, and chest. When the guard fastens the strap across Joe's chest, he pulls it very tight. Joe lifts his head and says, "Hey, man, you're cutting off my wind."

I say to the warden, "Can't you adjust that strap a bit to help him breathe?"

The guard looks scared and nervous. He looks at the warden. The warden's face is set. He says nothing, and the guard leaves. I'm standing right near Joe and he says, "Sister Helen, they got it so tight."

"They won't change it, Joe," I say. "It's the way it'll be. Try to take shallow breaths. It won't be long." He's looking at me, and I put my hand on his shoulder and say the final words he'll hear on this earth: "Christ's love surrounds you, Joe, and Lori's love, and all the love and prayers of the pope and the people of Italy. I'll take care of Lori."

A guard escorts me into the room where the witnesses sit in three tiered rows of plastic chairs. Above the viewing window is a sign: WITNESSES MUST REMAIN SEATED. PRESS IN BACK TWO ROWS. A curtain has been drawn across the window. Witnesses will be permitted to see Joe only after needles have been inserted into his arms and the saline solution is flowing. Everyone is silent. Everyone is watching the curtain. I am praying, *Oh, Christ, be near him now, help him, strengthen him.* I fold my hands in my lap and close my eyes. Lori is in the motel room. I pray for her. Everything is silent on the other side of the curtain. Time ticks by. I can hear the scribbling pen of a journalist sitting behind me.

The curtain is drawn back. Behind the gurney a blue plastic curtain hangs with two square holes cut into it, one small, the other larger. Through the small one runs the intravenous tubing. Both of Joe's arms are wrapped with elastic bandages to hold the IV in place. Four solutions will be injected: saline, which is already running, to open the veins; then sodium thiopental to put Joe to sleep; Pavulon, or pancuronium bromide, to paralyze his muscles and stop his breathing; and potassium chloride to stop his heart. I figure the bigger hole in the plastic curtain contains a one-way window for the death technician to see the effect of his work on Joe's body. I am at Joe's feet, facing him squarely. Since he is lying flat, I cannot see much of his face, only a bit of his chin and his nostrils. I cannot see his eyes.

A guard holds a telephone for Joe to say his last words: "This is the happiest day of my life. I married Lori today.

"Governor Allen, you have a wife and daughter, but tonight you're taking mine away from me. Governor, you're killing an innocent man.

"Eddie Schartner [Helen Schartner's son], I'm sorry about your mother, but I didn't kill her. I hope you find out the truth.

"Lori, I will love you through eternity."

I close my eyes and fold my hands in my lap and pray for God to take Joe quickly. Because of the tight strap, he cannot even draw one deep final breath of life. I pray for Lori. I pray for Joe's sister, Sheila. I pray for the people of Virginia. I pray for the governor and the courts and all who are participants in this man's death.

I open my eyes and see that a doctor has a stethoscope on Joe's chest, and I close my eyes again and wait for the warden's announcement to come. And soon it does: "Joseph O'Dell died at nine-sixteen p.m."

Guards lead me out ahead of the other witnesses to a waiting van. Outside in the parking lot, a huge array of media has assembled, no doubt because of the international attention Lori had marshaled for Joe's case. The lawyers Bob and Andy wait for me just outside the building. They look stricken. I take their hands in mine. "What we do now," I say to them, "is speak to the press. One of you should speak about the legal issues in his case and what happened to him in the courts."

This is a surprise for them. They didn't think they'd be allowed to speak to the press. It's a surprise for me, too. In Louisiana, anyone who has an opposing view is kept carefully away from the press conference that follows every state killing. It's a canned affair, with only the warden fielding questions. But here, with eight satellite dishes and a host of TV and radio affiliates as well as print journalists, the microphones are open to anyone who wishes to speak. As I step to the edge of the crowd, the warden is repeating Joe's final words: "This is the happiest day of my life. . . ." Standing before the phalanx of press, I introduce myself as Joseph's spiritual adviser and a friend of Lori Urs, and I tell them how this young woman fought so hard to get the courts and Governor Allen to do justice for Joe O'Dell. I say that I believe the killing of any human being, even the guilty, is morally wrong, but that the killing of Joseph O'Dell, a possibly innocent man, without allowing him DNA testing is doubly heinous. I point out the great contrast—that here in Virginia, Joe's killing is just one more state killing that people scarcely notice, while in Italy and the European Parliament and even for Pope John Paul II, Joe's killing has provoked outrage and resistance. I end by thanking the Italian people for their prayers for Joe and the ten thousand faxes and phone calls they made on his behalf to Governor Allen's office.

Later I will find out from Rino Piscitello, a member of the Italian parliament, that an estimated five million people in Italy stayed awake by TV sets and radios until 3:00 a.m. to follow the last hours of Joseph O'Dell's life.

When I walk into the hotel room, Lori is sitting in her bed, and when she sees me she begins to cry.

"What happened?" she asks, managing to compose herself. "Tell me everything."

And I tell her of Joe's last moments after he hung up the phone at 8:40 and how brave he was and full of dignity and composed and what his last words were, that he had said, "This is the happiest day of my life," and that he had ended saying that he would love her through eternity. She listens quietly, then bursts into tears, then listens, and I can sense in her the feeling—I've felt it myself—that when death comes it is so final, so irrevocable; you know that your loved one's sufferings are over, and there's a kind of peace in knowing that you can do no more. There's a peace in knowing that you left no stone unturned, no initiative untried, that you expended yourself without counting personal costs to do all you could to avert this death, to resist and uncover all the injustices, that you resisted with every fiber of your being.

"You succeeded in making Joe feel happy, Lori," I say to her. "Have you ever in your life heard of a man about to be killed who could say, 'This is the happiest day of my life'?" The words hit their mark. Lori seems calm.

Joe is to be buried in Palermo. She asks that I come with her, and I say, Of course I'll come, and I tell her that Joe had asked me to look after her and that he had said, "Y'all look like you belong together." We're Thelma and Louise, I say, and make her smile.

The Italian parliament is shouldering all of Joe's funeral expenses as well as the cost of flying his body to Palermo. First, his body is being shipped to Cox's Funeral Home in Norfolk, Virginia, where the Italian consulate is located. We fly to Norfolk and are met at the airport by Luciano Neri and Rino Piscitello, who drive us to the funeral home so that Lori can be there for the final sealing of Joe's casket. Lori doesn't want the coffin sealed because she wants to see Joe's face again when she gets to Palermo. The director is in a quandary over this and stretches his funeral director code of ethics to hand her a key to the coffin. The coffin is sealed by turning a key at the base, which rolls a metal covering over its length. As it slides slowly over Joe's face, Lori cries quietly.

I'm glad Luciano's here. He takes Lori by the arm and says, "Come, Lori, we're going to an Italian restaurant to eat." He's like a father to her—this gentle-faced man who stirred the Italian parliament to take action on Joe's behalf. I like him. I trust him. And I'm so glad he can help me accompany Lori.

The next morning, at the Italian consulate, we meet Vito Piraino, who has struggled through five days and nights of phone calls, faxes, memos, and letters to secure—and he waves it before us—"this tiny piece of paper that grants official permission to ship the body overseas." He had been the one to first call Governor Allen's office to request that Joe's body be turned over to the Italian consulate. To be sure, this was an entirely novel situation for the governor's assistants and just the beginning of Vito's adventure.

"Should I expect a problem?" he asked one of the governor's stunned aides. "I don't think you want an international incident fighting with us over the body of this man."

Luciano takes the hard-earned document from Vito and is instructed to show it when he leaves with the body from the United States and when he arrives with the body in Italy. I'll bet Vito will never forget Joseph O'Dell. Nor will officials in Virginia. It is the first time ever that permission has been sought for the body of an executed criminal to be flown overseas for burial in a place reserved for dignitaries. It reminds me of Joseph of Arimathea going to Pontius Pilate for permission to bury Jesus of Nazareth, also considered a despised criminal, dispatched by crucifixion by the Roman state.

The next day, we fly from Norfolk to Newark, where we'll catch our flight to Rome. A hearse from Cox's Funeral Home has driven Joe's body to Newark International Airport. When we arrive at the airport, Lori goes immediately to a phone to talk to Joe's lawyers about getting a court order to secure the sperm samples being kept in the district attorney's office. She and the lawyers are enacting a legal strategy to obtain the sperm samples, along with Joe's clothes and other belongings, as part of Lori's marital right to his estate. They talk about how crucial it is to move quickly to get a court order to freeze the evidence while they file the legal suit for possession. DA's offices are notorious for making evidence mysteriously disappear. And already prosecutors and attorneys for the commonwealth would have been alerted by Barry Scheck's statement at the press conference in Richmond of the intention to pursue postmortem DNA testing if the governor refused to order it done. While Lori is talking on the phone, I glance out the window—she does, too—in time to see Joe's casket on a conveyor belt making its slow way up into the belly of the plane.

We are on our way to Rome, accompanied by Rino and Luciano. Last night at the hotel in Norfolk, I had faxed a letter to Monsignor Gabriele Caccia, assistant to the secretary of state at the Vatican. He was the one who greeted Lori in January when she went to Italy to rally support for Joe, and he carried my letter to the pope. Lori told me how compassionate he was, and I know that it would be consoling for her, now so traumatized and grieving, to be in the company of such a kind, gentle man. I have his telephone number, so when we arrive in Rome I will call him to see if a visit is possible.

Lori needs desperately to sleep. She must be alert and coherent when she greets dignitaries and members of the press. She badly needs to withdraw from the currents of trauma and grief for a while. I am grateful when, on the plane, she sinks into a long, sound slumber, and when we arrive I can see she is poised and ready for what the day will bring her. A phalanx of media waits on the tarmac to get a photo of the plane arriving and Joseph's casket. Lori and I look at each other.

"Well, Thelma," I say, "looks like we're off to a roaring start."

Lori smiles and says, "We can handle it, Louise. It's all for Joe. Killing him and the injustice done to him by the courts was outrageous, so now I'll get a chance to tell his story to the world."

Welcome words. Lori's got her fighting spirit back.

Inside the airport, members of the Italian parliament and the assistant to the mayor of Palermo greet us and escort us to the VIP room. Luciano and Rino hold off media, promising that there will be a press conference later on. Soon after we arrive, a call comes from Monsignor Gabriele Caccia in the Vatican. "Come right away to the Vatican," he says. "Pope John Paul is just now arriving from Castel Gandolfo for a public audience, and we think we can arrange a private meeting for you with him immediately afterward."

We throw our suitcases into a taxi and rush across the streets of Rome to the Vatican, where we pick up a pass with our names on it at the guardhouse near the entrance. Then we go to the building where Monsignor Caccia awaits us. *Lori is right about him,* I think as I see for the first time his kind face.

At the airport Lori found time to change from her traveling clothes into a dress, but I'm still in pants and a baggy blouse. I say to Monsignor Caccia, "Please, can you find me a place where I might change my clothes? I can't meet the pope in pants."

"Noooo," he agrees readily, good Vatican man that he is, "you must not meet the pope wearing pants."

In a small parlor, right next to the large room where the pope will come to meet us, I accomplish the quickest change of clothes in my life. Panty hose (uncooperative and resistant on a hot, sticky July day), blouse, skirt, and last of all, my cross around my neck . . . but the chain on the cross breaks. . . . Oh, no, I can't meet the pope without my cross . . . nervous fingers tying a knot in the chain and pulling it over my head, only to have it stop squarely in the middle of my forehead. . . . Head too big, chain too short . . . hurry . . . untie and retie knot . . . ah . . . got it . . . run across the hall to the meeting room . . . what about my hair? Forget the hair, the pope doesn't give a hoot about women's hair.

Lori is already waiting in a large, straight-backed wooden chair whose arms curve into animal heads. I sit in a similar one. Our feet swing in the air. The chairs must have been built for giants. We wait. Lori says, "I just knew Monsignor Caccia would do this for us." I'm happy for Lori. It will help to take the edge off the horror of what has happened to Joseph. She has expressed more than once her amazement at the pope's speaking out for Joseph's life. She's wearing the pope's rosary around her neck, a gift given her through Monsignor Caccia when she was last in Rome.

We hear a slow footfall in the hall and the murmur of men's voices. I look for white in the doorway, but I see scarlet. A cardinal or some Vatican official comes in to announce that the pope is coming. Lori and I move near the doorway, and there he is—Pope John Paul II, dressed in a white soutane and that little white skullcap he always wears—walking slowly toward us, one shoulder lower than the other, one of his hands tucked into the wide sash around his waist, his face very pink, looking exactly like every photograph I've ever seen of him in schools, convents, and church halls.

He looks very tired, and my heart goes out to him. He walks right up to us, to Lori first, takes her hand in his, and says, "I prayed for Joseph at Mass."

Lori says, "I married him."

He nods, blesses her, and kisses her on the forehead. After he kisses her, she says, "Would you bless me again?" And the pope gently kisses her again.

I reach out my hand to him and thank him for speaking out against the death penalty and for helping the church to embrace a position against it. He nods, blesses me, and kisses me on the forehead. The burdens that he carries are written in his face and his stooped shoulders. As he turns to leave, I say to him, "Take care of yourself." Later, when Monsignor Caccia mails me the photographs of the visit (I never saw a photographer or remember a flashbulb going off), I see the two of us, hands pressed to our hearts, our feelings reflected in our faces.

He walks slowly out of the room, and we watch his plodding steps toward the door.

Then Luciano Neri takes Lori and me to meet with fourteen members of parliament who had been most active in the efforts to save Joseph's life. Lori tearfully thanks them and says that she has a mission to tell the world what happened to Joe O'Dell so that the United States can forever abolish the death penalty. "The forces of state government and courts were all stacked against Joe," she says. "You in Italy, you were our only light. You helped to give Joe hope, and, even more important, your efforts on his behalf gave him dignity."

We take the plane from Rome to Palermo. A crowd of well-wishers and reporters is waiting on the tarmac. Luciano directs Lori to walk a little toward the people to acknowledge them. She extends her hands and throws them a kiss, and they applaud. Lori greeting the crowd is the top story on the TV nightly news.

At the airport in Palermo, I meet Mayor Leoluca Orlando, who caused such consternation when he visited Joe in prison. Because of his battle against the Mafia, he must travel in a bomb-proof, bazooka-proof car, and he has four armed bodyguards around him at all times. He stands with us on the tarmac as Joe's casket is taken off the plane.

We go to the small church where the funeral will be tomorrow. Lori, Mayor Orlando, Luciano, and I walk slowly behind ten men carrying Joe's heavy bronze casket up a cobblestone path flanked by tall, graceful trees. After the men position the casket, Lori and I go in alone. She uses the key the funeral director had given her and opens the casket to see him for the final time. Her knees buckle, and the mayor puts his arm around her and says, "Be strong, Lori, be strong."

The next morning in the church, we sit in the first row near the casket and people stream in, bringing flowers and notes, leaning over and kissing Lori, clasping her hand, touching the casket, some of them crying. Some have brought their children, who look up at Lori with awe, offering a consoling kiss or a small clutch of flowers. Four men in dark suits and white gloves stand as honor guard around Joe's coffin.

Fifteen minutes before Mass begins, press photographers are allowed into the church. Luciano has briefed Lori beforehand about the photographers, so she is prepared for them. I notice how calm and poised she is. Her ardent but futile efforts to save Joe's life have captivated the hearts of the Italian people.

The little church is packed. Some, unable to get inside, stand on the steps, listening to the singing and snatches of the priest's words at the homily. Joseph O'Dell's life and death resembles that of Jesus, the priest says; both were innocent and executed by the state. Both endured humiliation, agony, and cruel suffering. But now we believe that Joseph O'Dell has joined Jesus in glory; life eternal has conquered earthly death.

When the priest finishes speaking, loud and sustained applause fills the little church. I can't help but contrast this funeral with the others I have attended of executed men: small clutches of family members huddled around the grave, dreading publicity of any kind. I remember that just before the funeral ceremony of Robert Lee Willie, there was a ruckus outside the funeral home when one of his aunts ran off a photographer, threatening to hit him with her shoe.

At the conclusion of the Mass, the priest sprinkles holy water on Joe's casket and the choir sings, "May the angels lead you into paradise. . . ." The pallbearers raise the casket to their shoulders and carry it out of the church. Using two white bands, the men slowly lower the casket into the grave, and once again the crowd applauds. Then the men put into place the memorial slab, on which is written in Italian and English:

JOSEPH ROGER O'DELL III
BELOVED HUSBAND OF LORI URS O'DELL
HONORARY CITIZEN OF PALERMO
KILLED BY VIRGINIA USA
IN A BRUTAL AND MERCILESS JUSTICE SYSTEM
BORN SEPTEMBER 20, 1941
DIED JULY 23, 1997

Lori Urs never faltered in her efforts to prove the innocence of Joseph O'Dell. After his death, she made one last attempt to gain possession of the evidence for DNA testing. As Joe's widow, she filed a legal suit demanding Joe's clothes and other personal effects as part of his legal estate. But the state of Virginia refused to relinquish the items, arguing that as state's evidence they were not subject to probate law. And once again the Virginia courts backed them up. Shortly after the court's decision in their favor, a state official announced that all evidence in the O'Dell case had been destroyed.[56]

On September 25, 2003, six years after the execution of Joseph O'Dell, I receive an e-mail message from Steven Watson, the jailhouse snitch who was so instrumental in putting Joe on death row. He had asked me to respond, and when I did so one more sad story of a human being under pressure in the criminal justice system came pouring out:

> AFTER THE ORDEAL WHICH OCCURRED IN VA, THANK GOD I GOT MY LIFE STRAIGHT AND IN 1983 MARRIED, HAD THREE CHILDREN, WAS MARRIED UNTIL 1989. AFTER TWO YEARS, I REMARRIED IN 1990, WE JUST CELEBRATED 14 YEARS. YOU KNOW WHEN I WAS IN JAIL WITH JOE ODELL, WE DID TALK A LOT, I AT THE TIME WAS FACING MANY YEARS IN PRISON, I WAS YOUNG, SCARED, NIEVE TO THE LAW. AT THE TIME THE ONLY THING ON MY MIND WAS TO FIND A WAY OUT OF THE TROUBLE I WAS IN. THEN I REMEMBERED THE THINGS THAT JOE AND I HAD SPOKE ABOUT, THE MORE I THOUGHT ABOUT IT THE MORE DETERMIND I WAS IN FINDING THAT ONE WAY OUT

OF MY MESS. I WAS NOT WORRIED ABOUT ANY ONE BUT MY SELF, THEN I CAME UP WITH THE SOLUTION, THAT IF I WOULD SAY THAT JOE DID CONFESS TO ME, I COULD TELL THE ATHOURITIES AND GET A PLEA AGREEMENT, NEVER DREAMING THAT I WOULD HAVE TO TESTIFY ON WHAT I TOLD THEM.... I WANT SO MUCH TO TELL THE REAL STORY AND I WANT SO MUCH TO SIT DOWN FACE TO FACE WITH YOU AND GIVE YOU THE TRUE FACTS OF WHAT OCCURRED THAT SENT A INNOCENT MAN TO HIS DEATH ALL BECAUSE WHEN THE TRUTH CAME OUT* I HAD THE STATE POLICE KNOCKING AT MY DOOR, TELLING ME THAT PERJURY IS TEN YEARS IN PRISON. THEN I BEGAN THINKING HERE I AM HAPPILY MARRIED WITH CHILDREN, AGAIN FACING TIME IN PRISON AND THIS TIME BECAUSE I WANT TO MAKE AMEND AND GET EVERY THING OUT AS IT SHOULD BE.... I WAS TOLD DO IT OR ELSE. IN MY CASE, TO DO A BAD THING I GOT REWARDED. TO TRY AND DO A GOOD DEED I WAS GOING TO GET PUNISHED ... ME I GET OFF JOE DIES. ITS NOT RIGHT ... ITS 4:30 AM....

*Lori Urs had persuaded Watson to recant, and local media had made his recantation public. But when he was threatened with imprisonment for perjury, Watson recanted his recantation.

I

When I see him in the New Orleans International Airport, I can't believe it's Supreme Court justice Antonin Scalia, fiddling with the headphones of his compact disc player. I figure he's flying back to Washington, D.C., and I guess where he's been: duck hunting with my brother Louie. They met nine years ago at the wedding of one of Justice Scalia's sons, and they've been hunting buddies ever since. They pack their guns and head to Pecan Island in Louisiana, where Louie cooks up seafood gumbo and jambalaya, which he says "Nino just loves." I'm amazed by the coincidence not only that my brother Louie and Scalia are friends, but that I should encounter the justice, who calls himself part of the "machinery of death," in my home-town airport. But here we are, Scalia and I, on a Sunday night in November 2002, Concourse A, Gate 7—meeting.

Louie tried to convince me that Justice Scalia is a devout Catholic: "Sis, he's got nine kids, you know he's a good Catholic."

I've also been told that Scalia attends one of the few parish churches that still offers a Latin Mass. Some Catholics have sought out more conservative churches using older forms of the liturgy, because they disagree with the attempt by the Second Vatican Council (1962–1965) to modernize the church by urging Catholics to worship in their own languages. Strict traditionalists prefer the Mass in Latin, the "universal" language, which they say promotes a unified church, run from the top down. They don't like the way Vatican II emphasized the church as the people of God and called on the hierarchy to share decision making with the laity. Traditionalists fear that the introduction of democracy into the American Catholic Church spells disaster. Better, they say, to have the teaching authority of the church solidly in the hands of the hierarchy, whose task it is to faithfully preserve and hand down the "deposit of faith," which is summarized in an official compendium, the Catholic Catechism. The main virtue required of the laity is obedience. Traditionalists abhor "cafeteria" Catholics who choose to obey only those church teachings that suit them.

As soon as I see Justice Scalia in the airport, I can't help but think of Dobie and Joe as they lay dying: Dobie struggling to control his fear, and Joe, in disbelief that the courts were letting him die without granting him the hearing he had sought for twelve years. Watching these men die, I learned an unshakable truth: The courts, including the Supreme Court, killed them every bit as much as the executioners who injected poison into their veins. And now I'm about to meet one of the justices who authorized these killings.

I walk up. "Are you Scalia?"

"Somebody has to be," he quips, shoving wires into the music case. I glance at his hands and wonder if he's right-handed. Is that the hand that signs all the rejected petitions that send people to their deaths? Justice Scalia has talked openly about his role on the Supreme Court as "part of the machinery of death," explaining that his vote, "when joined with at least four others, is in most cases the last step that permits an execution to proceed."[1]

Exactly.

In the cases of Dobie and Joe, Justice Scalia had voted with the majority to reject their petitions.[2] If he had voted differently, Dobie and Joe might have been granted federal hearings, which could have saved their lives. In my letter on behalf of Joseph O'Dell to Pope

John Paul II, I said that Catholic justice Antonin Scalia was part of the crucial 5–4 majority vote of the Supreme Court to reject O'Dell's petition.[3] Justice Scalia, I said, is "relentless in his pursuit of legalizing executions every way he can. He seems to have no trouble squaring executions with his Catholic faith. . . ."[4]

Justice Scalia has not yet raised his eyes to look at me. He is still fiddling with the headphones. "I'm Sister Helen Prejean. I'm Louie's sister."

"You're Louie's sister?" he says, looking up.

I know he's heard of my book, *Dead Man Walking.* Louie told me that on their first hunt a friend proudly told Scalia that "Louie's sister's" book had been made into a film with Susan Sarandon and Sean Penn. Scalia cut him off: "Just what we need, another anti–death penalty film by a bunch of liberals."

"Louie's a fine guy," Scalia says. "He even brings his rosary beads into the duck blind."

I'm not surprised. You can't find a more devout, prayerful Catholic than my brother. At a family dinner, when Louie first told us about duck hunting with Justice Scalia, I asked him if he knew about Scalia's voting record on death penalty cases, and he said they didn't talk about "court stuff," they just hunted.

I well understand that Louie wouldn't want to debate Justice Scalia about anything. I realized how powerful a debater Scalia is when I read his speech and his answers to questions at a death penalty conference at the University of Chicago on January 25, 2002.[5] His arguments dominated the conference, and the audience appreciated his humor. References to audience laughter permeate the transcript of the conference, and the nervousness of questioners who dared to challenge him was palpable.[6] I tell Justice Scalia that my brother has a big heart, always has; he has a job helping people with disabilities get homes and jobs.

"Get any ducks?" I ask.

"Not a one in the sky. None flying," he says.

I was returning home from a talk I had given at Georgetown University, Scalia's alma mater. A year ago, he spoke there as part of "Jesuit Heritage Week." He recalled his student days and praised Jesuit education for "not losing its soul" to "secularism." Afterward, a student asked how he squares his position on the death penalty with his Catholic faith.[7] Since Jesuits emphasize that church teachings on social justice are integral to Catholic faith, many students at Scalia's talk would have known of the numerous papal pronouncements calling for an end to the death penalty and would have studied the pope's encyclical on the subject[8] and the most recent change in the Catholic Catechism.[9] Scalia said he prefers the traditional view of Augustine and Aquinas, which upheld capital punishment. He said that since the recent teachings on capital punishment were not issued "ex cathedra" (strictly declared infallible teachings), he had given them his "thoughtful consideration" and decided to reject them.[10]

At my lecture at Georgetown, there was still a buzz about Justice Scalia's talk. Otto Hintz, a Jesuit who teaches theology, told me, "Irony of ironies. We invite a Catholic Supreme Court justice to address our students during Catholic Education Week, and he tells them he rejects church teaching on the death penalty. He thumbed his nose at the pope, the U.S. bishops, and the Catechism, claiming the teaching wasn't infallible. But not a single moral teaching of the church has ever been taught ex cathedra—not abortion, birth control, euthanasia—not one. So if that's Scalia's criterion, he can ignore 99.999 percent of the church's teachings. If our students used such a guideline, they'd be the most 'do your own thing' libertines you can imagine. I think Scalia used the ex cathedra argument as a loophole, and many of the students could see right through it. One student said, 'He's rationalizing so he can keep his job on the Court.' "

Maybe that's true. Justice Scalia has said publicly that if he believed the death penalty was immoral, he'd have to resign from the Court because he couldn't apply the law.[11] This, he said, is more honorable than those justices who "sabotage" the Constitution by imposing their "personal opinions." Scalia maintains that the Constitution clearly sanctions the death penalty in more than one place, and this is true. "No person shall be held to answer for a capital . . . crime . . . nor be twice put in jeopardy of life . . . nor be deprived of life . . . without due process of law. . . ."[12] "Nor shall any State deprive any person of life . . . without due process of law. . . ."[13]

Justice Scalia believes in a "fixed" constitutional text—sometimes he calls it "dead" or "enduring"—and he takes issue with those who see the Constitution as "living" or "evolving."[14] Such a view, he says, is treacherous because it leads people to "rewrite" the law, inserting their own opinions to make the Constitution say what they think it ought to say.

Among the "saboteurs" whom Justice Scalia sees obstructing the Constitution's clear mandate to impose the death penalty is Justice Harry Blackmun.[15] In 1994, after twenty years of upholding death penalty rulings on the Court, Blackmun, who concurred in the *Gregg v. Georgia*[16] opinion reinstating capital punishment in 1976, changed his mind and voted to overturn death sentences, saying that he now was convinced that the death penalty in its random application was unconstitutional. In *Callins v. Collins,*[17] Blackmun issued his famous dissent, saying that he could no longer "tinker with the machinery of death," a descriptive phrase Scalia appropriated for his own purposes.

My encounter with Justice Scalia in the airport is brief. After the preliminaries about duck hunting and what a good guy my brother is, I say to him, "Justice Scalia, I want to tell you something. I'm writing a book about two innocent men I've accompanied to execution, and I know what you said at Georgetown and in Chicago, and I want you to know that I'm taking you on in this book." I say this calmly, a simple declaration of intent.

He responds in a friendly way, jabbing his hand in the air: "And I'll be coming right back at you."

And that was that.

I walked down the concourse and out to the parking lot, a familiar trek for me. I travel in and out of New Orleans so often that most of the parking lot employees know me by name.

Justice Scalia and I couldn't be further apart. He provides the "legal groundwork" to send people to their deaths, and I resist his orders every way I can. He sits on his bench in marble chambers, and I sit in visiting stalls on death row. When he enters Court chambers in his black robe, everyone stands; and when he speaks, everyone listens. Years ago, when I first set out to give talks about the death penalty, I had to establish every inch of respect I could muster—and even now, after twenty years of public lecturing, an irate listener will still stand up and shout me down. I never know as I approach a lecture hall if protesters with signs will be waiting for me. Once, in Dallas, my host felt the need to hire an armed guard to accompany me. Justice Scalia attends Mass in a wealthy white suburban parish and sings Latin hymns. I attend Mass in an African American church and sing spirituals. Scalia and I both attended Catholic universities as undergraduates, but he got his graduate degree at Harvard Law

School and I got my "higher" degree in an inner-city African American housing project in New Orleans. When Scalia sends people to their deaths, he never sees their faces. But I see their faces as they turn to look at me when they are being killed. Scalia works mostly behind the scenes in the Court, while I live my life in public, traveling around the country, giving on average 120 lectures a year in Rotary Clubs, universities, churches, and synagogues. Scalia quotes the Bible to justify government's "divine authority" to kill "evildoers," and I summon the words and example of Jesus, who transformed the mandate of "an eye for an eye" by urging forgiveness, even of enemies.

When William Faulkner received the Nobel Prize for Literature, he said the only thing "worth writing about" is "the human heart in conflict with itself."[18] For twenty years, I have lived in conflict by becoming involved on both sides of the death penalty—with death row inmates and their families and with the families of murder victims. In visiting the condemned and accompanying them to execution, I've had to deal with my own feelings of revulsion and outrage at their unspeakable crimes. By accompanying murder victims' families in their search for healing, I've had to confront my powerlessness in the face of their irrevocable loss. I know I can never feel the outrage and sorrow these families feel. No one I've loved has been murdered. And I resist feelings of guilt whenever these families press me to agree with them that executing their loved one's murderer is a necessary act of "justice." Nor have I personally experienced the grief of Betty Williams, Dobie's mother, who had to stand by helplessly as the state prepared to kill her son.[19]

Justice Scalia says: "My morality and religious beliefs have nothing to do with how I vote."[20] His task as a justice, he says, demands that he scrupulously keep "personal predilections, biases, and moral and religious beliefs" out of the process when he interprets the Constitution. But I wonder whether he, too, has doubts.

II

Justice Scalia has said that if his moral beliefs opposed the death penalty, he would resign from the Court, but judging from his remarks about his religious beliefs at the Chicago conference, it doesn't seem likely that he'll face such a dilemma. He also said bluntly that for him the constitutionality of the death penalty is not a "difficult and soul-wrenching question." I find this morally troubling, because I can't help wondering how any human being could be called upon to decide life or death for his or her fellows and not break a moral sweat. But after reflecting on Justice Scalia's interpretation of chapter 13 of Paul's Epistle to the Romans, which he explicated in Chicago, I understand why Justice Scalia never breaks a moral sweat as he upholds one death sentence after another. In fact, the way he interprets Romans 13 unveils one of his foundational religious beliefs, which has everything to do with the way he approaches death sentences.

Justice Scalia's choice of chapter 13 of Paul's Epistle to the Romans is itself revealing. Steeped in Catholic tradition, he knows that from the time of the early church, this passage from Romans has been interpreted by Christians as a sound biblical basis for establishing the right of civil authority to kill criminals, and if he had used this passage to prove his point sixty or so years ago, no Catholic theologian or church official would have disagreed with his interpretation. But thanks to the leadership of Pope Pius XII, Catholics have a more enlightened methodology for interpreting the Bible. Through his 1943 encyclical, *Divino Afflante Spiritu,* Pius XII encouraged Catholics to look deeper than the literal meaning of biblical passages by taking into account the literary form as well as the historical situation of biblical passages. But Justice Scalia either has no knowledge of this approach to biblical exegesis or he disagrees with it. His interpretation of Romans 13 is indistinguishable from that of fundamentalist preachers, who use this passage to argue that "God's wrath on evildoers" not only justifies the death penalty, it demands it.

Scalia prefaced his remarks on the Epistle to the Romans by first drawing a crucial distinction between what is expected morally of Christian individuals and what is expected of governments:

> The death penalty is undoubtedly wrong unless one accords to the state a scope of moral action that goes beyond what is permitted to the individual. . . . Few doubted the morality of the death penalty in the age that believed in the divine rights of kings, or even in earlier times. St. Paul had this to say . . . "Let every soul be subject unto the higher powers, for there is

no power but of God. The powers that be are ordained of God. Whosoever, therefore, resisteth the power resisteth the ordinance of God. . . . For he is the minister of God to thee for good. But if thou do that which is evil, be afraid, for he beareth not the sword in vain, for he is the minister of God, a revenger to execute wrath upon him that doth evil."[21]

Here's how Justice Scalia interprets Romans 13:

The core of [Paul's] message is that government . . . derives its moral authority from God. It is the minister of God with powers to revenge, to execute wrath, including even wrath by the sword, which is unmistakably a reference to the death penalty. Paul, of course, did not believe that the individual possessed any such powers . . . he said, "Dearly beloved, avenge not yourselves, but rather give place unto wrath, for it is written, vengeance is mine, saith the Lord." And in this world, the Lord repaid—did justice—through his minister, the state.[22]

Along with Genesis 9:6 (the man who sheds blood will have his own blood shed) and Exodus 21:25 (an eye for an eye), Romans 13 tops the list of biblical passages frequently invoked in support of the death penalty—and not just by preachers (or Supreme Court justices). I recently received a scathing letter from a man who used Romans 13 to criticize my work, reminding me that "God gives government the sword" for a purpose, and saying that my focus on death row prisoners was therefore misplaced. "Instead of crying for murderers and rapists, why don't you think about the victim?" my correspondent asked, noting that he was praying for me to be forgiven for my "hatred of justice."

In selecting Romans 13 to drive home his theological position, Justice Scalia has exercised a high degree of selectivity. Anyone can flip through the Bible and find words to make a point; it's called proof texting, and it salts and peppers death penalty discourse in the United States, especially on radio talk shows. I must confess that when I first began debating the death penalty, I used to indulge in some hefty proof texting myself. Once in a discussion about whether or not Jesus would "pull the switch," I argued that Jesus refused to impose the death penalty on an adulterous woman even though Mosaic law prescribed the death penalty; and I thought I had clinched my argument by quoting Jesus's words: "Let the one who is sinless cast the first stone." But, like Scalia, I too was off the mark. I failed to take into account the literary genre of the biblical passage I quoted, which in John's Gospel is told as an "entrapment" story, meant to show Jesus's wisdom in besting his adversaries, not his ethical pronouncement about capital punishment.

Public officials are as apt as anyone to use the Bible to make a point. I once witnessed the president of the Louisiana District Attorneys Association argue on behalf of the death penalty before the judicial committee of the state legislature, armed not with legal precedent, but with these words of Jesus: He who lives by the sword dies by the sword (Matthew 26:52), an odd choice since it's clear from the context that Jesus was cautioning his apostles not to use their swords to defend him lest violence beget violence. It is a theme Catholic bishops are fond of stressing in their pastoral letters.[23]

However, serious scriptural analysis of Paul's Epistle to the Romans, which must take into account the political and social situation of Rome around 57 CE when Paul wrote the letter, yields an entirely different interpretation from Scalia's. Did Paul really intend to give God's unqualified endorsement to an empire that demanded worship of its emperor as a god (which for Christians was idolatry) and that in a few years under Nero would feed Christians to lions and set their pitch-covered bodies on fire to light night games in the Colosseum? If Scalia had turned to chapter 13 in the book of Revelation instead of to Paul's Epistle to the Romans, he would have found words that scathingly denounce the Roman government as the "beast," certainly not God's appointed "minister." Do the words *execute wrath . . . of the sword* refer "unmistakably," as Scalia claims, to government's divine right to execute individuals?

The historical context of verse 2 in Romans refers not to crimes of individuals, but to "rebellion" or "riots" that had occurred in Rome among various Jewish sects and had led Emperor Claudius to expel Jews from Rome a few years before Paul wrote his letter.[24] Roman authorities regarded Christian Jews as one more extremist sect, and at least some Roman authorities would remember that their founder had been crucified by sentence of a Roman judge. Also in Rome's volatile mix at the time Paul wrote the letter were widespread civil agitations due to the empire's oppressive tax collection practices. No wonder, then, that Paul would admonish the Christian community to keep a low profile and subordinate themselves to the governing authorities.

In his proof-texting mode, Scalia saw the words *wrath of the sword* and leaped to the conclusion that they refer "unmistakably" to government's right to impose the death penalty on individuals. But careful literary analysis yields a far different interpretation. Why, if Paul was referring to capital punishment, did he not use the word *rhomphaia* ("broadsword"), which his readers would readily identify as the weapon used by the Romans to inflict capital punishment? Instead, Paul used the word *machaira* ("dagger" or "short-bladed knife"), widely interpreted as a symbol of Rome's military authority to keep the peace, in much the same way that a police officer's gun or badge represents "law and order" today. Nor, upon examination of the text, does the word *execute* in verse 4 ("execute wrath") mean the infliction of capital punishment the way we use the term *execute* today. In this text, *execute* means "to perform," as in "execute the plan." In fact, the verb *execute* is completely absent in the original Greek text and had to be added for the English translation to make sense.[25] In light of serious biblical analysis, Justice Scalia's interpretation of Romans 13, driven by his polemical bent, provides a hint of what we can expect when he interprets constitutional text.

In quoting this passage, Justice Scalia divides the spiritual legacy of Jesus into distinct jurisdictions: Government officials can kill with God's blessing, but individuals can't—which means that only individuals and not the state must take seriously Jesus's teaching never to meet hatred with violent retaliation. But the early Christian community so internalized Jesus's abhorrence of violence that they refused to join the military and understood that Jesus's exhortation to love the "least" among us was to be practiced by social institutions as well as by individuals. They took to heart Jesus's images, such as leaven in dough, by which he taught them to transform the society in which they lived. Jesus's challenge to his followers continues today. When governments oppress and deny people justice, Christians are expected to transform those governments, not blindly obey them as

"God's minister." My friends in Murder Victims' Families for Human Rights say, "When the state kills, it kills in my name." A passive population under a regime with the power to kill is fascism.

Justice Scalia's facile identification of divine authority with government goes against the prophetic biblical tradition, which began with Moses's resistance to the Egyptian pharaoh to lead the Hebrews out of slavery. The first liberating insight of the Hebrew prophets was that social systems and their rulers had Yahweh's blessing only if they practiced justice and cared for outcasts like the "orphan and the widow." Scalia, however, identifies government as God's "minister," no requirements asked, free to kill "enemies" at will—however they choose to define them. Nigeria, for example, demands that a woman convicted of the crime of adultery be stoned to death. If a child is born as a result of her unlawful act, she is allowed one year to wean her infant before she is taken away to be stoned.[26]

Amnesty International has amply documented that whenever governments are given absolute power to kill "enemies" they invariably kill the weak, the poor, the misfits, and the disenfranchised. Justice Scalia's God is a God of wrath, who desires punishment and even death for "evildoers." In *Callins v. Collins,* Scalia laments: "How enviable a quiet death by lethal injection" compared to the tortured death the perpetrator inflicted on his victim.[27]

Justice Scalia says that Christians "[are] more likely (than nonbelievers) to regard punishment as deserved." Here his theology is Anselm's view of atonement, which holds that suffering willingly embraced restores the sinner's relationship with God,[28] as if God's offended sense of justice can be placated only by human suffering. But what kind of God is that?

Justice Scalia's strict belief in the "doctrine of free will" underlies his absolutist view of individual responsibility. With God's grace, he explained, every person may "resist temptations to evil," a belief that is "central to the Christian doctrine of salvation and damnation." He rejects the "post-Freudian secularist [who] is more inclined to think that people are what their history and circumstances have made them, and there is little sense in assigning blame."[29] He believes that this "secularist" mentality plays a key role in Europeans' rejection of the death penalty.

Justice Scalia's doctrine of absolute free will takes too little account of damaging experiences that befall human beings, such as

sexual and physical abuse, alcoholic parents, drug addictions, aban-
donment, poverty, or mental retardation. For Scalia, few "mitigating
circumstances" reduce individual culpability for crimes. His cold
legal calculus scrutinizes only the individual's act in isolation from
personal history. He sees as empty "excuses" any attempt to show
that a human being who has been subjected to violence since childhood might one day explode into violence against others. Such a
rigid approach makes compassion impossible.

Not only does Justice Scalia judge behavior out of all context, he
reads the Constitution without acknowledging the influence of his
own moral values, and he quotes scripture without taking into
account the historical situations its authors were addressing. Such
compartmentalized thinking is the way machines work, not human
beings.

"These passages from Romans," Scalia writes, "represent the
consensus of Western thought until quite recent times . . . regarding
the powers of the state. That consensus has been upset . . . by the
emergence of democracy. It is easy to see the hand of almighty God
behind rulers whose forebears, deep in the mists of history, were
mythically anointed by God or who at least obtained their thrones in
awful and unpredictable battle, whose outcome was determined by
the Lord of Hosts, that is the Lord of Armies. It is much more difficult to see the hand of God or of any higher moral authority behind
the fools and rogues—as the losers would have it—whom we ourselves elect to do our own will. How can their power to avenge, to
vindicate the public order, be any greater than our own? So it is no
accident, I think, that the modern view that the death penalty is
immoral has centered in the West . . . the domain of democracy.
Indeed, it seems to me that the more Christian a country is, the less
likely it is to regard the death penalty as immoral. Abolition has taken
its firmest hold in post-Christian Europe and has least support in the
church-going United States. I attribute that to the fact that for the
believing Christian, death is no big deal."[30]

Forgive me, but I'm flabbergasted at the arrogance of a man who
says "death is no big deal" when it's not his child who's being put to
death or his father, or his wife, or himself—personal catastrophes that
he can't imagine. I cannot recognize Scalia's God, much less worship
such a God. Who can kneel in awe before the "Lord of Armies," a
military God whose divine authority is recognizable not in demo-

cratic leaders, but in kings, of all people, so many of whom were venal, arrogant men who sacrificed thousands of lives in their petty wars?

III

I've lived on the ground. For twenty years, I have encountered death row inmates and victims' families, guards and governors, lawyers and prosecutors, journalists, talk show hosts, and audiences across the country, learning all along the way about law, the Constitution, and the way the death penalty works—or doesn't work.

When I started out as a young Catholic nun teaching religion and English in junior high at St. Frances Cabrini in New Orleans, I never thought I would enter the surreal world of government killing chambers. I was profoundly naïve about the criminal justice system, the courts, and the horrendous sorrow of murder victims' families. Only when I lived among poor people did I become involved with death row prisoners. It took me a long time to realize that following the way of Jesus meant involving myself in the lives of the poor. For a long time, I thought Christianity meant prayerfulness, charity to the needy, and obedience to the teachings of the Catholic Church. Charity was the most important virtue, but its practice was directed to individuals, never to systems of oppression. It was up to "political activists" to change systems. I thought of myself as a nun, not an activist. I was a spiritual presence in the world. I prayed for the poor and left it to God to take care of them.

In the late 1970s, serious discussion arose in my religious community, the Sisters of St. Joseph of Medaille, about the dire struggles of the poor and disenfranchised. Why, some sisters were asking, were so few of us involved with issues of social justice? I said, because "we're nuns, not social workers. It's not up to us to change what has always existed in the world. Some will always be rich and some always poor. Didn't Jesus say, 'The poor you will always have with you'?"

I had learned that life on earth was a transitional affair, anyway. We were all just "passing through" on our way to heaven. In such a view, what do earthly concerns matter? So what if we polluted the air and water or chopped down rain forests? What did it matter if others suffered on earth, if they died young or had no medical care or a decent-paying job? The unspoken theology was that if people were poor, it must be God's will. And if that was so, then certainly it was not God's will for poor people to organize themselves to obtain justice.

But then I woke up. One day in June 1980 at a conference with my religious community, I heard a talk by Sister Marie Augusta Neal. She spoke about Jesus, and I can still remember the words she said that changed my life: "Jesus preached good news to the poor, and integral to the good news he preached was that they would be poor no longer."

Poor no longer.

Suddenly I got it.

Poverty is not God's will. It is caused by humans, and it must be changed by humans. The quest for social justice isn't only what "political activists" do, it's what Christians must do. I wanted more than anything to follow the way of Jesus: If Jesus aligned his life with poor people, so would I. But I realized I didn't know poor people. I was like the schoolgirl who wrote an essay, "The Poor Family," in which she said, "Once there was a very poor family. The mother was poor, the father was poor, the children were poor, the butler was poor, the gardener was poor, and the chauffeur was very poor."

So I went into neighborhoods where poor people lived, which in New Orleans isn't hard to do. Almost half the city's inhabitants, most of them African Americans, live in poverty. In 1981, following the trajectory of my new spiritual insight, I moved from a manicured lakefront suburb into the noisy, chaotic St. Thomas Housing Project among poor African Americans. I lived in an apartment with four other Catholic sisters, and we worked at a place called Hope House. We were the only whites in the neighborhood, and the kids called us "Sister." In fact, they called any white person they saw in the project "Sister," even Brother Joe Porter, who pointed to his beard and said, "Look, I'm a brother," which led the kids to call him "Sister-Brother."

Geographically, I had traveled less than five miles. Spiritually, I had crossed a galaxy. After I moved into our apartment in St. Thomas (I checked to make sure my bed was below the windowsill in case stray bullets came through the window), I was shocked at the contrast. I couldn't believe that this was also America. It seemed that I had changed countries: gunshots in the night or in broad daylight, blood on sidewalks, open drug deals, pregnant teenage girls, horrific encounters between young men and police, plenty of funerals and weeping mothers, and, for most young male residents, greased tracks straight into Angola Prison. Every family in St. Thomas seemed to have a relative in prison. Young men in St. Thomas talked about "doing time" the way my Catholic students talked about going to college.

In the early 1980s, the rage for incarceration began to further dominate American crime policy, resulting in a fourfold increase in the prison population. We now lead the world in our per capita incarceration rate. Two million–plus people currently occupy cells in state and federal prisons—1 in every 142 Americans. The criminal justice system claims 1 in 3 African American males ages twenty to twenty-nine and significant numbers of other minorities.[31] Each year, prisons disgorge into society the equivalent of the population of Seattle, many of whom are drug or alcohol abusers who received no treatment while incarcerated.[32] George W. Bush's "war on drugs" continues to spend two thirds of its budget toward punishment rather than treatment.[33]

I worked as a teacher at Hope House's Adult Learning Center, and it was here that I realized how privileged my life had been. My father was a lawyer, my mother a registered nurse, and we lived in a big, two-story house with servants (African American, of course), went to Catholic schools (all white, of course), and traveled extensively during summer months. Kids were coming into the learning center who had never ventured out of their neighborhood, except maybe to take a bus downtown to shop. Some came into the learning center having gone as far as eleventh grade in school. They stumbled through third-grade readers. Girls only sixteen years old came to classes with toddlers in tow. Attendance was erratic. Some family crisis or other always seemed to be going on in people's lives.

I thought of my excellent high school education at St. Joseph Academy in Baton Rouge. Before I graduated, I knew how to speak in public and to conduct meetings according to Robert's Rules of Order. I could read books and understand them. I had disciplined study habits. I felt confident that I could accomplish whatever goals I set, and everywhere I turned I had resources.

The young people in St. Thomas were, in theory, "free" to follow the great American dream; and despite the strong pull of criminality all around them, they were expected to know "the difference between right and wrong." Sometimes I'd hear inspiring stories about young African Americans who swam against fierce currents of poverty to graduate from college or become president of a bank. But not often. Success stories stood out because there were so few of them.

In St. Thomas, I began to read the newspaper through a new lens. I couldn't help noticing that whenever white people were murdered it was always front-page news, but when black people were killed the news evoked barely a five- or six-line article on the back pages.

I also read the Gospel stories about Jesus with a different bent. I noticed that he chose the company of outcasts. He touched lepers, ate meals with "sinners," and included women among his closest friends. And when the crowds came to him, trying to touch him, eager to hear his message, he was moved with compassion, because he saw they were "like sheep without a shepherd." He directed his fiercest anger at the religious hierarchy, calling them "blind guides" whose legalism led them to "strain out a gnat and swallow a camel," neglecting the "weightier matters of the law: justice and mercy. . . ." Law, he taught, was always to be tempered by compassion, and the Gospels amply record that it was compassion that drove him to preach all through Galilee and Judea, reaching out to the downtrodden and demoralized, whom he affectionately called "the least of these." I was shocked to realize that Jesus was a layman. Out of respect, people called him "Rabbi," but he was not born into the priestly caste. He was a carpenter, struggling to survive like every other Jewish peasant. Jesus lived on the ground, close to ordinary people, and they came to him in droves because he spoke to them directly from the experiences of his spirit-led life. More than half of his images and parables came from the natural world—clouds and wind, seeds and soil, sparrows and vultures, rocks and rivers.

As I joined with St. Thomas residents to protest the injustices they suffered at the hands of police, landlords, employers, and banks that "redlined" them,[34] I understood better why Jesus ignited such controversy. If he had preached only a "spiritual" message detached from social concerns, he might have lived to be an old man, tending a prize fig tree in his backyard. Instead, as the prophets Isaiah, Jeremiah, and Amos had done, he radically opposed the society of his day, not only by preaching, but by inaugurating a new kind of community that erased distinctions of "righteous" and "unrighteous" and welcomed everybody, even despised tax collectors, who collaborated with the Roman oppressors. "The last will be first," Jesus said, and showed his followers the meaning of leadership by washing their feet. He spoke out fearlessly and engaged in prophetic action, such as the "cleansing of the temple," an event of such importance that all four Gospels record it. According to the accounts, Jesus strode into the Jerusalem temple, whip in hand, and drove out the "moneychangers," turning over money tables as he went. Such a dramatic critique of the temple cult could not have been more disturbing to the temple priests, whose livelihood came from sacrificial offerings and other forms of religious taxation. Immediately following the temple incident, Mark ominously remarks, "When the chief priest and scribes heard [of] it, they kept looking for a way to kill him." The face-off in the temple culminated in a series of confrontations in which Jesus denounced religious leaders for oppressive taxation. "[You] tithe mint and rue and herbs of all kinds and neglect justice and the love of God" (Luke 11:42).

Life among struggling African Americans in St. Thomas gave me new eyes. I realized that if Jesus lived on earth today, he'd choose to live in a neighborhood like this. But mostly I was grateful that I had awakened to these new dimensions of Christianity. I read the lives of modern prophets such as Martin Luther King, Mahatma Gandhi, and Dorothy Day, whose faith impassioned them to transform society without resorting to violence. But not without controversy. Dorothy Day was fond of saying that the heart of the Christian Gospel was to "comfort the afflicted and afflict the comfortable."

When I went to live in St. Thomas, I realized how oblivious I had been to the sufferings of African Americans living right at my doorstep. When I made the move, friends and family and the sisters in my community feared for my safety, and my good Catholic mama at Mass prayed aloud for her "daughter in the ghetto."

I began to pray differently, too. Before, I had asked God to right the wrongs and comfort the suffering, but once in St. Thomas I realized that God had entrusted these tasks to me.

IV

Justice Scalia says, "I look at a text. I take my best shot at getting the fairest meaning of that text and, where it is a constitutional text, understanding what it meant at the time it was adopted."[35]

Can he do that? Can any human being ever read a text without bringing in personal convictions that color the text's meaning? Reading is a complex experience. There's the text itself and its placement in the document, the historical situation in which it was written, the author's presumed intent, and then there's the reader, who brings to the text emotions, beliefs, opinions, biases, attitudes, personal relationships (calm or turbulent), and maybe even the condition of his or her digestive system (dyspeptic or benign). Slobodan Milošević and Nelson Mandela may both read the words *human rights* and come away with radically different interpretations. Hitler, when he read the word *cruelty,* evidently did not think it described his treatment of Jews, Gypsies, the mentally retarded, and homosexuals. Justice Brennan inferred from the Eighth Amendment's prohibition against "cruel and unusual punishment" that the premeditated taking of any human life violates human dignity.[36] He called death in the electric chair the modern equivalent of "burning at the stake."[37] Another example is Justice Blackmun's earlier reading of the words forbidding "cruel punishment," which allowed him to affirm death sentences despite his personal revulsion for capital punishment. Like Justice Scalia, he felt it his duty to "apply the law" as the Constitution mandated. But when Blackmun finally dissented and declared the practice of the death penalty "unconstitutional," he was reading the very same constitutional text, though now after twenty years of frustrated efforts to apply guidelines he himself had helped to write.

Blackmun, of course, knew that the Framers of the Constitution acknowledged the death penalty, but he also took into account constitutional requirements added by the Framers to protect citizens facing death, such as "due process," "equal justice under law," "a speedy and fair trial," a right to "face one's accusers," an "impartial jury" of one's peers, and adequate defense counsel. If these protections were afforded defendants, Blackmun asked, why were some defendants sentenced to life imprisonment and others, whose crime seemed identical, sentenced to death? This element of "random and capricious" application of the death penalty had so troubled the Court that it declared the death penalty unconstitutional in *Furman v. Georgia* (1972).[38] Four years later, the Court reinstated the death penalty in *Gregg v. Georgia* (1976),[39] in a decision that included reforms intended to eliminate the randomness. But the unpredictable way the death penalty is imposed today is as arbitrary as it was when the Supreme Court declared it unconstitutional.

At any rate, it is clear in Blackmun's dissent in *Callins* that he had begun to read the Constitution with a different bent. Watch that word *read*. When we engage in the mysterious, open-ended act of reading a text, we're prisms, not mirrors. Everyone reads from a point of view. Like anyone else, Scalia perceives reality through the prism of values he holds dear, whether he's draped in the solemn black robe of his office or not. He has a bent all right, which I am learning as I read and meditate on the revelatory speech he gave at the Chicago conference. Actually, he has two bents: One is the philosophical disposition that shapes his interpretation of the Constitution, and the other is his theological understanding, which arises from his belief in a God of retribution who invests government with divine authority to punish "evildoers."

When Justice Scalia reads the Constitution, he finds that the Framers sanctioned the death penalty, and he believes that their words today mean just what they meant at the time. For him, the Constitution is not a "living" document to be interpreted by successive generations as the Old and New Testaments, for example, have been variously interpreted. Instead, its meaning is fixed by the Framers' intent, as if that intent were perfectly transparent on its face, requiring no further discussion. The Eighth Amendment forbids "cruel and unusual punishments," and it is clear that the Framers did not consider the death penalty "cruel" since they sanctioned its use in the Fifth Amendment of the same Bill of Rights that contains the prohibition against "cruelty."

Moreover, Justice Scalia argues that the Framers did not restrict the death penalty, and since they did not restrict it, neither may the Court. In fact, the death penalty has been imposed for an assortment of crimes, including rape, horse thievery, arson, even witchcraft. According to Scalia, if a state legislature or Congress wanted to hang thieves, rapists, or arsonists, the Supreme Court cannot stop them. The Supreme Court, he insists, errs in its attempts to restrict the death penalty, such as its proscription against death for the crime of rape[40] and the Court's exclusion of juveniles from death for crimes committed under the age of sixteen.[41] The age limit of sixteen, Scalia points out, is well above what existed in common law when the Constitution was written (boys as young as fourteen were hanged for stealing). Scalia also argues against unlimited use of "mitigating factors"—circumstances in the defendant's life that recommend mercy.[42]

When the Court rendered *Atkins v. Virginia* (2002),[43] declaring it unconstitutional to execute mentally handicapped persons, Justice Scalia disagreed so vehemently that he read a summary of his dissent from the bench. According to Scalia, *Atkins* is another example of the Court's imposing its "personal opinion" upon the Constitution and thwarting the Framers' intent. He points out that the Framers, following "common law," specified only that "idiots" were excused from culpability for their crimes, not mildly retarded people; and to prove his point, Scalia supplied the eighteenth-century definition of "idiot" as a person who "cannot account or number twenty pence, nor can tell who was his father or mother, nor how old he is, etc., so as it may appear that he hath no understanding of reason. . . ." Unlike "idiots," Scalia contends, mentally retarded offenders "know the difference between right and wrong." In addition, he says, the Framers would not have considered execution of mentally handicapped persons "cruel" or "excessive," because during the late eighteenth century, the only punishments "always and everywhere" considered "cruel" were the "rack and the thumbscrew."[44]

Such icy sophistry reveals someone profoundly separated from the human family. Justice Scalia never met Dobie Williams or any of the thirty-five "mildly retarded" human beings already executed by state governments because *Atkins* came too late to save them.[45] He never met Jerome Bowden, a thirty-three-year-old African American with the mind of an eight-year-old, whose execution so disturbed the Georgia legislature—the state known as the "buckle" of the "death belt" for its readiness to kill—that it voted to establish Georgia as the first state to prohibit the execution of mentally handicapped people.[46] Bowden was killed for the murder of Kathryn Stryker, but the only incriminating evidence against him was his confession, which was typed by police because Bowden could not read or write. As the warden and guards were about to strap him into the electric chair, Bowden said, "I want to thank the people of this institution for taking such good care of me."[47] It would be good if

Scalia met the prison officials who have the sorrowful task of carrying out the killings he authorizes. They probably don't know much about the Framers' intent, but they know that killing a man with the mind of an eight-year-old is an unconscionable act of cruelty, regardless of the eighteenth-century definition of idiocy or cruelty.

To justify the reversal of *Penry v. Lynaugh* (1989),[48] in which the Court had upheld the death penalty for mentally handicapped persons, the Court referred to eighteen state legislatures that had passed statutes forbidding execution of mentally retarded persons and declared that a "firm consensus" of an "evolving standard of decency" had emerged among the American people. Justice Scalia sourly called it "riding a trend."[49] My heart sank when I read in *Atkins* that Louisiana is one of the few states that in the last decade have killed people with an IQ under 70. One quivering human reality embedded in that cold statistic is Dobie Williams, whose IQ was 65. Under *Atkins,* he could have been spared. He came so close. *Atkins* was issued just a few years after he was killed.

I read *Atkins* while writing this book in the beach house of some friends, on the Gulf of Mexico. When I read the tragic timing of the Court's decision, I got up and walked along the beach. Sorry, Dobie. When Louisiana killed you, it was constitutional. Now it's not. I sketched out on the brown sand the name *Dobie Williams,* an ephemeral memorial that would soon fold into the sea with the tide. If Justice Scalia walked this beach and saw Dobie's name, he probably wouldn't recognize it. This name and this life, along with hundreds of others whose deaths he routinely authorizes, would mean nothing to him. The more I learn about Scalia, the more it seems fitting that he describes himself as a machine that dispenses death.

Though Justice Scalia insists that the Constitution is not "living" and does not "evolve," he recognizes that the "moral standards of decency" of societies do evolve, "but the instrument of evolution," he said in his Chicago speech, "is not the nine lawyers who sit on the Supreme Court of the United States, but the Congress of the United States and the legislatures of the fifty states, who may, within their own jurisdictions, restrict or abolish the death penalty as they wish."[50] Since legislators may do this only with a popular mandate, Scalia urges citizens who believe the death penalty should be abolished to devote themselves to the education of their fellow citizens to effect legislative reform.

I agree with Justice Scalia that educating the public is crucial if we're ever going to put government killing behind us—I devote my life to that purpose—but I disagree that legislation is the only way to abolish the death penalty, much less a realistic possibility in the foreseeable future. The southern states, which perform over 80 percent of the killing,[51] are the least likely to strike the death penalty from their code of criminal law. The "string 'em up and hang 'em high" southern legislators read the same Constitution that Scalia reads and insist, like him, that the death penalty is absolutely constitutional. These legislators win elections by being "tough on crime," and the legacy of slavery in these states casts a long shadow.

I reject the constitutionality of the death penalty because I've seen close up how the death penalty operates. The Supreme Court could declare the death penalty unconstitutional tomorrow morning if it were willing to confront the unfair patterns that have emerged during the last twenty-five years of state killing.

This constitutional discourse we're engaging in here—I by writing and you by reading—is a precious exercise of our citizenship, vital to our democracy, because it's our Constitution—we the people "own" it, and we must never leave its interpretation solely in the hands of "experts" like legal theorists or lawyers or even Supreme Court justices. The Constitution gives the people a voice with which to respond to the Supreme Court, which may misinterpret or even betray it outright. In *Plessy v. Ferguson* in 1896,[52] for example, the Court ruled 7–1 that the "separate but equal" Jim Crow laws, which went so far as to forbid African Americans to drink from water fountains labeled "White," did not violate the constitutional mandate of "equal justice under law." For fifty-five years, the Supreme Court upheld this apartheid until it ruled in *Brown v. Board of Education*[53] that, in practice, "separate" never meant "equal." *Plessy* is one of the worst examples of "bad law" ever issued by the Supreme Court. Under its long burden, African Americans suffered humiliation, hostility, and violence.

Yet racial attitudes continue to infect Supreme Court justices, as they infect everybody else, no less today than in 1896. As late as 1987, *McCleskey v. Kemp*[54] admitted the existence of racial "discrepancies" in the application of the death penalty but declared them "inevitable" and offered no remedy. What if *Brown* had said that racial discrepancies in the education of children are "inevitable"?

Notice that in *Brown,* the Supreme Court came to its decision through principled, constitutional arguments based on the Fourteenth Amendment's guarantee of "equal protection" of the law. What was relevant was the evaluation of lived experience under "Jim Crow" regarding the constitutional requirement of "equal justice under law."

When the Court reinstated the death penalty in *Gregg* in 1976, it laid out reforms intended to eliminate the random application of the death penalty. The Court ruled in *Furman* that a punishment randomly applied is cruel. And if there is any sure characteristic we know about how government death is imposed, it is its weird, unpredictable, arbitrary application. Annually a mere 2 percent or less of the fourteen thousand or so persons who kill are selected to die; and while it is true that some of these perpetrators have committed the "worst of the worst" murders, most were condemned to death because of their race, the race of their victim, or bad luck in drawing an abysmally inept lawyer. Consider also that over 90 percent of criminal cases are decided in plea bargains and never see a jury trial.[55] While some guilty defendants are allowed to plead to life, many more innocent ones are cowed into pleading to avoid the death penalty. Criminal courts, overwhelmed with the sheer number of cases, resort to "bargain basement" justice, in which it is easy for prosecutors to pare down defendants' rights by telling them that if they plead guilty, they will be spared the death penalty. The death penalty is not always on the table, but it's there often enough, and prosecutors admit openly that they use the threat of death to obtain confessions, thus avoiding long and costly trials. A bill in the Texas legislature to introduce life-without-parole sentences for felony murders has met defeat mostly because of strenuous objections by prosecutors. They fear that jurors, considering life-without-parole sentences as an alternative to death, would return far fewer death sentences.

Arbitrariness in the application of law is a silent invitation for biases and prejudices to exert invisible influence that thwarts "equal justice under law." It is no secret that in this country the impact of the death penalty has always fallen heavily on poor people and minorities, especially in the South. As we have seen in the cases of Dobie Williams and Joseph O'Dell, poor people don't have resources to make the law work for them, and people of color are powerless in the face of racist practices that infect the justice system at every turn.

If it can be called a justice system at all. When nine in every ten criminal cases are decided extrajudicially in the visiting rooms of jails and the back rooms of courthouses, guess who suffers the most discrimination?

The crux of the constitutional debate is this: If, despite twenty-five years of attempted reform, the death penalty is still imposed randomly, the practice of the death penalty is unconstitutional as surely as if the Framers had explicitly forbidden its use.

At the conference in Chicago, when a questioner asked Justice Scalia about this unfairness, he replied, "Do you want to have a fair death penalty? You kill, you die. That's fair."[56]

Denny LeBoeuf, my friend and a criminal defense attorney, is angry when I tell her that Justice Scalia said, "You kill, you die." "It's crass intellectual dishonesty for a Supreme Court justice to say this at a public conference, where the people in the audience may not have the time or the legal skill to refute him. Scalia knows that this formula does not offer reasonable norms to assess degrees of culpability."

V

My coming to live in the St. Thomas Housing Project was an awakening. And now that I was awake, I was ready to act. I was receptive to the casual invitation I got one January day to write letters to Patrick Sonnier, a convicted murderer on Louisiana's death row. I didn't know much about the death penalty, but I knew I had come to St. Thomas to serve poor people, and I figured that if this man was on death row, then surely he was poor. Around the neighborhood I'd heard, "Capital punishment means them without the capital get the punishment." Everybody knew rich people never go to death row. So I wrote to Patrick, thinking that writing letters was all that was expected of me. I never dreamed that two and a half years later, Patrick Sonnier would be electrocuted in Louisiana's killing chamber and that I'd be there with him, praying and telling him to look at my face when they killed him. I had never seen anyone deliberately killed. As guards strapped him into the electric chair, his eyes searched among the witnesses and found mine. As he left this earth, mine was the last face he saw. I left the killing chamber in shock, and driving home afterward, we had to stop the car so I could vomit.

I had also never been exposed to the searing pain of murder victims' families. Patrick Sonnier and his brother Eddie were convicted of killing a teenage couple. The seventeen-year-old boy, David LeBlanc, and the eighteen-year-old girl, Loretta Bourque, were found lying facedown in a deserted field with bullet holes in the backs of their heads. I was horrified. I could think of nothing more cruel. Prosecutors had no trouble convincing juries that the murderers deserved death.[57] Patrick Sonnier's jury was convened on Monday, and by the following Monday he had been found guilty of murder and sentenced to die in the electric chair.

When he was executed, the community said, "Good riddance. The scum had more kindness shown to him than he showed to his young victims." The hostility directed at him also found its way to me. "Who's the bleeding heart liberal (probably Communist) nun holding this scumbag's hand? Why doesn't she give comfort to the victims' families, where it belongs?" Headfirst I catapulted into the firestorm of public debate. For six weeks, angry letters poured into the New Orleans newspaper.

I let the controversy rage over me. I could hear in people's anger their deep moral outrage and fear. Patrick Sonnier's execution, legitimized by the Louisiana Legislature and approved by the U.S. Supreme Court, seemed right to most people. Patrick Sonnier had killed, and he deserved to die. It was simple retributive justice. It was American. "I'll be happy to pull the switch and fry this monster myself," said one irate citizen. "If you kill, you die."

But there was a quiet place in my soul. I had seen close up what it means for the government to kill a human being. I had also seen the effect such killings have on those who have to carry them out. In the death house, a guard pulled me aside and whispered, "I'm not happy, ma'am, about doing this, but it comes with the job. I got a wife and kids." I had listened to the anguished soul of Major Kendall Coody, the supervisor of Louisiana's death row, who had participated in five state killings. He said that afterward he couldn't eat and sat in his recliner chair, unable to sleep. He knew the crimes of every man on the Row, some of them "horrendous," but he also knew each of the men personally, which is a serious occupational hazard for someone who has the job of killing them.

I knew one important truth that the irate citizens of Louisiana did not know: I knew Patrick Sonnier. Through visits and conversations, letters and phone calls, I came to know that there was more to this human being than his terrible deed. I came to realize a truth that has never left me: Every human being is worth more than the worst act of his or her life. I was horrified by Patrick's crime. I still am. But I had waited with him in the last hours as guards shaved his head and eyebrows and the calf of his left leg, where the electrode would ground 1,900 volts of electrical current—and the final touch of shame, the diaper that the guards put on him before they took him to kill him. When they had finished with him, he looked stripped and fragile, like a bird without feathers, and anger flickered as he said, "I'm a grown man, and I have to leave this world with a diaper on." I had come to know his soul, and he told me that on the Row at night, when the lights were dimmed, he would fall to his knees by his bunk with his Bible and pray for the slain teenagers and their parents. "Nobody was supposed to get killed," he told me. As he walked to the death chamber, he handed me his Bible and I saw words he had underlined from Psalm 31:

> I am the scorn of all my adversaries, a horror to my
> neighbors;
> I hear the whispering of many as they plot to take my
> life;
> In you, O God, I seek refuge. . . .

For two and a half years, I had sent him books to read, listened to him, cared for him, prayed with him, and watched him learn and grow. He told me once: "It figures I'd have to come to prison to find love." As I waited with him during his final hours, he kept thanking me. Patrick Sonnier's brutal crime was unspeakable. But he was a human being.

In the storm of controversy around Patrick's execution, there was one criticism against me that stung. It was true that over the years as I visited Patrick, I had not reached out to the victims' families. I avoided them partly because I had never faced such extreme grief, and I wasn't sure how to comfort people in such pain. But it was also cowardice. I was afraid of the families' anger and rejection. I was offering counsel and solace to the killers of their children, so how could they not see me as an enemy? Reaching out to them would only upset them further, I told myself, assuming that every victim's family must be solidly for the death penalty. Better to stay away.

When I did meet them, my assumptions were shattered.

Lloyd LeBlanc, the father of the murdered teenage boy, David, said to me, "Sister, why didn't you come to see us? You can't believe the pressure we're under with this death penalty." He reached out to me in friendship, and I continue to visit and pray with him. David was murdered in 1977, and now, twenty-five years later, Lloyd and his family still suffer the pain of his loss. I will always remember the words of a man whose daughter had been killed in the Oklahoma City bombing: "Can we agree not to use that word *closure* anymore? There's not a day of my life that I won't remember how my daughter died."

I do not pretend to comprehend the pain these families suffer. As I attended murder victims' support groups, I realized how alone many of them feel. People tend to stay away from them for the same reason we back away from raging fires. Standing helpless in the presence of such unspeakable pain is not easy for any human being. Parents whose children are murdered suffer an "incurable wound," as the prophet Jeremiah described it. To lose your child to a savage murder, your parental love unable to protect your child, is unbearable. One night, coming from a Parents of Murdered Children support group, I made a decision to help victims' families. In a sea of sorrow, it was a small act, but real. With others I secured funding, office space, a telephone, and a Mennonite volunteer coordinator, and a murder victims' support group, Survive, came into being. Later, I became an honorary member of Murder Victims' Families for Human Rights. Each member of this group lost a loved one to murder, and each has found a way to face the loss without demanding the death of the perpetrator. Their accounts of navigating their way from vengeance to compassion are among the most riveting I have ever heard.

As I descended into personal tragedies of murder and its aftermath, I learned there were victims on both sides. The mother of Patrick Sonnier also suffered an "incurable wound." She bore the humiliation of her son's execution and the hatred of her townspeople. Vicious calls drove her to disconnect her telephone. At the grocery store, the fierce, accusing whispers came, so she retreated into her house. Sometimes in the morning she picked up the bodies of dead animals thrown on her front porch during the night. She couldn't stop the hatred, which mingled with her own deep remorse for having failed her children. When the government kills human beings, it sends a signal that such criminals are no better than vermin. The family of the condemned are often treated like vermin, too. Patrick Sonnier's little daughter had to change schools because of the taunts of her classmates, and when a kind aunt asked if she'd like to take ballet lessons, she said, no, she thought she'd better take karate.

When I walked out of the execution chamber on the night of April 5, 1984, I didn't know that my life had changed. In the deep of night, a guard drove me in a van to the gates of the prison, and I could see clusters of amber lights from camps scattered across the vast eighteen-thousand-acre prison. I thought, *The people of Louisiana are sleeping, but if they could be brought close to see what happened here tonight, they would realize that we must find an alternative to government killings.* I didn't realize it then, but a mission was being born inside me that would shape the rest of my life. I had been an eyewitness to state killing, and what I had seen had set me on fire. Most people would never see what I had seen on this night unless I took them there. My resolve to share my experience was bolstered by trust in the basic goodness and decency of the American people. My mission began. I talked to whoever would listen.

I quickly became known as the "death penalty nun," and in the first years the audiences were small—ten, twelve people—and arguments were hostile. But through dialogue, I learned how to help audiences navigate their way through the fiercely ambivalent emotions that the death penalty evokes: outrage at murders of innocent victims and horror at the cold protocol of government killing. As I talked to audiences, I discovered that most people had scant information about the death penalty, most of it obtained from media sound bites or politicians' rhetoric. Not many knew that death sentences are imposed on very few murderers—2 percent or less.[58] This means that almost all murder victims' families—98 percent—never get the "justice" that politicians promise. Most were shocked to learn that capital cases, which some prosecutors call the "Cadillac of the criminal justice system," cost on average double or triple that of life imprisonment.[59] Nor did the great majority of people know that all states impose life without parole or long-term imprisonment for those convicted of capital murder.[60] Real life sentences. This is a crucial fact, because safety is one reason people support the death penalty. They fear that criminals will be paroled and kill again. For most people, the assurance that dangerous criminals will be imprisoned for life is enough for them to forgo the death penalty. Public opinion polls over the past ten years have consistently shown that when citizens are given a choice between death and life without parole, close to 50 percent choose life.[61] Many people, I discovered, are ambivalent about the death penalty. Few have reflected deeply about it, and most are wary of government's ability to efficiently run any program or manage public funds fairly or control their own bureaucrats, much less manage who should live or die.

In addition to my talks, I began to write guest editorials for newspapers, then magazine articles, and then my first book, *Dead Man Walking: An Eyewitness Account of the Death Penalty in the United States*. When *Dead Man* was published in 1993, my publisher, Random House, sent me on a book tour to cities around the country and set up media interviews. But my publisher and I knew that it would be a miracle if a book on such a grim topic, written by a Catholic nun, became a best-seller.

But, like a child, a book has a life of its own and goes where it wants to go—into bookstores and schools and into public consciousness, and the next thing you know, your life is public, too. During the two years it took to write *Dead Man*, I felt I wasn't doing real work like the other sisters, going out into their ministries each day. I was alone, day after day, tapping out page after page of words. Writing is like praying, because you stop all other activities, descend into silence, and listen patiently to the depths of your soul, waiting for the true words to come. When they do, you thank God because you know the words are a gift, and you write them down as honestly and cleanly as you can.

Miracles happen. One day sometime late in 1994, the actress Susan Sarandon telephoned me. She happened to be in Memphis and was reading *Dead Man* while filming *The Client*, which would bring her to New Orleans. We went to a great Cajun restaurant, the Bon Ton, ate crawfish étouffée, and talked about making a film. Susan was the midwife. She felt the urgency of making a film on the death penalty that would provoke serious reflection and debate. It took her six months to persuade her partner, Tim Robbins, to read *Dead Man*, but when he did, he saw its potential and invited me to their home in New York, where he and Susan and I sat in their living room and talked about what the film might be. Tim, from the beginning, knew that the film should be not a polemic, stacked with anti–death penalty arguments, but a journey to help the audience grasp the visceral, complex issues that surround the death penalty. He told me in our first conversation that he thought the deepest moral question about the death penalty is not whether we should execute the innocent. "Everybody knows it's wrong to execute innocent people," he said, "but what about the guilty ones who have done unspeakable crimes? Aren't we justified in executing them?"

The film opened in theaters in December 1995. People formed long lines to see it. Most film critics praised it. Theater managers reported that when *Dead Man* ended, audiences stayed in their seats all the way through the credits and then filed out of the theater in silence. I rejoiced in the success of the film and its likely impact. Public discourse is the soul of a democratic society and the way its people evolve morally. Without it we'd still be flogging disobedient slaves in the public square and white male property owners would be the only ones allowed to vote.

Susan received an Academy Award for her role in the film, and *Dead Man Walking* went out to the whole world. My nephew Steve, visiting his brother Don in Kathmandu, saw a homemade sign in the window of a little hole-in-the-wall café that read, "*Dead Man Walking* tonight."

My book hit the *New York Times* Bestseller List for eight months, was translated into twelve languages, and introduced the phrase *dead man walking* into television shows, editorials, political cartoons, and the commentary of late night comedians. I didn't know a book could have such power. People called to invite me to speak in universities, civic clubs, and churches. I responded to as many invitations as I could, and I still do. In the last six years, I believe I have traveled and spoken more than any politician who ever ran for national office.

After the film, the opera of *Dead Man Walking* premiered in San Francisco in October 2000, opening further public discourse on the death penalty. I'm not much of an operagoer, but I know that music can take us into unsuspected places of our hearts. I was glad when I heard the aria "My Journey," which my character sings, because that's what it's always been for me, a journey, ever since I entered the lives of poor people and wrote the first letter to Patrick Sonnier on death row.

Learning about death penalty law has been a big part of my journey. When I said to Justice Scalia that I was going to "take him on," it was not because I knew more about the law than he did. That would be nonsense. But I have seen state killing close up and the grossly unfair way it is meted out to innocent and guilty alike.

When I began visiting Patrick Sonnier, we talked about everything except the legal issues of his case. He trusted that his appeals lawyer knew what he was doing, and so did I. I knew that inept doctors could kill you, but I didn't realize that incompetent lawyers can also get you killed. And I really trusted the appeals courts to be fair. Didn't the United States have the best justice system in the world? Didn't emerging democracies all over the world look to our Constitution as a model? Wasn't the shining ideal, "Equal Justice Under Law," emblazoned on the marble portals of the U.S. Supreme Court building?

When in late November 1983 the Fifth Circuit Court of Appeals turned down Patrick's federal habeas corpus petition, I made a desperate telephone call to Millard Farmer, a champion defense attorney, to beg his help.[62] I had heard that Patrick's last recourse lay with the U.S. Supreme Court, which had begun to deny death row petitioners on a regular basis. Shortly after the Fifth Circuit denied Patrick's appeal, the state of Louisiana killed Robert Wayne Williams in "Gruesome Gerty," the state's electric chair, the first execution in twenty-two years.[63] Then, just a few months later, they executed John Taylor,[64] and suddenly I realized that unless the courts stopped the process, Patrick might be the next one killed.

I can still remember my relief when I heard Millard's gravelly Georgian voice: "Okay, we'll 'hep' you." Naïvely, I thought that no matter how far along Pat's case had progressed in the courts, a good appeals attorney like Millard could save his life. Patrick once mentioned that his trial lawyer "wasn't too good," which proved to be a stunning understatement. I would later learn that during the nine months Patrick was in jail awaiting trial, he received no correspondence or even a phone call from his court-appointed attorney. He had been brought before a judge for pretrial hearings alone, with no lawyer to advise him. Immediately before trial, his lawyer had met with him for only two half-hour periods. No wonder the trial ended so quickly. But once Millard Farmer took the case, I thought he'd point out the miserable quality of Patrick's defense and the appeals court would see the injustice and order a new trial. I couldn't have been more wrong.

When Millard agreed to help Patrick, I sent him two large packages of trial transcripts. He spent hours reviewing the transcripts, then drove eight hours from Atlanta to New Orleans to pick me up, and we headed to Angola Prison to see Patrick. As we rode, I learned that the courts are a system of gates that shut like one-way turnstiles. Once you come out, you can't go back. For appeals courts to review a case, Millard explained, the trial attorney must raise formal objections during trial; otherwise the courts rule that the defendant has "waived" rights of appeal. "Every time a defendant's constitutional rights are in question, the defense attorney should be objecting," Millard explained, and ticked off some of those rights: an opportunity to face accusers, protection from unwarranted search and seizure of one's property, an impartial jury of one's peers, provision of defense attorneys for the indigent, and, throughout all these proceedings, "due process" and "equal justice under law."[65] "Those last three—a lawyer, due process, and equal justice—are the big ones," Millard said, holding up three fingers, "especially in the southern death belt, where race and poverty still play a huge role in determining who dies." How, he asked, could we claim "equal justice under law" when it was "as clear as the nose on your face" that prosecutors usually sought the death penalty for the murder of whites but rarely for the murder of black people, especially when one black person killed another black person? "First there was slavery, then lynching, and now the death penalty," he said. "It's all about whites trying to control the black people, but now it's legalized." He said he thought that "hands down," the death penalty is the single most important civil rights issue of the day.

As we drove, Millard told hair-raising stories of defending impoverished black clients in small Georgia towns. One time when he was defending a black client on capital charges, he had walked out of the courthouse to his rental car and found a bullet hole in the back fender. The "good ol' boys" in the town, he said, "didn't take kindly" to his coming into town to defend a black man. When he reported the assault to the police, showing them the bullet hole, the policeman wrote "alleged bullet hole" on the report.

During another trial, the judge habitually addressed whites in the courtroom by their surname but called Millard's black client "Willie." Millard objected and asked the judge to address his client as he addressed the others, but the judge dismissed the objection and warned Millard not to raise it again. When the judge once again addressed his client by his first name, Millard not only objected but told the judge that his behavior was racist. And the judge's response? I asked. Millard smiled and said, "He threw me in jail overnight for contempt of court."

I liked Millard Farmer from the moment I met him. I admired his courage and his fierce dedication. Every one of his clients, including Patrick Sonnier, was too poor to pay him, so he defended them free of charge. This meant scrabbling for funds. But I had learned as soon as I started working at Hope House that working for social justice always meant scrabbling for funds.

When I told Millard about the dismal performance of Patrick's defense lawyer, he shook his head and said he'd include "ineffectiveness of counsel" in the federal habeas corpus appeal, though he was almost certain the courts would reject it, citing "abuse of the writ" (of habeas corpus). He explained that the court would object because the petition came after so much time had elapsed. "Abuse of the writ," Millard explained, prevented defendants from filing issues piecemeal, which would keep cases before the courts indefinitely. He agreed that courts needed "finality," but he would include "ineffectiveness of counsel" in the petition anyway, hoping that some fair-minded judge might understand why the issue was filed late. Millard explained that Patrick's inexperienced appeals attorney had failed to see the importance of the "ineffectiveness" issue and so hadn't filed it.

On April 5, 1984, six months after Millard and I had this conversation, the state of Louisiana killed Patrick Sonnier in the electric chair, and Millard sat by me and held my hand as we watched him die. Millard was as shaken as I. He had never lost a death row client. But I had summoned him too late. By the time he took Patrick's case, all the invisible one-way gates in the courts had closed. Still, he did everything he could to save Patrick's life. When his efforts in the courts failed, he turned to Governor Edwin Edwards to grant clemency. On the afternoon of Patrick's execution, Millard went to the Governor's Mansion and pressed for a personal meeting with the governor, but Edwards refused to see him and sent two legal aides in his stead. Undeterred, Millard stayed on in the mansion, mingling unnoticed among guests at a social event, looking for an opportunity to talk with Governor Edwards. Only when that effort failed did he telephone Patrick in the death house to tell him that he was going to die, apologizing profusely for his failure. Twenty years later, I still remember Patrick's response: "No, Mr. Millard, no, you didn't fail me. It's the justice system, it stinks real bad."

VI

Many people believe that the U.S. Supreme Court's attempt to craft a death penalty free of the arbitrariness of the past has failed. But more disturbing are the revelations that the system cannot even be relied upon to convict the right people. Since reinstatement in 1976, for every 8 persons executed, 1 wrongfully convicted person has been released from death row.[66] As of October 2004, 117 wrongfully convicted persons from twenty-five states have been released from America's death rows, and no one will be surprised if tomorrow's evening news carries yet another such story. It seems that our "machinery of death" can't achieve accuracy, much less master the finer points of constitutional protection. In light of the awareness that the "best court system in the world" is so seriously flawed, let's take stock of the Supreme Court's death penalty rulings and where they've brought us. Citizen scrutiny of the Court couldn't be more timely. Death penalty law issued by the Supreme Court over the past twenty-five years is confusing, contradictory, and full of surprising reversals. In the course of just thirteen months, between 1971 and 1972, the Court found that the death penalty was being constitutionally applied under the Fourteenth Amendment[67] yet unconstitutionally applied under the Eighth Amendment.[68] Then, four years later, they were ready to allow executions to resume based on largely untested statutes from Georgia,[69] Texas,[70] and Florida.[71] Current death penalty law stems from the Supreme Court's decision in *Gregg v. Georgia* in 1976.[72] The Court ruled the death penalty constitutional, and also ruled that the arbitrary application they had found in

Furman had been cured by the new procedures in Georgia's law. The Court's guidelines were meant to reserve death sentences only for the "worst of the worst" murders. What made the Court think it could enable jurors to distinguish between "ordinary" murders and the "worst of the worst" murders? Aren't all murders stunningly extraordinary in their singular and irrevocable impact? What grieving family would think of referring to the murder of their loved one as "just an ordinary murder"? The very concept is difficult to understand, much less apply. The closest parallel to the *Gregg* guidelines might be the Supreme Court's attempt to define obscenity, which says: You know it when you see it. If only the Court, while deliberating its attempted reforms in *Gregg,* had taken to heart Justice John Marshall Harlan's caution in *McGautha v. California* that any attempt to formulate "guiding standards" for weighing degrees of guilt was "beyond present human ability."[73] It wasn't possible, Harlan said, to formulate such guidelines in "language which can be fairly understood and applied." A stunning understatement.

The truth is, after twenty-five years of implementation, nobody—state legislators, prosecutors, judges, even U.S. Supreme Court justices—really knows what "worst of the worst" murders are. And in the practical realm, there are examples all over the place. Take Gary Ridgeway, known as "the Green River killer," for example. He pleaded guilty in Seattle (November 2003) to murdering no fewer than forty-eight women, yet he was not given the death penalty. And why not? Because prosecutors promised him life in exchange for information about his victims and where they were buried.

Furman v. Georgia (1972),[74] which declared the death penalty unconstitutional, hit the country like a thunderbolt. The ruling reduced the death sentences of about six hundred people who had been convicted of murder or rape and led many to think that the end of the death penalty in America was imminent.[75] In the twenty years preceding *Furman,* as the civil rights movement unfurled and crime seemed manageable, executions had dwindled, then stopped altogether. In 1957, for the first time in American history popular support for the death penalty fell below 50 percent,[76] which led Supreme Court justice Potter Stewart in *Witherspoon v. Illinois*[77] to regard unswerving death penalty supporters as a "distinct and dwindling minority."

In *Furman,* the Court found the death penalty unconstitutional, not because it was inherently "cruel," but because it recognized that the "random" and "capricious" way death sentences were meted out made it "unusual." Examining hundreds of capital cases, the Court could find no rationale to explain why some defendants received death sentences for crimes that seemed almost identical to crimes for which defendants received life imprisonment. The sheer randomness led Justice Stewart to state that getting a death sentence was like "being struck by lightning." The Court also recognized the troubling pattern in the way minorities and poor people bore the brunt of death sentences.

If the Court had paid closer attention to the geography of the six hundred death row inmates freed from death sentences in *Furman,* it might also have noticed a troubling pattern. Two thirds of the six hundred condemned occupied cells in the Deep South, mostly in Texas, Florida, Georgia, and Louisiana. And every one of the eighty-one condemned to die for rape (invariably of white women) was also in the South.[78] The Court could have asked why, although all states were governed by the same Constitution, such a small handful of states accounted for more death sentences than all the other states combined. But evidently the Supreme Court thought it could correct those disproportions. The Court thought the solution lay in clearer guidelines to help juries sort out the "worst of the worst" murderers, for whom the death penalty was solely intended.

In *Gregg,* the Court set out two reforms: guidelines for juries in sentencing and the division of death penalty trials into two distinct phases, one for determining guilt or innocence and the other for sentencing. The Court had a lot riding on the proposed new jury guidelines in *Gregg.* It had put states on notice that for death penalty statutes to be constitutional, they must include "checklists" of aggravating circumstances surrounding a murder, and mitigating evidence of all kinds must be allowed. Such "objective" criteria, the Court claimed, would help jurors better weigh degrees of culpability. Was the murder intentional? Was the murder carried out in a particularly vicious way? State statutes could also designate mitigating factors that might evoke mercy: Was the murder provoked? Were the defendant's mental abilities impaired? Was the defendant very young?

Florida, which had the most people on death row when the old laws were thrown out in *Furman,* was the first to pose a new death penalty statute.[79] It listed as aggravating factors a murder that was "especially heinous, atrocious or cruel."[80] The Florida Supreme Court approved the new statute, stating that "the meaning of such terms is a matter of common knowledge" and "an ordinary man would not have to guess at what is intended."[81] But just in case further clarification was needed, the Florida Supreme Court explained that "heinous" means "extremely wicked and shockingly evil," and "atrocious" means "outrageously wicked and vile."

Thus began a quagmire of words.

The U.S. Supreme Court shortly realized that such broad terminology could sweep in almost any murder as "aggravated," thereby raising the prospect of the arbitrary application that *Furman* had condemned. There was no way that the Court could review the facts of every one of the hundreds of death penalty cases that would come before them. Instead they left the job to the states, and the results could make your head spin.

Many horrendous murders came before the Florida Supreme Court: a victim beaten to death with a hatchet, another stabbed and left to painfully bleed to death, and the murder of three people who were first tied up and then shot in the head. The Florida court found none of these murders "especially heinous." Yet they upheld other far less bloody murders.[82] One such case involved a young man, a former convict and drifter, who had picked up a hitchhiker who along the way forced his driver to have sexual relations, bullied him into playing Russian roulette, and stole his money. During a fight that ensued, the driver shot and killed the hitchhiker. The jury determined that the crime was "especially heinous, atrocious and cruel" and the court sentenced the driver to death, and the Florida Supreme Court upheld the death sentence.[83]

No matter how many adjectives are thrown into state death statutes, the only real aggravating circumstance has to do not with modifiers but with nouns, not with the circumstances surrounding a murder but with who was killed and who did the killing. Since *Gregg,* eight of every ten persons executed for murder had white victims.[84] Economic class also plays a key role in determining death sentences. District attorneys, who must calculate cost, court time, and personnel resources, must decide which murder cases are worth the expense of the death penalty. The murder of one minority by another may not help a DA's next election. When "nobodies" are killed, law enforcement seems hardly to notice, much less vigorously prosecute the perpetrator.

I first learned about the low status of African American murder victims when I attended meetings of Survive, a support group in New Orleans comprising primarily African Americans. Of the forty or so families, not only had none of them seen the murderer of their loved one charged with a capital crime, not one had seen a case brought to trial. In some cases, there had not even been an investigation of the murder.

State death penalty statutes invariably include certain categories of citizens, whose lives are so valued that their murders qualify as a "death eligible" offense. Law enforcement officials usually top these lists along with children, then the lists vary. Some states include firefighters and other public officials; and state judicial committees constantly face new proposals to include other valued citizens on the list. If the murder of firefighters is death eligible, why not nurses or teachers? What about postal employees or city maintenance workers? If the murder of a twelve-year-old is a capital offense, why not thirteen-year-olds or any juvenile? This forces another question: Which murders do not justify the death penalty? Winos? Prostitutes? High school dropouts? Drug addicts?

If aggravating factors have been impossible to interpret, what about mitigating circumstances, which *Gregg* also required juries to consider? In 1978, after only two years of attempts to narrow the choices that juries had to make, the Supreme Court justices realized they had to open the door much wider if they were to allow for human differences. It was the case of Sandra Lockett that forced the dilemma.

Lockett, assigned as the driver in a team of burglars, waited outside a pawnshop in the getaway car while her accomplices robbed the place. Contrary to plan, the robbers killed the pawnshop owner, which made Lockett an accomplice to murder. Lockett went to trial, was found guilty of abetting murder, and was sentenced to death. Her lawyers argued before the U.S. Supreme Court that Lockett's situation as "getaway driver" ought to be considered a legitimate mitigating factor. After all, she hadn't killed anyone and never thought that anyone would be killed. It was not the plan to kill someone. So why weren't these mitigating circumstances equal to others that the legislature had approved? The weary Court ruled in *Lockett v. Ohio*[85] that no state statute could limit mitigating circumstances; the jury must be allowed to consider anything that might move them to show mercy. "Unguided discretion" was back, at least on the mitigation side of the death penalty equation.

As if the process of death sentencing was not inscrutable enough, what happens when jurors are asked to decide life or death by weighing mitigating circumstances against aggravating circumstances? What if the defendant, who committed an unspeakably outrageous crime, also suffered an outrageously abused childhood and is mentally ill? Consider the case of John Brooks of Louisiana, who shot and killed six people and who, during trial, said to a surviving victim, "I should have killed you when I had a chance." His mother told the jury that when she became pregnant with John at the age of thirteen, she thought she had a "bad case of worms" and so had beat on her stomach to drive the worms out. And as the tragedy of John Brooks's childhood unfolded, the prebirth beating proved to be a harbinger of many other beatings from other hands to come upon the little boy who was "not right in the head." What juror could be expected to follow a purely rational process to decide life or death for John Brooks? And what happens to jurors' hearts and minds when they are brought face-to-face with the weeping mother of the victim, begging them to "do justice" for her slain child, and the weeping mother of the defendant, begging them not to vote to kill her child?

Delma Banks Jr., who is black, was convicted of killing white sixteen-year-old Richard Whitehead and sentenced to die. The day before Banks's scheduled execution, the two mothers, Ellean Banks and Jackie Whitehead, were interviewed on National Public Radio.[86]

> Mrs. Whitehead: Like his daddy, Wayne loved bowling. Him and his brother started bowling when they were—couldn't even pick up a bowling ball, they were so heavy. He was just a sweet, innocent kid.
>
> Ms. Banks: Delma was a very kind person, took everybody to be his friend. He didn't think that there was no bad people. White and black; he just loved people.
>
> Mrs. Whitehead: I could think about a certain day of the month; they found him on a certain day.

We buried him on a certain day. And that day might pop up in any given month, it would just bring it all right back. It was like you just relive it. It's there and you never forget it.

Ms. Banks: It's not a day pass that I don't think about it. I feel like I have been on death row right along with Delma for twenty-two years. When he first went in there, he said, "Mama, here I am in here. I'm listening to these men brag about who dey done kill. I haven't killed anybody and look where I am!"

Mrs. Whitehead: I don't think I've ever questioned that he did it. Maybe we can just have some peace after almost twenty-three years.

Ms. Banks: I was sitting there at my desk. The telephone ring; Delma was on the other end. And he said, "I hate to tell you this, Mama." He said, "They wanna know who gonna be at my execution. They wanna know who gonna claim my body. They wanna know what I wanna die in and what I wanna eat for my last meal."

Mrs. Whitehead: I'm going to be a witness. But I tell him, I said when it actually comes time, "I really don't know if I can go in there."

Ms. Banks: I gotta be there. I gotta be a witness. I gotta be in there with him. I want him to see my face, tell him, "I love you. I love you," at the last.

Mrs. Whitehead: I think when a parent has to bury a child, it's quite devastating. And in that respect I can feel for how Ms. Banks would feel right now.

Ms. Banks: I've spent many sleepless nights thinking about what they going to do to my son; put him on that table and take his life. Twenty-two years and then they want to execute him. How can I say good-bye? (sobbing) I'm sorry. (sobbing) I can't make it if he don't. I can't make it.

Mrs. Whitehead: When something like that happens, it makes you remember to tell people that you

do love—tell them a lot that you love them, 'cause
they can walk out the door and never come back.[87]

The modern era of the death penalty has been presided over largely
by Justice William Rehnquist, who took over the reins of chief justice in 1986. In 1953, Rehnquist was a clerk at the Supreme Court
when Julius and Ethel Rosenberg were about to be electrocuted at
Sing Sing. He wrote a now famous memo saying, "It is too bad that
drawing and quartering has been abolished."[88] A Nixon appointee,
Rehnquist came to the Court in 1972 in time to dissent strongly
from *Furman,* which had declared the existing death penalty unconstitutional. In 1992, he intervened personally to ensure that the execution of Robert Alton Harris in California would go through.
During the twelve hours immediately preceding Harris's killing, four
separate stays of execution were issued by the U.S. Court of Appeals
for the Ninth Circuit. When the fourth stay of execution arrived,
Rehnquist was so exasperated that he not only overturned the stay,
but issued a direct order: "No further stays of Robert Harris' execution shall be entered except upon order of this court."

No further stays of execution unless ordered by the Supreme
Court? The chief justice of the highest court just put the
Constitution on its head. No matter how late at night it is or how
grumpy he feels, should he take it upon himself to order a lower
court to stop interpreting the Constitution and filing appeals? That's
their job. It's what lower courts are supposed to do. And the role of
the Supreme Court is to decide about those petitions once presented;
perhaps to disagree and rule against them, but certainly not to order
a court to stop doing what the Constitution mandates them to do,
especially at the eleventh hour. This incident illustrates, I think, just
how much emotionality and sheer ideology distort judgment in the
death penalty debate. Even the chief justice is not immune.[89]

Throughout the 1980s and into the early 1990s under
Rehnquist's leadership, the Supreme Court issued a series of death
penalty rulings that blocked almost every avenue of constitutional
appeal once open to death row inmates.

In *Strickland v. Washington* (1984),[90] the Supreme Court opened a
gaping loophole through which egregious examples of "ineffectiveness of counsel" could safely sail. The Sixth Amendment of the
Constitution promises to provide an attorney to citizens brought to

trial who cannot afford to hire one—about nine out of every ten defendants in capital cases[91]—and while the Constitution doesn't specify qualifications for these attorneys, the spirit dictates that appointed counsel is reasonably competent. *Strickland* established that for a defense lawyer to be declared ineffective, the condemned must demonstrate not only that his lawyer was incompetent, but also that without the lawyer's mistakes there was a "reasonable likelihood" that the outcome of the trial or sentencing would be different. With so many variables at work in juries' decisions, this was an impossible criterion. *Strickland* so shut the door to "ineffectiveness" claims that for fourteen years the Supreme Court did not find a single instance of "ineffectiveness" among the many claims of death row petitioners.

Effective representation is absolutely key. Poor people's inability to get decent defense—as the stories of Dobie Williams and Joseph O'Dell show—should alone have been sufficient to stop this punishment in its tracks. No matter what other death penalty reforms are undertaken, if defendants on trial do not have defense competent enough to challenge the prosecution's evidence, the adversarial system of arriving at truth crumbles, and wrong verdicts are inevitable. Justice Ruth Bader Ginsburg recognized the centrality of the defense issue: "People who are well represented at trial do not get the death penalty," Ginsburg said in support of a moratorium on executions. "I have yet to see a death case among the dozens coming to the Supreme Court on eve-of-execution stay applications in which the defendant was well represented at trial."[92] Dobie's trial lawyer, Michael Bonnette, was so inept that he failed to conduct forensic testing on the blood evidence, sat by passively as an all-white jury was seated to decide the fate of his black client, and offered virtually no mitigating evidence at the sentencing portion of the trial. His performance was so abysmal that a federal district judge, who rarely decided in favor of death row petitioners, overturned Dobie's death sentence, declaring that having a defense lawyer like Bonnette was like having no lawyer at all. But the Fifth Circuit overturned the district court judge's decision on technical grounds, arguing that the revelation of errors came too late under the Antiterrorism and Effective Death Penalty Act. The Fourth and Fifth Circuit courts (the federal appeals courts responsible for such states as Texas, Louisiana, and Virginia) routinely deny claims of "ineffectiveness of counsel," even when petitioners demonstrate that during trial their lawyers were drunk or on drugs.[93] Defense lawyers joke that in death penalty cases, the courts approve the performance of any defense lawyer who can pass the "mirror" test: Hold a mirror under a lawyer's nose, and if signs of breath appear, then yes, say the courts, you have a lawyer.

But recently—very recently—the Fifth Circuit and the Supreme Court at last found a case in which they could acknowledge that Texas had gone too far in allowing abysmal representation.[94] Calvin Burdine's court-appointed lawyer, Joe Frank Cannon, in full view of everyone in the courtroom, had slept during his client's trial. Unsurprisingly, Texas, where the quality of representation of capital defendants is so poor that a third of the lawyers who represented defendants sent to death row had been sanctioned for legal misbehavior,[95] upheld Burdine's conviction and sentence. Ten other clients of Cannon's also received death sentences.

A three-member panel of the Fifth Circuit at first ruled that the sleeping lawyer was not ineffective because it was not known exactly when during the trial the lawyer had dozed off.[96] Members of the panel reasoned the lawyer may have dozed off during boring parts of the trial. The panel's ruling was so outrageous that it precipitated a hearing before the entire Fifth Circuit, which for a death penalty case was a rare occurrence. At last, even the Fifth Circuit court had to agree that a defense lawyer who slept during his client's murder trial was ineffective.[97] Meanwhile, the "sleeping lawyer" story hit the national news and became an issue during the Bush-Gore presidential debates. When Texas governor George W. Bush, who presided over the killing of 152 prisoners, was asked what he thought about the sleeping lawyer, he chuckled. Nor would he later concede that even one convicted prisoner on Texas's death row might have been wrongfully convicted.

In *Stanford v. Kentucky* (1989),[98] the Supreme Court ruled that sixteen-year-olds could be killed by the government—a great irony, since American youngsters under age eighteen are legally prohibited from fighting in combat, voting, purchasing alcohol or tobacco, signing legal contracts, or witnessing executions. The reason given for excluding juveniles from such activities is their lack of maturity, which is why most countries adhere to the worldwide standard of protecting minors from execution. Besides the United States, the exceptions are countries like the Congo, Iran, Nigeria, Pakistan, and Saudi Arabia, and even some of these countries are reforming their laws. The world carried out fifteen executions of juvenile offenders between the years 1997 and 2001. The United States killed nine of the fifteen. The United States is the leading executioner of juveniles in the world and far out of sync with the human rights practices of most other countries.[99] Studies consistently show that juveniles who commit murder have often themselves been victims of abuse, which argues for the state's duty to heal and rehabilitate rather than kill them.[100] By mid-2003, there were seventy-eight juveniles on death row in thirteen states, twenty-eight of them in Texas. In refusing to ratify the UN Convention on the Rights of the Child, the United States gave as its main objection that it would be required to abandon the killing of juvenile offenders. Only two countries in the world—the United States and Somalia—have refused compliance with this treaty.

In *Ford v. Wainwright* (1986),[101] the Supreme Court did rule that the Eighth Amendment's proscription against "cruelty" prohibits killing the insane but provided no definition for determining insanity. As a result, states have set standards that make it almost impossible for a death row inmate to be found insane, and in fact, few have been spared under *Ford*. Recently, Texas executed Kelsey Patterson despite a recommendation from the state's notoriously harsh parole board that his sentence be commuted and despite the fact that he suffered from severe paranoid schizophrenia and had been found mentally incompetent on related charges.[102]

The Court compounded the problem for the mentally ill by holding that should insane death row inmates be restored to sanity through therapy or medication, the state could still kill them. This puts psychiatrists in the surreal situation of being called upon to "cure" clients so the state can kill them. In Arkansas recently, both state and federal courts allowed the state to forcibly medicate Charles Singleton with psychotropic drugs against his will to restore a suitable level of sanity.[103] The U.S. Supreme Court refused to review the issue, and Singleton was executed in 2004. At the time of his execution, he was voluntarily taking his medication and did not want further appeals filed.

In *Herrera v. Collins* (1993),[104] the Supreme Court ruled that even if a defendant has new evidence of innocence, he or she has no right to a federal hearing and must abide by the state's statutory cutoff date, which in Virginia was twenty-one days after trial and in Texas thirty days after trial. To gain a hearing after the statutory time has expired, a defendant must present a "truly persuasive demonstration of 'actual innocence.' " *Herrera* played a direct role in Joseph O'Dell's killing by the state of Virginia. It affirmed Virginia's outrageously short twenty-one-day cutoff date for presenting new evidence, which prevented O'Dell from ever getting a state hearing on DNA evidence. And when he tried to get a federal evidentiary hearing, he was told that federal courts are not required to hold evidentiary hearings if state courts have not held hearings, another ruling of the Rehnquist Court (*Keeney v. Tamayo-Reyes*).[105] The flood of DNA exonerations has caused some courts to rethink the validity of such unreasonable barriers, but the Court's decision in *Herrera* still stands.

In *Murray v. Giarratano* (1989),[106] the Supreme Court ruled that the Sixth Amendment's right to counsel did not extend to postconviction appeals. This means that once a death verdict has been upheld by the state's supreme court, the condemned loses the service of an attorney. This results in the dire situation that Patrick Sonnier and many other indigent condemned persons faced upon their arrival on death row: Two letters await them, one from the courts confirming their death sentence and the other from their attorney terminating his or her service. Some states provide funds for postconviction defense, but not all, and of those that do, it's usually not enough. Legislators in "death belt" states, who must allot the funds, do not look kindly upon defense lawyers who file what they see as "endless, frivolous appeals to delay executions and thwart justice."

Congress also has helped to shut the door on habeas corpus appeals. In 1996, the Antiterrorism and Effective Death Penalty Act for the first time in history set a one-year deadline for filing a federal habeas petition after state appeals had been completed.[107] More drastically, the AEDPA declared that federal courts were no longer allowed to exercise their independent judgment on the fairness of a defendant's trial. The new standard required federal courts to grant relief to death row petitioners only when state courts "unreasonably" applied federal law in denying a defendant's appeal. An accusation of "unreasonableness" is as serious for a court as the accusation of "malpractice" for a doctor. When higher courts overturn the rulings of lower courts, the disagreements are almost always about aspects of law or procedure about which reasonable jurists can disagree. It is extremely rare for a higher court to find a lower court decision so bizarre and irrational as to deem it "unreasonable." Since the AEDPA, the Fourth and Fifth Circuit courts, which almost always side with state courts against death row petitioners anyway, have upheld virtually every state court ruling in death cases. The AEDPA has guaranteed that federal courts would become nothing more than rubber stamps to state court rulings.

In the same year that Congress enacted the AEDPA, it delivered another devastating blow to death row petitioners by defunding federal resource centers, which had provided at least a modicum of post-conviction defense.

Finally, in reviewing the Rehnquist Court's death penalty rulings, we come to the most shameful of them all: *McCleskey v. Kemp* (1987).[108] In this ruling, the Court acknowledged that racial disparities permeate death penalty sentencing but refused to provide reforms. Even more than *Strickland* has blocked poor people from mounting successful claims of "ineffectiveness of counsel," *McCleskey* has blocked people of color from challenging racial discrimination in death sentencing.

The issue of racism in the application of the death penalty had arisen earlier in 1972 in *Furman v. Georgia,* but the Court had skirted that issue in its opinion. The evidence of racism in the way death had been disproportionately meted out to black men convicted of raping white women could not have been more striking. Of the 455 men executed for rape during the years 1930–1968, 405 were black, mostly in southern states.[109] Not a single white man was executed for rape over the forty-two-year period from 1930 to 1972 in Louisiana, Mississippi, Oklahoma, Virginia, West Virginia, and the District of Columbia. Yet when the Court addressed the issue of the death penalty for rape in *Coker v. Georgia* (1977),[110] it made no mention whatsoever of racial disproportion. Instead the Court ruled the death penalty for rape unconstitutional because it found the punishment excessive for a crime that was not murder.

But the best opportunity for the Supreme Court to address racism in death sentencing arrived in the petition of Warren McCleskey, a black man in Georgia who had been sentenced to die for killing a white person. In preparing McCleskey's petition, a law professor, David Baldus, conducted the most comprehensive study of racial impact on public policy ever undertaken in the United States. Baldus examined more than two thousand murder cases in Georgia throughout the 1970s and took into account 230 nonracial factors such as circumstances of the crime, social profiles of offender and victim, and economic and political variables.[111] The results were irrefutable, and the Supreme Court in *McCleskey* was forced to acknowledge the existence in capital sentencing of "a discrepancy that appears to correlate with race." The Baldus analysis demonstrated that people charged with killing whites had odds of being sentenced to death that were 4.3 times as high as for those who killed blacks. The study showed that the death penalty was handed down in 22 percent of cases involving black defendants who killed whites but in only 1 percent of cases involving black defendants who killed other black people. Baldus cited one judicial circuit in Georgia where even though 65 percent of homicide victims were African Americans, 85 percent of the cases in which the district attorney sought the death penalty involved cases in which whites had been murdered.

The Baldus study was later credited by the U.S. government's General Accounting Office, which scrutinized twenty-eight studies of racial bias in capital sentencing and found them to be "remarkably consistent" in their conclusion that killers of whites are more likely to receive the death penalty than killers of blacks.[112] The GAO found the factor of race present "at all stages of the criminal justice process," including the prosecutor's decision to charge a defendant with a capital offense or the decision to proceed to trial rather than plea-bargain. The research projects they reviewed took into account factors such as prior criminal records, heinousness of the crime, and number of victims.

When faced with similar empirical evidence of racism in housing and employment, the Supreme Court relied on legislative remedies; but not so in the administration of the death penalty. The Court had hoped that clearer statutory guidelines regarding aggravating and mitigating circumstances would channel the jury's discretion and alter the discriminatory pattern of death sentences. But clearly the guidelines were not working. The Baldus study provided the hard empirical data that revealed that what affected the imposition of death sentences was not just the circumstances surrounding a murder, but quite prominently the race of the victim in the underlying murder.

Faced with the irrefutable evidence of the Baldus study,

McCleskey gave the Supreme Court the opportunity to address the problem of race in the death penalty in a definitive way. But in its narrow 5–4 ruling in *McCleskey v. Kemp,* the Court not only ignored the consequences of the race studies, it did something worse: It legitimized racial discrimination in the application of the death penalty, declaring racial disparities "an inevitable part of our criminal justice system." To declare an evil "inevitable" sanctions its use as unchangeable and acceptable. In betraying the noble constitutional promise of "equal protection of the law," *McCleskey* says to every American man, woman, and child of color: Do not expect justice here.

Justice Lewis Powell wrote the lead opinion of *McCleskey,* joined by Justices Rehnquist, Scalia, White, and O'Connor. Later, when Powell retired from the Court, he said *McCleskey* was the one decision he regretted; but it was too late.[113] At the time of *McCleskey,* a political cartoon appeared depicting a judge presiding in a courtroom, in which the words *Equal Justice Under Law* were prominently displayed. Behind the judge were two doors that had signs over them. One door was marked WHITES, the other BLACKS, like signs in public places during Jim Crow.

McCleskey demanded of petitioners that they demonstrate intentional racial bias against them by the prosecutor. This is impossible. Human attitudes and motives are invisible and can be only guessed at, not demonstrated by empirical means. In other civil rights arenas, the Supreme Court considered the concrete effects of racially biased attitudes. When, for example, a black plaintiff sues landlords or realtors for housing discrimination, he or she can demonstrate a pattern of discriminatory activity: X number of black people were denied an opportunity to buy a house, whereas white persons of comparable financial means were allowed to buy. Patterns of behavior are concrete and demonstrable. Personal prejudicial intent is not. The members of the Supreme Court certainly knew this and in *McCleskey* even openly admitted that attempting to correct patterns of racial discrimination in the application of the death penalty would be too disruptive of the entire criminal justice system. It certainly would be—just as desegregating schools and public facilities had been disruptive. Standing up to racial injustice is always disruptive, especially in the United States, which for over two hundred years built its economy and social customs on the subjugation of black slaves. But aren't such self-corrections, despite the disruptions they cause, precisely what courts are for? Isn't that why the constitutional ideal "Equal Justice Under Law" has been chiseled into the front portico of the U.S. Supreme Court building?

At the time of this writing in 2004, the Supreme Court has yet to acknowledge the culture of racism it legitimized in *McCleskey.* Until the Court reverses *McCleskey,* district attorneys will have free rein to press hard for death sentences for those who kill whites, while neglecting to similarly prosecute those who murder blacks. And in a related issue, many prosecuting attorneys have been able to eliminate most or all people of color from juries in capital trials without fear of reversal by higher courts. Although the Supreme Court has outlawed such practices in *Batson v. Kentucky* (1986),[114] prosecutors have been able to circumvent the law by offering reasons other than race for eliminating each black juror. Attempts by DAs to deliberately exclude blacks from juries in criminal trials had become such a part of the culture in DA's offices, especially in the Deep South, that it was assumed to be normal and fair. A district attorney's manual surfaced in Dallas that cautioned prosecutors, "Do not take Jews, Negroes, Dagos, Mexicans or a member of any minority race on a jury, no matter how rich or well educated."[115] Although dated, such blatant documentation indicates the climate of racism that existed and still persists in some places.

We are not too far removed from a time when racism completely dominated social attitudes and the law, especially in the South, which is where close to 90 percent of executions are carried out today. The story of Emmett Till, a teenage African American boy from Chicago who was visiting relatives in Mississippi in 1955, epitomized the seething hatred that existed. According to one account, Emmett went into Roy Bryant's general store one summer day and bought some candy, and as Carolyn Bryant rang up the sale on the cash register, he "wolf whistled" at her, touched her on the arm, and said, "Bye, baby," as he left the store. Emmett's accompanying friends became frightened and quickly hustled him away from the store. As rumors of the incident spread, Emmett's aunt and uncle, with whom he was staying, became concerned for the boy's safety and thought of sending him back to Chicago, then thought that if he stayed quietly in the house, the incident would blow over. But a few days after the incident, Roy Bryant and his half-brother, J. W. Milam, came in the early hours of the morning and dragged Emmett from his aunt and uncle's house. His body was eventually found floating in the Tallahatchie River, and his mother insisted on an open-casket funeral so that "all the world [could] see what they did to my son." He had been savagely beaten and castrated, had an eye gouged out and a finger cut off, and been shot in the head. Milam and Bryant were arrested and tried before an all-white jury, who acquitted them. A year later, they told their story to William Bradford Huie of *Look* magazine, in exchange for which they were paid $4,000. In the interview, Milam talked openly about the murder:

> As long as I live and can do anything about it, niggers are gonna stay in their place. Niggers ain't gonna vote where I live. If they did, they'd control the government. They ain't gonna go to school with my kids. And when a nigger even gets close to mentioning sex with a white woman, he's tired of living. I'm likely to kill him. . . . I stood there and listened to that nigger throw that poison at me, and I just made up my mind. "Chicago boy," I said, "I'm tired of them sending your kind down here to stir up trouble. Goddamn you, I'm going to make an example out of you, just so everybody can know how me and my folks stand."*[116]

Stories of young black men made to suffer for not staying in "their place" continue to this day, as the trial, sentencing, and execution of Dobie Gillis Williams exemplifies.

Who decided Dobie's fate?

An all-white jury.

Who defended him?

A lawyer so unethical that he was later barred from practicing law.

Who upheld the legality of it all?

*In July 2004, federal authorities announced they were reopening the investigation of the murder of Emmett Till. Although J. W. Milam and Roy Bryant are deceased, investigators are questioning witnesses who know of others involved in Till's abduction and killing. See www. picayuneitem.com/articles/2004/07/30/news/11fbi.txt and www.kansascitykansan.com/ articles/2004/08/04/news/local/news4.txt.

Every appeals court in the United States, including the U.S. Supreme Court.

In a strange twist of irony, what happened to Dobie Williams, the "Many black," inside the Colfax courthouse, was mirrored a short distance outside the courthouse by a historical marker that stated that during the "Colfax Riot" on April 13, 1873, "150 Negroes" and "three white men" were killed. If Negroes only had been killed, it is doubtful that such a memorial would have been erected. Then, as now, the killing of whites is what elicits attention and concern, especially if the perpetrators happen to be persons of color.

The end of July 2003 marked the execution of the three hundredth African American since judicial killing was authorized in 1976. Of these, over 6 of every 10 (62 percent) had been found guilty of killing white victims.[117] Although African Americans make up 12 percent of the American population, they account for more than 40 percent of those condemned to death. Of those executed since *Gregg,* 1 in every 3 has been African American. The legacy of slavery is evident not only in the imposition of a disproportionate number of death sentences on African Americans, but also in their mass incarceration in jails and prisons. More African American males are currently incarcerated in America—4,834 per 100,000—than were incarcerated in South Africa at the height of apartheid—851 per 100,000.[118] In the days of Jim Crow, African Americans were prevented from voting through the use of "poll taxes" and "literacy tests." In Alabama today, 31 percent of the black male population, having been incarcerated, have permanently lost the right to vote. Also in that state, African Americans, who account for 70 percent of the executions between 1976 and 2000, make up 26 percent of the population.[119]

On federal death row, the impact of race is even more disproportionate than it is in states. Currently, more than two thirds of those condemned to death in the federal system are nonwhite.

The Supreme Court's *McCleskey* ruling, still in place today, has made it almost impossible for a person of color on death row to demonstrate racial prejudice during his or her trial.

But not every death penalty decision handed down by the Supreme Court under Rehnquist has been bad. In recent years, several positive developments have emerged. Some people believe that the spate of innocent people walking off death row in Illinois and around the country has contributed to a more cautious approach by the Court. In any case, there have been a few notable reversals, or at least refinements, of previous decisions.

In the year 2000, despite the restrictions of *Strickland* and the AEDPA, the Court ruled for the first time that a death row inmate had been given ineffective assistance of counsel. The Court reversed Terry Williams's death sentence[120] because his attorney failed to investigate the copious mitigating evidence in his childhood. With better representation, Williams was resentenced to life in prison.

In 2002, in *Atkins v. Virginia*,[121] the Court finally exempted the mentally retarded from the death penalty, reversing its previous position from 1989 because the justices found that a national consensus had formed against such executions. In the same year, in *Ring v. Arizona*,[122] the Court gave broader powers to juries in determining death sentences. As a result, many inmates whose cases had been decided solely by judges were now required to receive new sentencing hearings.

In two death cases from Texas, *Miller-el v. Cockrell* (2003)[123] and *Banks v. Dretke* (2004),[124] the Court gave partial relief to the defendants because of prosecutorial misconduct. Thomas Miller-el's case involved allegations of racial bias in the selection of the jury; in Delma Banks's case, the prosecutors withheld key evidence. Miller-el is being given a chance to appeal the adverse rulings from the lower courts; Banks will be given a new sentencing hearing.

And in *Wiggins v. Smith* (2003),[125] the Court reversed the Fourth Circuit and held that the state court had indeed been unreasonable in not finding ineffectiveness of counsel for Kevin Wiggins. In *Wiggins,* the Court took an unprecedented step to begin reform of their own slack requirements for efficiency of counsel in capital cases, going so far as to cite the American Bar Association standards, which now require, among other things, that defense attorneys in capital cases hire (at the state's expense) mitigation experts to conduct a thorough review of defendants' backgrounds (another ruling that might have saved Dobie's life had it happened sooner).

But for every positive decision of the Court, there were others that pointed the other way, and in virtually all of the cases just cited, a hard-line group of justices dissented from the majority ruling.

McCleskey together with other Supreme Court death penalty rulings of the past fifteen years have so restricted appeals on nearly every front that death row petitioners can lose access to almost all the protections promised them by the Constitution. This massive imposition of technical barriers to appeals, engineered by the Supreme Court and Congress, virtually assures that innocent people will be killed along with the guilty. Yet every ruling of the Supreme Court that has eviscerated these constitutional protections has been perfectly legal.

But legal doesn't necessarily mean moral. Laws have a way of legitimating prejudice, which unleashes brutality even in normally mild, respectable citizens. During the Nazi era, stories abounded of German citizens who revealed Jewish neighbors' hiding places to the Gestapo or who spat on Jews they happened to pass on the street. *Plessy v. Ferguson,*[126] which upheld racial segregation for many years in the South, played a part in the way that I, a little white girl, could sit at the front of the bus, laughing and talking with my white friends, without a twinge of conscience or concern about the black people forced to sit in the back of the bus. Good laws encourage people to be respectful of one another. Bad laws encourage meanness and cruelty, even to the point of making it acceptable to kill "undesirables" among us.

No wonder some African Americans call the death penalty "legal lynching."

The Trappist monk Thomas Merton said, "When the world ends, it will be legal."

VII

After twenty years of trying to make death penalty jurisprudence square with constitutional requirements, Justice Harry Blackmun finally gave up, declaring: "From this day forward I no longer shall tinker with the machinery of death."[127] Blackmun was driven to the forbidding image by frustration with the Court's reliance on "mechanical logic" in its deliberations on death penalty cases. By the early 1990s, members of the Court had grown impatient with the steady stream of petitions from death row prisoners—many filed only hours before execution—and so had installed procedural rules that screened out virtually every death penalty petition as soon as it hit the Court. Justice Blackmun saw that the Court had come to rely too heavily on purely extrinsic requirements, such as the time or manner in which petitions were filed, instead of looking at the constitutional claims that lay at the heart of the petitions. The "mechanical logic" troubled Justice Blackmun, not only because the procedural rules contradicted the spirit of the law, but because they insulated his colleagues from moral responsibility. The justices could claim that the procedures, which allowed no exceptions, legally prohibited them from considering the merits of death cases and thus relieved them of responsibility for the executions that inevitably followed.

Justice Blackmun, appointed by President Richard Nixon to the Supreme Court in 1970 because of his strong law-and-order philosophy, had arrived at his startling dissent in *Callins* through a long and painful odyssey. Signs of Blackmun's frustration with the Court's approach to death penalty cases began to surface in dissents in several cases prior to *Callins*.

In *Coleman v. Thompson,* a case in which the defendant, despite substantial evidence of innocence, had been barred from federal review because his attorney filed a notice of appeal three days past the state's deadline, Blackmun wrote: "The Court today continues its crusade to erect petty procedural barriers in the path of any state prisoner seeking review of his federal constitutional claims. Because I believe that the Court is creating a Byzantine morass of arbitrary, unnecessary and unjustifiable impediments to the vindication of federal rights, I dissent."[128]

In *Sawyer v. Whitley,*[129] Blackmun voiced his "ever-growing skepticism that, with each new decision from this Court constricting the ability of the federal courts to remedy constitutional errors, the death penalty really can be imposed fairly and in accordance with the requirements of the Eighth Amendment."

Blackmun's dissent in *Herrera v. Collins* brought his frustration to a boil. Shortly before his scheduled execution, Herrera, contrary to procedural requirements, had filed a second writ of habeas corpus, alleging he was not guilty of the crime and outlining the evidence he could show in federal court if given a chance at federal review. Earlier, the Supreme Court had ruled that defendants who failed to raise such a claim during their first habeas hearing thereby waived their right to a further hearing and on these grounds had rejected Herrera's petition.

Justice Blackmun wrote:

> I have voiced disappointment over this Court's obvi-
> ous eagerness to do away with any restriction on the
> State's power to execute whomever and however
> they please. I have also expressed doubts about
> whether, in the absence of such restrictions, capital
> punishment remains constitutional at all. Of one
> thing, however, I am certain. Just as an execution
> without safeguards is unacceptable, so too is an exe-
> cution when the condemned prisoner can prove that
> he is innocent. The execution of a person who can
> show that he is innocent comes perilously close to
> simple murder.[130]

Justice Blackmun, however, was no ideological rogue. Like Justice
Scalia, he too sought to interpret the Constitution according to the
"Framers' Intent," but he discerned that intent in a wider context.
As Blackmun saw it, the Framers of the Constitution, while
acknowledging the fact of the death penalty, never intended that it
be applied whimsically or unfairly, which is why they took pains to
spell out a Bill of Rights to protect individuals who might be brought
before the far-reaching powers of the state. Finally, Justice Blackmun
had come to realize that the Court on which he served was hope-
lessly bogged down in a quagmire of its own making.

After struggling for two decades to square death penalty law with
the Constitution, Justice Blackmun finally realized the heart of the
Court's dilemma: "It seems that the decision whether a human being
should live or die is so inherently subjective—rife with all of life's
understandings, experiences, prejudices and passions—that it
inevitably defies the rationality and consistency required by the
Constitution."[131]

But Justice Blackmun came to realize that the Court was never
going to be able to make death penalty law constitutional because it
was trying to reconcile two irreconcilable goals: consistency in cases
(the reason behind guidelines and procedural rules) and attention to
the unique characteristics of each case (ungovernable by formal
rules).

Declaring in *Callins* that "the death penalty experiment had
failed," Justice Blackmun thereafter dissented from every case affirm-
ing a death sentence until he retired later in the term.

VIII

When Justice Scalia made his remarks in Chicago, only one man in the audience stood up to him. "My name is David Bates," he said. "I'm a formerly incarcerated individual, served ten years in prison, was falsely accused of a crime, tortured, beaten. I'm worried because this [conference] seems more like a joke. You have innocent people on death row right now, who have been forced to sign confessions, who have been tortured, suffocated, beaten, and it's like this is a tea party here. I'm scared that you're a justice. I'm honest. I'm scared. I'm worried."[132]

Shortly before David Bates stood up, Justice Scalia remarked that during his fifteen years on the bench, he had seen "only one [death penalty] case" that raised "a little doubt" about guilt. The vast majority of appeals that came before the Supreme Court, he said, involved nothing more than "foot faults" of prosecutors.[133] Scalia uttered these unpardonably callous words in Illinois, of all places, which by December 1999 had been compelled to release thirteen wrongfully convicted men from death row. When evidence had set the thirteenth man free, Governor George Ryan, a pro–death penalty Republican, declared a moratorium on executions and mandated a thorough study of the death penalty system, a decision supported by 64 percent of the people of Illinois.[134] One year after David Bates raised concern for the innocent men on death row who had been coerced into signing false confessions, Governor Ryan pardoned Madison Hobley, Stanley Howard, Aaron Patterson, and Leroy Orange, from whom police had extracted confessions through beatings and by placing plastic bags over their heads. Each man had spent at least twelve years on death row. When he pardoned them, Governor Ryan declared that their cases were "perfect examples of what is so terribly broken about our system" and called the Illinois criminal justice system "inaccurate, unjust and unable to separate the innocent from the guilty, and at times very racist."[135] He blamed rogue cops, zealous prosecutors, incompetent defense lawyers, and judges who rule on technicalities rather than on what is right.

It took courage for David Bates to stand up in that assembly and face off with a Supreme Court justice, or perhaps it was outrage at cruelty and injustice. The memory of the beatings was what made Bates stand up, especially since he knew there were others like him, innocent, but worse—innocent on death row and facing execution. At that polite, intellectual conference he stood up, the only speaker that day who knew personally what the broken, flawed criminal justice system does to people. Bates spoke with an authority that cut through the jocular atmosphere, confronting everyone with hard realities, because he's been there, he's lived on the ground.

I

After a quarter century of experience with the death penalty, there are promising signs that Americans are beginning to abandon its use. Not according to Justice Antonin Scalia's rigid standard, which says that legislation alone reveals a national consensus to end the death penalty. In southern death belt states, anti–death penalty legislation is going to be the *last thing* to happen, and even then only under federal mandate. Unlike Justice Scalia, I see a wider framework for discerning "evolving standards of decency." I look at what people actually do—how they act—more than what they say. In the spiritual life I'm much more interested in people's spiritual practice than I am in their professional beliefs. "Annunciations are frequent. Incarnations are rare," St. Basil said in the fourth century, a sentiment that today might be translated as "*Say-so* is easy; *do-so* is difficult." So when we look beyond political rhetoric and opinion polls to focus on how the death penalty is actually implemented in the United States by real people, an interesting picture emerges.

The death penalty in the United States is experiencing a period of consistent decline for the first time in twenty-five years. Even as debate rages about the flaws in the justice system and how to fix them, the vast majority of American citizens in practice have already begun to shut down the machinery of death.

In 2001, the number of executions began to drop: from a peak of 98 executions in 1999, down to 66 in 2001, 71 in 2002, and 65 in 2003. The number of death sentences also began to drop from a peak of 320 death sentences in 1996 to 231 in 2000, 163 in 2001, 159 in 2002, and 143 in 2003.[1] Although the death penalty is currently legal in thirty-eight states, a dozen southern states account for eight out of ten government killings, so that if we add the twelve states that forbid all executions to the twenty-six states that rarely kill, we find that thirty-eight out of fifty states are letting the death penalty slip into disuse.[2]

Prosecutors, now more wary of convicting the innocent and aware that capital trials cost four to six times more than ordinary trials, seek the death penalty less often. Unlike other criminal trials, capital cases require two trials, one for determining guilt or innocence and another for sentencing, usually followed by eight or ten years of appeals. And now, because of the Supreme Court ruling in *Wiggins v. Smith* in 2003, the state must foot the bill for the services of mitigation specialists for all defendants facing capital charges.

Orange County, California, is an excellent example of the decline in death sentences. Well-known for producing juries that side with prosecutors on death penalty cases, Orange County in 2002, for the first time in ten years, failed to hand down a single death sentence. Even Philadelphia's district attorney Lynne Abraham, known for seeking the death penalty in 80 percent of eligible murders, in 2003 won only one death sentence in forty-five capital trials. During a recent budget presentation to the city council, which has passed a resolution calling for a moratorium on state executions, council members vigorously challenged Abraham about such a large expenditure of public funds to achieve a single death sentence.[3]

Federal death penalties are also in decline. In 2002, prosecutors failed to persuade juries to impose death in fifteen of sixteen federal capital trials. Over a five-year period—1995–2000—60 percent of federal prosecutors did not seek a single death sentence, leaving a clutch of firebrand federal prosecutors in five districts[4] to accrue 42 percent of the total number of death penalties. The distribution of the federal death penalty shows an even more pronounced pattern of racial discrimination than the states. As of April 2004, twenty of the twenty-nine persons condemned to death in the federal system have been people of color. Given its sporadic application, few federal executions are actually carried out (as of 2003, only three). No doubt the "trophy execution" was that of convicted Oklahoma City bomber Timothy McVeigh. But at a staggering price. By the time McVeigh recited his last unrepentant words, "I am the master of my fate," the government had spent $82.5 million to investigate and prosecute and over $15 million for defense.

The scarcity and unevenness in the application of the federal death penalty clearly troubles U.S. attorney general John Ashcroft, who uses the power of his office to pressure local federal prosecutors to seek the death penalty, even when they have judged a death sentence unwarranted.[5]

As death sentences and executions decline in most of the nation, the eagerness of many southern states to execute becomes glaringly apparent. In 2003, southern states performed 89 percent of executions. From 1976 to 2003, the South carried out 81 percent of all executions, the Northeast less than 1 percent, the West 7.1 percent, the Midwest 10.8 percent.[6] Contrast that with California—the state with over six hundred prisoners on death row, the largest death row in the country—which has executed only ten persons since the state reinstituted the death penalty twenty-five years ago. And in Colorado, despite aggressive efforts by prosecutors in over one hundred cases to obtain death sentences, only a single person currently occupies a death row cell.

Geographic disparity in the application of the death penalty is most pronounced when we compare the number of executions in Texas with that in the rest of the nation. In 2002, when fewer states conducted executions than in any year since 1993, Texas executed thirty-three people, accounting for almost half of government killings.

Six years after the Supreme Court's decision in *Gregg v. Georgia* cleared the way for the reintroduction of the death penalty, Texas had *140 people* on death row. New York, six years after its death penalty was reinstated, had *6 people* on death row. After reinstatement of the death penalty, it took nearly twenty years for Texas to carry out one hundred executions, but only five years to reach two hundred, and three years to reach three hundred. As of August 2003, Texas carried out 39 percent of all U.S. executions.

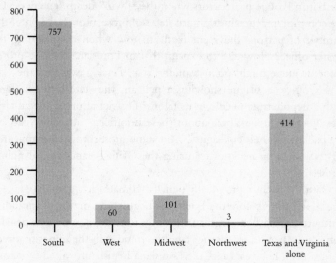

NUMBER OF EXECUTIONS BY REGION SINCE 1976

Source: Death Penalty Information Center, July 23, 2004
Note: Federal executions are included in the state where the crime occurred.

Maybe Texas has its own customized edition of the Constitution. Or maybe a very large concentration of the nation's "worst of the worst" killers happens to reside in the Lone Star State. Texas officials claim that similar murders occur in other states but Texans are simply more efficient in carrying out the law.[7] The "efficient" part is definitely true. The "why" takes more reflection.

How can fifty states, each bound by the same Constitution and Supreme Court guidelines, implement the death penalty so differently? Isn't this the capricious and arbitrary application of capital punishment that the Supreme Court attempted to correct in *Gregg v. Georgia*? The Supreme Court can tinker with death penalty guidelines all it wants, but patterns of implementation clearly show that who is killed and who is spared is determined largely by local culture—"our way of doing things here"—and not by law. In *Miller-el v. Cockrell* (2003), which widened the scope of evidence the Court may consider in establishing whether or not discrimination in jury selection takes place, Justice Anthony M. Kennedy referred to the "culture" of the Dallas (Texas) District Attorney's Office, asking if "happenstance" could explain why nine out of ten eligible black jurors were turned away.

What, other than "culture," can explain the celebratory meals of the Baton Rouge prosecutors when they "win" death sentences? Or the common practice in southern states of prosecutors boasting of the number of persons they sent to death row when campaigning for higher office? How else to explain that in Louisiana today, a prosecutor or judge might point proudly to a "Prick" award on the wall of his office, a plaque showing a pelican, the state bird, in flight with a hypodermic needle in its talons? District attorneys, even after they become judges, brag about these unofficial "atta boy" pats on the back from their colleagues. And some prosecutors have appeared for trial wearing neckties featuring the Grim Reaper or a dangling noose.

Within such a pro–death penalty climate, it's going to take a long, long time before the Louisiana Legislature, or any of the other southern "death belt" legislatures, votes to strike down death penalty statutes. In fact, in my home state, the trend is in the opposite direction. Only a few years ago, the Louisiana Legislature voted to *expand* the death penalty to include the crime of raping a child, even though the death penalty for the rape of an adult was declared unconstitutional by the Supreme Court twenty-seven years ago. The Louisiana legislators who passed the death-for-rape statute knew what they were doing. In a climate where most of their constituents accept capital punishment with the air they breathe and the mosquitoes they swat, the politicians knew their "tough on crime" legislation would play well in the next election. For that matter, the members of the Louisiana Supreme Court, who are also elected to office—or removed if they vote too often against the grain of their constituents—may have calculated that it would be far better to uphold the highly questionable statute and suffer the slight indignity of having their decision overturned by the Supreme Court than to suffer the ultimate humiliation of being unseated from office by disgruntled voters.

II

In 1992, Barry Scheck and Peter Neufeld, using DNA testing, proved that a New York truck driver had spent eleven years in prison for a rape he didn't commit. By 2003, Scheck and Neufeld along with other innocence projects had used DNA testing to free more than 130 wrongly convicted people from prison. (Scheck offered the highly sophisticated form of DNA testing on the evidence in Joseph O'Dell's case, but the Virginia courts refused to allow it.)

DNA provided the first tangible evidence that the criminal justice system was seriously flawed. As Scheck and Neufeld point out in their book, *Actual Innocence*,[8] before DNA testing, those trying to prove wrongful convictions had the almost impossible task of attempting to get witnesses to recant or real perpetrators to confess.

Realizing the unwillingness or inability of appeals courts to screen out the innocent from the guilty, citizens organized some forty pro bono Innocence Projects, modeled on Scheck and Neufeld's prototype at New York's Benjamin N. Cardozo School of Law. Most of these projects are staffed by students and supervised by professors.[9]

Despite the system's so-called safeguards, DNA testing proved that innocent people were being sentenced to death, and this prompted a grassroots reexamination of capital punishment.

On January 11, 2003, Illinois Republican governor George Ryan, a longtime proponent of the death penalty, found its administration so troubling that he pardoned four persons on death row and commuted (most to life without parole) the sentences of the remaining death row inmates—167 men—the largest mass commutation of death sentences by a politician in modern times.

Governor Ryan's journey from death penalty proponent to principled opponent was not easy. As a member of the Illinois Legislature, he had voted with the vast majority to reinstate the death penalty and as governor had not hesitated to sign death warrants. But three years before his historic act of commutation, Ryan had announced a moratorium on executions in Illinois, declaring, "I cannot support a system which, in its administration, has proven so fraught with error and has come so close to the ultimate nightmare, the state's taking of innocent life." He set up a bipartisan committee to conduct a thorough review of the death-sentencing system and two years later took to heart its eighty-five recommendations of reform. Only after the legislature refused to implement even one of his three proposed death penalty reform packages did he take his unprecedented step. In announcing the pardons and commutations, Ryan said he was well aware that most Illinois death row inmates were guilty; but, given the flawed system, he also knew that some were innocent, and killing even one innocent man was "unconscionable."

Governor Ryan told of his reaction to the exoneration of death row inmate Anthony Porter: "I watched in surprise as freed death row inmate Anthony Porter was released from jail. A free man, he ran into the arms of Northwestern University Professor Dave Protess, who poured his heart and soul into proving Porter's innocence with his journalism students. [Porter] was 48 hours away from being wheeled into the execution chamber where the state would kill him. It would all be so antiseptic and most of us would not have even paused, except that Anthony Porter was innocent of the double murder for which he had been condemned to die." To his opponents, who claimed that the release of Porter and the others proved that the justice system was working, Ryan responded: "A system that's so fragile that it depends on young journalism students is seriously flawed."

Stories of exonerated death row inmates, coming from twenty-five states, continue to find their way onto the nightly news. In Louisiana, John Thompson was acquitted of the murder of a hotel executive after being confined on death row for eighteen years. In a stroke of luck, the appeals attorneys who worked pro bono on Johnson's case for fourteen years uncovered a crime lab report that showed that the blood type of the robber, found on the victim's pants, did not match Thompson's. Prosecutors had withheld the crime lab report and made a deal with the other original suspect in the murder in exchange for his testimony implicating Thompson. In the tragic case of Frank Lee Smith of Florida, DNA testing, which exonerated him, was not done until after he died of cancer while still on death row, where he had spent fourteen years.

Public concern about the death penalty is reflected in the extensive coverage of the issue in the media. Since 1981, the number of news stories about the death penalty has doubled every five years. A growing number of newspaper editorial boards, even in death belt states such as Texas, Florida, and Georgia, have called for a moratorium on executions. *The New York Times* has called for abolition of the death penalty everywhere, declaring that the time has come for America to dismantle its "machinery of death."

In popular culture, reflection on the death penalty has also deepened. Thanks to the bold, talented contribution of Tim Robbins, Susan Sarandon, and Sean Penn, the film *Dead Man Walking* exemplified that a morally complex and controversial subject could be a resounding box office success. In the wake of *Dead Man Walking*, a stream of films exploring the issue of the death penalty followed: *Last Dance, True Crime, Eye for an Eye, The Chamber, The Green Mile, Monster's Ball, The Life of David Gale*, and *Monster*. Television network programs such as *West Wing* and *The Practice* began to feature serious treatments of the death penalty. One segment of *West Wing* ended with the president, after consenting to an execution, kneeling in the Oval Office and praying, "Forgive me, God, for I have sinned."

Justice Virginia Long of the Supreme Court of New Jersey called for a moratorium on the death penalty in that state, declaring, "It is time for the members of this Court to accept that there is simply no meaningful way to distinguish between one grotesque murder and another for the purpose of determining why one defendant has been granted a life sentence and another is awaiting execution."[10]

Judge Jed Rakoff of the U.S. District Court of New York declared the federal death penalty unconstitutional, stating, "The best available evidence indicates that, on the one hand, innocent people are sentenced to death with materially greater frequency than was previously supposed and that, on the other hand, convincing proof of their innocence often does not emerge until long after their convictions. It is therefore fully foreseeable that in enforcing the death penalty a meaningful number of innocent people will be executed who otherwise would eventually be able to prove their innocence. It follows that implementation of the Federal Death Penalty Act [passed by Congress in 1994] . . . *creates an undue risk of executing innocent people, and thereby violates substantive due process.*"[11]

Former Florida chief justice Gerald Kogan, who participated in over a thousand capital cases as prosecutor, defense attorney, and judge, said, "There is no question in my mind . . . that we certainly have in the past executed those people who either didn't fit the criteria for execution in the State of Florida or who, in fact, were factually not guilty of the crime for which they have been executed."

In May 2000, the New Hampshire Legislature became the second state legislature to vote to abolish the death penalty since its reinstitution in 1976. Although New Hampshire's governor vetoed the bill, the vote nevertheless signaled a dramatic change of sentiment about the death penalty among lawmakers.

A year before New Hampshire's historic vote for abolition, the Nebraska Legislature became the first in modern times to approve a moratorium on executions while a study was conducted. The prime sponsor for the bill was Senator Kermit Brashear, a Republican who favors the death penalty but is concerned about fairness in the way death is meted out. Although the Nebraska governor vetoed the bill, the Nebraska Legislature voted to override the portion of the governor's veto that would have halted the study of the death penalty. The comprehensive two-year study scrutinized the role of race, economic status, and other factors in approximately 1,500 homicide cases in Nebraska since 1973 and found that criminals are more than three times as likely to receive the death penalty if they murder someone relatively rich. The study also found that prosecutors in urban areas were more likely to pursue the death penalty than prosecutors in suburban and rural areas.[12]

Departing from his long-held pro–death penalty views, Republican delegate Frank D. Hargrove Sr. of Virginia stunned his fellow lawmakers by declaring, "One of the responsibilities of government is to protect the public. I have voted for the death penalty over the years numerous times. . . . But now that we have life without parole, I believe that addresses the [public safety] situation without a sentence that is irreversible. . . . This eliminates the possibility of the awful mistake."[13]

Columnist George F. Will, a strong death penalty supporter who once called a community's desire for execution a "noble" sentiment, was shaken by the book *Actual Innocence* and wrote:

> Conservatives, especially, should draw this lesson from the book: Capital punishment, like the rest of the criminal justice system, is a government program, so skepticism is in order. Horror, too, is a reasonable response. . . . You will not soon read a more frightening book. It is a catalog of appalling miscarriages of justice, some of them nearly lethal. Their cumulative weight compels the conclusion that many inno-

cent people are in prison, and some innocent people have been executed."[14]

Leaders of many U.S. religious denominations add yet another indicator of evolving standards of morality in our society. In 2004, as governors in Minnesota and Massachusetts attempt to reinstate the death penalty in their states, their strongest opponents are Catholic bishops. Once silent on the issue of capital punishment, Catholic bishops now call press conferences, give media interviews, phone and visit legislators, and encourage Catholics in the pews to do the same.

In the Los Angeles archdiocese, Cardinal Roger Mahoney sent every local parish a pastoral letter explaining the recent anti–death penalty development in church teaching and exhorting priests and congregations to work actively to end the death penalty. Included in the packet was a petition calling for a moratorium or freeze on executions while a two-year study of the faulty system is undertaken.

In March 1999, the fifty-five U.S. Catholic bishops issued "A Good Friday Appeal to End the Death Penalty," their most unequivocal statement yet of opposition to the death penalty. The bishops released the statement on Good Friday, a day when Christians recall Jesus's execution at the hands of the Roman state; and in their appeal, the bishops called on "all people of goodwill and especially Catholics, to work to end the death penalty . . . and . . . to support victims of crime and their families. . . ."

As of June 2004, 111 municipalities have called for a moratorium on executions. As of May 2002 in North Carolina alone, 21 municipalities and 1,055 businesses and organizations had passed moratorium resolutions.[15] On May 3, 2004, the New Haven (Connecticut) Board of Aldermen took an additional step and became the second local government in the nation to call for complete abolition of the death penalty.

As public discourse on the death penalty heats up, Gallup polls show a drop in popular support for the death penalty from 80 percent in 1994 to 65 percent in 2000. Following the events of September 11, 2001, support for the death penalty rose during 2002 and early 2003 but then slipped back to the lowest recorded level in twenty-five years—64 percent.[16] Yet even these numbers are misleading. When citizens are asked to choose between death and life without parole, support for death falls to 50 percent or less. Understandably, people are horrified by heinous murders, but when they are offered even a minimum of information about the death penalty—its impotence in deterring crime, its cost (on average two to three times more costly than life imprisonment), its application to less than 2 percent of murderers, its deadly mistakes—support drops precipitously. When I did research for *Dead Man Walking*, I learned that since the 1930s, when pollsters first registered public opinion on the death penalty, a majority of Americans have said they favor its use (except for a few short years in the 1960s when support dropped below 50 percent). But as I have learned in my twenty years of dialogue with the American people, this unreflected response arises more from the spleen than from the brain.

In 1972, Justice Thurgood Marshall in *Furman* argued that "informed public opinion" about the death penalty is, in fact, anything but informed: "The American people are largely unaware of the information critical to a judgment on the morality of the death penalty. . . . If they were better informed they would consider it shocking, unjust and unacceptable."

Citizens would consider the death penalty even more shocking if they could see it close up. But the death penalty is designed to make sure that doesn't happen. Executions are almost secret rituals, which only a handful of citizens are allowed to watch. All efforts to make executions public have failed. I believe that is a calculated decision. Warden Burl Cain, who held Dobie Williams's hand and prayed for him even as he nodded to the executioner to kill him, told me, "Let the public see what they are calling for. Let them see what it means to kill a man. Believe me, we'd see support for the death penalty go way down. I've said this publicly."

The widespread use of lethal injection masks the reality of death. But recent medical discoveries show that pancuronium bromide, one of the drugs used in the deadly cocktail, paralyzes persons being killed, which makes it impossible for them to cry out if they are in pain. Some veterinarians have testified they no longer use pancuronium bromide when euthanizing animals because if the medicinal procedure malfunctions, the animal cannot register distress. One woman on whom the drug was used while undergoing eye surgery told of being so paralyzed that she could not so much as "lift a finger" or cry out that she was in excruciating pain throughout the two-hour procedure. In a recent conversation, Gary Clements, a capital defense attorney in Louisiana, explained to me that the sole purpose of the drug is to make executions easier for witnesses because it spares them the anguish of seeing a person twitching and groaning as he or she goes into cardiac arrest. The drug, he said, serves no real function other than to mask distress.

But try as they might, state officials are never going to completely mask the death they impose. Every human being is a wild card, quirky and unpredictable, especially when he or she is led forcibly into a room to be strapped down and killed. Government officials would like the condemned to walk meekly to the death chamber, but that doesn't always happen. Above all, wardens and execution teams don't want a Leandress Riley or a Lewis Williams Jr. execution scene on their hands.

Leandress Riley was an African American man executed in San Quentin's gas chamber in 1953. He was small, weighing eighty pounds, and he was terrified. The guards carried him screaming and struggling into the gas chamber, where with great difficulty they strapped him into the metal chair and bolted the door. But just before they dropped the cyanide pellets into the vat of acid, Riley pulled his slim wrists out of the restraints and jumped up; he began to race around the inside of the chamber, beating frantically on the glass windows, where witnesses and media watched, horrified. Prison officials had to stop the process, open the chamber, and strap him in again. This happened three times. Word has it that none of the guards who participated in Riley's execution ever worked another execution.

Lewis Williams Jr., an African American man lethally injected by the state of Ohio in 2004, also did not go quietly to his death. Convicted of the murder of Leoma Chmielewski in 1983, he had occupied a cell on death row for twenty-one years.

The day before the execution, Williams had talked quietly with his lawyers and read his Bible. But when officials offered him the "special" meal the night before his execution, he refused, saying that he found sustenance in "the word of God." And when the twelve guards came for him the next morning, he struggled all the way to the preparation room, where officials waited to insert IVs into his arms. Williams kept shouting, "I'm not guilty, I'm not guilty, God, please help me, God, hear my cry!" It took nine guards to lift him from his knees, pry his hands loose from the edge of the table, and strap him down. One guard standing by his head alternately restrained Williams and patted his shoulder to comfort him. After the IV lines were inserted into Williams's arms, four guards carried him into the execution chamber as he shouted, "God, help me, please help me," a prayer he repeated when asked for a last statement as he was strapped onto the gurney in the death chamber. Standing behind a window about five feet away, his sixty-six-year-old mother, Bonnie Williams, wept and cried out, "My boy, my boy."[17]

Reginald Wilkinson, director of the Ohio Department of Rehabilitation and Corrections, said, "I would say it was disturbing. . . . It was probably as traumatic as anything our staff has gone through." And in an unusual move, Ohio attorney general Jim Petro publicly offered condolences to the Williams family along with the Chmielewski family.

I remember my conversation with C. Paul Phelps, head of the Louisiana Department of Corrections when Patrick Sonnier was executed in 1984, who explained to me how he tried to design a "humane" execution process. The protocol strictly prohibited any expression of emotion by "either side" during the entire execution process. Phelps said to me, "Don't take this wrong, but the process is meant to be almost clinical." I recognized that he was protecting himself. It's not easy to design a process to deliberately kill a fellow human being, even if you're doing something approved by law. When I asked Phelps if he would witness an execution, he answered, "Never in a million years."[18]

III

"Laws which are intended to moderate the ferocity of mankind, should not increase it by examples of more barbarity."

So wrote Cesar Beccaria in his *Essay on Crimes and Punishments* in 1764. Beccaria's arguments against capital punishment are still relevant today. Why pick and choose a few people to hang, Beccaria asked, when imprisonment is available? "It is not the intenseness of the pain that has the greatest effect on the mind," he argued, "but its continuance; for our sensibility is more easily and more powerfully affected by weak but repeated impressions, than by a violent but momentary impulse."

Beccaria also probed the moral implications of government killing, pointing out the "pernicious" effects of the death penalty on societies that practice it.

Beccaria was joined in his critique by several other writers of the Enlightenment—Montesquieu, Rousseau, and Voltaire—who put great store in rationality and systemic ordering and could not help noticing the haphazard way death sentences were meted out. Like Beccaria, they argued that the best deterrent to crime was the certainty of punishment rather than its severity. In the 1780s, this argument gained cogency as a growing prison system gave American society a practical way to incapacitate dangerous criminals and make society safe without government killings. Imprisonment has led the majority of countries around the world to eliminate capital punishment, a process that continues today. Of the 195 countries in the world, only 78, including the United States, still practice it (as of June 2004).

My heart goes out to the jurors in capital trials. They are ordinary souls, regular folks; yet they are called upon to decide the undecidable. They must stand before the white-hot fire of unspeakable crimes, look into the eyes of tormented victims' families and the equally tormented eyes of perpetrators' families, and render a verdict of life or death.

I remember a juror in New Orleans who got caught in the throes of this moral dilemma. To protect his identity, I shall call him the Anguished Juror.

He voted for death for a defendant, even though his conscience urged him to vote for life. He said the defendant "didn't look right," but the man's inept defense lawyer presented no information about his client's mental handicap or the brain damage he had suffered. When jurors met behind closed doors to decide upon a sentence, emotions were running high because the defendant's guilt was clear and the murder was especially heinous. The Anguished Juror recounted how his fellow jurors took a preliminary tally to determine what the sentence would be. A death sentence required unanimity. He said, "They were going round the circle and everybody was saying 'death, death, death' until it came to me, and I said, 'Hey, let's let the guy live; he'll be in prison the rest of his life.' " The juror said he was amazed at the anger heaped on him from the other jurors. He said he thought that jurors "would, you know, calmly and rationally discuss the pros and cons, and it would be like a democracy with every person free to vote his conscience." As it turned out, he was the only juror who had voted for life. The others wanted death, and in the end he, too, voted for death. In the years afterward, he lamented that he had not held true to his conscience, and he told his son, "Always do what your heart tells you is right, no matter what pressure people put on you."

By the time competent appeals lawyers investigated the condemned man's mental condition and arranged for a brain scan, the only forum left was the governor's pardons board. The Anguished Juror attended the hearing and begged the governor's appointees not to kill this man, because if, as a juror, he had been told about the defendant's mental handicap, he would never have voted for death, and without the jury's unanimity the death sentence would never have been given in the first place. Unmoved, the pardons board voted to uphold the execution. The appeals lawyer told me that on the night their mentally retarded client was killed, the Anguished Juror, drunk and weeping, telephoned to apologize once again for his failure of courage. He said that he had been given false information by other jurors, who told him that if the defendant got a life sentence, he would serve only seven or ten years and get out of prison and kill other people. It wasn't true. Life without parole for first-degree murder was solidly in place in Louisiana in the 1980s, but at that time the jurors were not allowed to know this.

Beccaria was right. The death penalty's most "pernicious" effect is on those who practice it. While theories of justification for the death penalty sound righteous, its implementation taints everyone it touches, especially when politics is thrown into the mix. Prosecutors, out to win a case at all costs or win an election, hide or manipulate evidence. Judges in capital cases may ignore defendants' constitutional rights. In the tiny percentage of murder cases in which the death penalty is handed down, the victims' families wait ten or fifteen years for the execution to come. The promised healing seldom comes at all. And on both sides of this terrible "death for a death" ordeal, mothers anguish: mothers of the perpetrators in the death house, who say a final good-bye to their children; and mothers of the victims, their children ripped from them, who grieve inconsolably—before and after the execution of the perpetrator. Some guards on "strap down" teams, who carry out the final acts of killing, return home afterward unable to sleep or eat or talk to their children about "Daddy's work."

Nor are the souls of U.S. Supreme Court justices exempt from the death penalty's pernicious effects. Justice Antonin Scalia, who claims to leave his moral beliefs outside the courtroom door, unashamedly identifies himself as part of the machinery of death. Chief Justice William Rehnquist, in his rush to expedite executions, shouts, "Get on with it!" and leads the charge in paring down condemned persons' access to constitutional protections. And in a fit of temper, he abuses his judicial power by ordering a lower court: "No further stays . . . of execution . . . except upon order of this court!" And Sandra Day O'Connor, who publicly laments the dismal state of defense counsel for poor defendants, herself penned the majority opinion of *Strickland,* which for almost twenty years made it very difficult for the condemned to demonstrate "ineffectiveness of counsel," and for twenty years approved case after case of abysmal lawyering at the trials of men and women condemned to death. In addition, O'Connor, in her enthusiastic endorsement of federalism, which turns judicial power over to states, has played a key role in investing states such as Texas with all the power they need to punish criminals as they see fit. Texas, with its long legacy of slavery, "sees fit" to target mostly African and Mexican Americans as the "criminal element," especially if they have committed crimes against white people. In September 2003, the execution of Larry Allen Hayes in the Texas death chamber made history. Among the hundreds of executions that have been carried out in Texas since the death penalty was resumed after *Gregg,* Hayes was the first white person to be executed for having murdered a black person. The law as it is written might be considered "neutral," but the people who implement the law are anything but neutral.

Nowhere is the "pernicious" effect of the death penalty more manifest than in the morally bankrupt reasons politicians give in its defense. Most politicians claim to favor restricted use of the death penalty, reserving it for the perpetrators of "the worst of the worst" crimes, which by now we know is impossible to determine. Many also claim that they support death for the sake of the victims' families. Such families, they say, deserve to see "justice" done. They claim that "closure" for victims' families demands that the government kill the perpetrator while offering victims' families front row seats to witness the "act of justice." Such a claim, that killing perpetrators is done for the sake of victims' families, is unique to U.S. politicians. The leaders of other countries, such as China, which carries out over half the world's executions each year (criminals are lined up by the hundreds in stadiums and shot), are more candid.[19] They simply say the law demands death. They talk forthrightly about retribution.

Surely American politicians must know that the *real* way to help murder victims' families is to make available victims' support groups and compensation funds. At the state level, victims' assistance for medical care, counseling, lost wages, and funeral expenses is almost always underfunded.

To see the "pernicious effect" of the death penalty at work in a politician and a state, look at Governor George Pataki and the state of New York. During his campaign for governor in 1994, Pataki pushed hard for the death penalty, claiming it would deter future murderers. Upon being elected, Pataki initiated a bill in the New York Assembly to reintroduce the death penalty. The bill was successful: In 1995, New York once again had a death penalty statute on its books. But implementing the statute proved to be almost impossible—and very costly. Over a nine-year period, hundreds of potentially capital cases were processed, netting a total of five persons on death row by 2004 at a staggering cost to taxpayers of $170 million. Recently, the New York Supreme Court found the death penalty statute unconstitutional and overturned it, which puts the legislature and the governor back to square one.[20] It's sickening to think how that $170 million could have been spent on real anticrime measures, such as helping at-risk kids or making available drug rehabilitation clinics to indigent youth.

Pardons boards, which governors set up ostensibly to dispense mercy to the condemned "where warranted," are seldom merciful. Before capital punishment became so politicized, governors dispensed mercy in 15–30 percent of the cases of those condemned to death. But for the past twenty years, grants of clemency have been extremely rare, and then almost always because of widespread public awareness of possible innocence. Only then do politicians feel "safe" enough to commute sentences or grant pardons. Illinois governor George Ryan's conscience-driven act of massive commutations stands out in sharp relief because it is so rare. While writing *Dead Man Walking,* I interviewed Howard Marcellus, a former chairperson of the Louisiana Board of Pardons and Paroles, and learned why pardons boards invariably uphold death sentences no matter what new information they receive. I told Marcellus's story in *Dead Man* because he was a political appointee who first acted out of political expediency but then had a change of heart. Over the objections of Governor Edwin Edwards, Marcellus asked to witness the execution of Timothy Baldwin, whose appeal for clemency he had voted to deny, even though he harbored grave doubts about his guilt. Marcellus wept when he told me how, like the Anguished Juror, he had succumbed to group pressure to deny clemency for Baldwin. Marcellus was the first person I met who was willing to tell me honestly how the pardons board operated. He said that when he accepted the governor's appointment to the board, his "marching orders" were very clear: Be *loyal* to the governor. What did that mean? I asked Marcellus. It meant, essentially, uphold death sentences no matter what new information is presented to you; say that the courts have thoroughly reviewed these cases and you're not going to second-guess the courts; keep these cases far from the governor, he doesn't want to be put in the public spotlight.[21]

In the twenty-first century, the investiture of absolute power over life and death in an individual governor represents the last vestige of the "divine right of kings." No power on earth is greater. Or scarier. Especially when such power is entrusted to politicians, motivated more by "expediency" than by conscience. Perhaps that's why Cesar Beccaria called the death penalty's corrosive effects on a society "pernicious." The dictionary defines *pernicious* as "that which does great harm by *insidiously undermining or weakening*." (italics added) Faced with a pending execution, no governor wants to appear callous about human life. So governors appoint pardons boards and meet with legal counselors, who siphon off the political heat of controversial cases. All governors claim to agonize over death penalty decisions. All claim to scrutinize every possible angle of the cases of condemned persons facing execution under their watch.

W. Bush during his six years as governor of Texas presided over 152 executions, more than any other governor in the recent history of the United States. Bush has said: "I take every death penalty case seriously and review each case carefully. . . . Each case is major because each case is life or death." In his autobiography, *A Charge to*

Keep, he wrote, "For every death penalty case, [legal counsel] brief[s] me thoroughly, reviews the arguments made by the prosecution and the defense, raises any doubts or problems or questions." Bush called this a "fail-safe" method for ensuring "due process" and certainty of guilt. He might have succeeded in bequeathing to history this image of himself as a scrupulously fair-minded governor if journalist Alan Berlow[22] had not used the Public Information Act to gain access to fifty-seven confidential death penalty memos that Bush's legal counsel, Alberto R. Gonzales, presented to him, usually on the very day of execution. The reports Gonzales presented could not be more cursory. Take, for example, the case of Terry Washington, a mentally retarded thirty-three-year-old man with the communication skills of a seven-year-old. Washington's plea for clemency came before Governor Bush on the morning of May 6, 1997. After a thirty-minute briefing by Gonzales, Bush checked "Deny"—just as he had denied twenty-nine other pleas for clemency in his first twenty-eight months as governor. But Washington's plea for clemency raised substantial issues, which called for thoughtful, fair-minded consideration, not the least of which was the fact that Washington's mental handicap had never been presented to the jury that condemned him to death. Gonzales's legal summary omitted mention of Washington's mental limitations and the fact that his trial lawyer had failed to enlist the help of a mental health expert to testify on his client's behalf. When Washington's postconviction lawyers shouldered his defense, they researched deeply into his childhood and came up with horrifying evidence of abuse. Terry Washington, along with his ten siblings, had been beaten regularly with whips, water hoses, extension cords, wire hangers, and fan belts. This was mitigation of the strongest kind, but Washington's jury never heard it.

Bush wrote in his autobiography that it was not his job to "replace the verdict of a jury unless there are *new facts or evidence of which a jury was unaware* or evidence that the trial was somehow unfair." (italics added) But new information about a mentally retarded man's battered, abused childhood that his jury never got to hear—wouldn't that qualify?

When Berlow directly asked Gonzales if he read the clemency petitions, he replied that he did so "from time to time." But Gonzales's summaries clearly indicate that he sided with the prosecutors. One third of his summary of Terry Washington's case is devoted to a detailed description of the gruesome aspects of the crime, while he fails to mention Washington's mental limitations and his miserably ineffective defense lawyer. In response to Berlow's direct question, Gonzales admitted that his conferences with Bush on these cases typically lasted no more than thirty minutes. Berlow confirmed this for himself when he looked at Bush's appointment calendar for the morning of Washington's execution and saw a half-hour slot marked "Al G—Execution."

To distance himself from his legal and moral responsibility for executions, Bush often cited a Texas statute that says a governor may do nothing more than grant a thirty-day reprieve to an inmate unless the Texas Board of Pardons and Paroles has recommended a broader grant of clemency. But anytime he wanted to, Bush could have commuted a sentence or stopped an execution. By the end of his governorship Bush had appointed all eighteen members of the board of pardons. He could easily have ordered a thirty-day reprieve and gotten word to the board that he had doubts about the fairness of a case and wanted an investigation and hearings. But the Texas Pardons Board is a farce. At least the Louisiana Board of Pardons and Paroles meets and holds hearings. True, they too routinely deny clemency, but they at least give the appearance of being a real, working board. The full Texas Pardons Board never meets to consider a death sentence. A few of them call one another on the phone. Sometimes. No one knows if the clemency appeals are even read.

In the Henry Lee Lucas case in 1998, Bush showed where the real power lay. He intervened with the Texas Pardons Board before they had a chance to make a recommendation, and after his intervention, the board handed him the decision he wanted: a 17–1 vote for commutation of Lucas's death sentence. The Henry Lee Lucas case gained national attention when it came to light that Lucas had been condemned to death for a Texas murder he couldn't possibly have committed, since he wasn't in the state at the time. Additionally, it was clear that Lucas would never be a threat to society because he was already serving six life sentences for other murders, which he may or may not have committed, since on a fairly regular basis he confessed falsely to hundreds of murders. Bush pointed out that jurors at his trial "did not know" certain facts that later came to light.

To make sure that he never had to examine death sentences seriously, Governor Bush used a legal tactic similar to the one used by the U.S. Supreme Court to block death row petitioners' access to constitutional claims: He restricted the standard for clemency so severely that no petitioner could qualify. He stated that since the courts had "thoroughly examined" every nook and cranny of a death row petitioner's claims and found no grounds for injustice, it was not his place to "second-guess" the courts. In his autobiography Bush wrote, "In every [death] case I would ask: is there any doubt about this individual's guilt or innocence? And, have the courts had ample opportunity to review all the legal issues in this case?"

But, of course, the courts would already have reviewed and rejected the legal issues of death row petitioners' cases before they landed on Bush's desk. As governor, Bush was literally the court of last resort for a condemned man or woman, vested with authority to dispense mercy or withhold it, according to his personal judgment. Unlike the courts, he was not restricted to pure legalities. As far back as 1855, the Supreme Court saw compassion and mercy as central to the exercise of gubernatorial clemency. This means that governors and their boards are free to consider *any basis for mercy:* mental handicaps, mental illness, childhood abuse, incompetence of defense counsel, remorse, racial discrimination in juries, signs of rehabilitation. Not uncommonly, such new facts of mitigation come to light only years after the trial, facts that the trial jury never heard and which appeals courts, following "procedural logic," routinely refuse to consider. In the Lucas commutation, Bush well knew how to use "new facts" that the trial jury "did not know" to persuade the Texas Pardons Board to do his bidding. It was not a lengthy, morally complex process. Bush stated his request and his board delivered.

If the jury who sentenced Karla Faye Tucker—another Texan whose death warrant Bush signed—had known of her drug-ridden childhood prostitution, would they have found mitigating circumstances to spare her life? And if, as her jury considered "future dangerousness," they could have been made aware of the potential for good in her character that would later make her such an exemplary prisoner, would they still have voted to kill her? The jury, deprived of foresight and thorough investigation into Karla Faye's childhood, did not have access to these "new facts," but George W. Bush did. In the Lucas case, when "new facts" presented themselves, Governor Bush requested the Texas Pardons Board for commutation. But when "new facts" in Karla Faye Tucker's case came to Bush's attention, he turned away, claiming that he was bound to follow the courts' decisions.

Berlow writes, "The fact that the courts have rejected a defendant's legal claims arguably places an added burden on the governor as the conscience of the state . . . to conduct a scrupulous review."

How, then, could Bush's legal counsel, Alberto Gonzales, systematically neglect to provide mitigating evidence or "new facts" that the petitioners' juries had never heard?

Easily. Once we realize that the "review" was a political game.

Gonzales produced exactly the kind of clemency review his boss wanted—a purely formal exercise, which never seriously entertained the possibility of real clemency for anyone. By the time Bush left the governor's office, he had denied clemency in all cases and refused to commute from death to life imprisonment a single death sentence but one—that of Henry Lee Lucas, because knowledge of Lucas's innocence of the murder for which he was about to be killed had become the subject of such national scrutiny that Bush could not afford politically to ignore it. Besides, the Lucas case emerged during the 2000 presidential campaign, when Bush had begun to portray himself as a "compassionate conservative."

By the time Bush had served as governor for a little over five years, he had presided over the executions of 130 men and 1 woman. Using the "thirty-minute formula," the clemency petitions of the men were denied with dispatch, but the plea for clemency by the woman, Karla Faye Tucker, presented a special challenge. By the time Tucker climbed onto Texas's lethal injection gurney, whispering, "Lord Jesus, help them to find my vein," her name had become a household word, not only in the United States, but around the world. Larry King's in-depth interviews with her on CNN made people feel they knew her personally.

Her crime could not have been more brutal. She had killed two people with a pickax as they lay helplessly in bed. But now people were talking about her fate, as arguments for and against clemency for condemned killers crystallized with new intensity.

The argument in favor of clemency for Karla Faye Tucker went like this:

Yes, she's guilty of a horrible crime—she killed two helpless people with a pickax—but she seems genuinely remorseful for her crime; she seems to have undergone a genuine, life-changing religious conversion. Even the warden and corrections officers attest that for fourteen years she's been a model prisoner. Couldn't she spend the rest of her life helping other prisoners to change their lives? Is a strict "eye for an eye" always called for?

On television screens across America, people saw Karla Faye Tucker's beautiful face as she talked about reading the Bible in her prison cell (she admitted *stealing* the Bible, not realizing it was free for the asking) and discovering Jesus, who "changed my life." In following Christ, she said, she had truly been made into a "new creation."

If only Karla Faye Tucker had not been so sincere, so *human*.

When Bush was presented with the Karla Faye Tucker case, a woman hadn't been executed in Texas in more than a hundred years. What was a "compassionate conservative" governor to do, especially one who claimed to be "born again"? Bush the politician knew that once he included religious conversion as a qualifier for clemency, his legalistic formula—stand behind court verdicts no matter what—would go up in smoke: others facing execution could claim that they too had been "born again" and so deserved clemency. Trapped in this political quagmire, he'd surely be accused of "second-guessing" the courts, and pro-death constituents would be displeased. Better, like Justice Scalia, to stick to the tried-and-true formula of retribution, which justified the sentence of death without reference to whether or not criminals changed their lives while awaiting execution. Retributive justice was just that—justice. You did the crime, you paid the price. By refusing to show favoritism, Bush would demonstrate the moral "toughness" required of a national leader. He could show that he "followed the law" even though his personal sympathies pulled him in another direction. This meant that no matter how strong the opposition to her execution, Karla Faye Tucker had to die.

But it was hard to kill her.

During her interviews with Larry King, she had looked directly into the camera and in a soft voice, in her unwavering, guileless tone, told the story of her life, presenting, for the first time, horrific childhood experiences her jury had never heard. Her chance for a loving, nurturing family had been shattered early on by her parents, who fought and finally divorced, leaving young Karla Faye and her older sisters to fend for themselves. Karla Faye first smoked pot with her older sisters when she was eight years old. By the time she was thirteen, she was shooting heroin. A year later, she dropped out of school and followed her mother into prostitution. She knew how to fight with her fists. She moved in and out of turbulent relationships with men. There were always drugs. There was always violence.

On the night of June 11, 1983, Karla Faye and friends began a weekend bash of heroin, cocaine, and pills. Two days later at 3:00 a.m., sleepless and high on drugs, Karla Faye Tucker and her boyfriend, Danny Garret, entered the apartment of Jerry Lynn Dean, whom Karla Faye had met two years earlier when he dated her best friend. There had always been animosity between them. On the night of the murders, Karla Faye's original plan had been to steal Dean's motorcycle, but once she was inside the apartment, robbery escalated into a frenzied act of double murder. Deborah Thornton, who shared Dean's bed that night, became an unwitting victim. Afterward, still high on drugs, Karla Faye bragged to friends that the killings aroused her sexually.

When arrested, Karla Faye Tucker readily confessed to the murders and implicated Garret. The jury sentenced Karla Faye Tucker to die. Johnny Holmes, the Harris County district attorney, was proud that he obtained more death penalties than any other DA in Texas. For Holmes, Karla Faye Tucker's death sentence was just one more political trophy. Holmes could brag that he was an "equal opportunity" district attorney, unafraid to impose tough sentences on women.

I visited Karla Faye Tucker and the other women on Texas's death row in October 1997, four months before her execution. I had been invited by Pam Perillo, Karla Faye's friend, who told me in a letter how she had watched Karla Faye change. She said that when Karla Faye had first arrived at the Mountain View Unit, "she had the foulest mouth you can possibly imagine" and would "snarl" at anyone who tried to befriend her. "She was far from the Lord," Pamela said, "definitely *not* saved."

In his autobiography, Bush claimed that the pending execution of Karla Faye Tucker "felt like a huge piece of concrete . . . crushing me." But in an unguarded moment while traveling during the 1999 presidential campaign, Bush revealed his true feelings to journalist Tucker Carlson. Bush mentioned Karla Faye Tucker, who had been executed the previous year, and told Carlson that in the weeks immediately before the execution, Bianca Jagger and other protesters had come to Austin to plead for clemency for Tucker. Carlson asked Bush if he had met with any of the petitioners and was surprised when

Bush whipped around, stared at him, and snapped, "No, I didn't meet with any of them." Carlson, who until that moment had admired Bush, said that Bush's curt response made him feel as if he had just asked "the dumbest, most offensive question ever posed." Bush went on to tell him that he had also refused to meet Larry King when he came to Texas to interview Tucker but had watched the interview on television. King, Bush said, asked Tucker difficult questions, such as "What would you say to Governor Bush?"

What did Tucker answer? Carlson asked.

"Please," Bush whimpered, his lips pursed in mock desperation, "please, don't kill me."

Carlson was shocked.[23] He couldn't believe Bush's callousness and reasoned that his cruel mimicry of the woman whose death he had authorized must have been sparked by anger triggered by Karla Faye Tucker's remarks during the King interviews. When King had asked her what she planned to ask Governor Bush, Karla Faye had said she thought that if Bush approved her execution, he would be "succumbing to election year pressure from pro–death penalty voters."

Election year pressure?

Bush was receiving thousands of messages urging clemency for Tucker, including one from one of his daughters. "Born again" evangelists such as Pat Robertson and Jerry Falwell, normally ardent pro-death supporters, urged him to commute Tucker's sentence. When Pope John Paul II urged Bush to grant mercy to Tucker, Bush responded disingenuously in a letter to the pope, saying, "Ms. Tucker's sentence can only be commuted by the Governor if the Texas Board of Pardons and Paroles recommends a commutation of sentence." On several occasions, Bush stated publicly that in deciding Karla Faye Tucker's fate, he was seeking "guidance through prayer," adding that "judgments about the heart and soul of an individual on death row are best left to a higher authority."

But there was no way Bush could avoid the godlike power thrust on him as governor. When Russian president Vladimir Putin declared that life-or-death judgments should be "left to the Almighty," he meant that such supposed judgments, even if they are believed to be divine, cannot properly be discerned and administered by flawed human agents. This recognition led him to oppose government executions. But while Bush claimed to leave the judgment of Karla Faye Tucker to God, in reality he exercised his own political judgment and authorized her death.

Karla Faye's death hit me hard. During my visit with her, she and Pam Perillo sat with me in a small chapel and talked together for an hour. Karla Faye said that she wasn't afraid of dying, but she dreaded the long car trip with the guards to Huntsville. Once before, when they had accompanied her to a court hearing, they had taunted her and delayed when she asked them to stop so she could "go to the bathroom." She said she had "delicate intestines" and a delay in getting to a toilet could prove "disastrous." "During those rides," she explained, "the guards have you in their power. Some are kind, but others are mean and not fond of me because I've gotten so much publicity."

How human, I thought. *Here she is, facing death on a gurney, and she's worried that the guards won't let her get to the toilet.* It reminded me of an incident recorded in the account of the martyrdom of Saint Ignatius of Rome, in which the saintly bishop, upon arriving at the Colosseum, where hungry lions awaited, bumped his shin as he stepped out of the carriage. The man was about to be torn apart limb from limb and the hagiographer felt the need to record that he *bumped his shin?* Yet there it is, the incident forever recorded, one small glimmer of the saint's vulnerable humanity.

When I heard Karla Faye's anxiety about getting to a toilet, I knew it was related to her sense of dignity. A woman, even as she is escorted to her death, does not want to soil herself. Dobie Williams refused a wheelchair so he could walk "on my own two legs" to his death. Joseph O'Dell refused tranquilizers so he could face death "awake and alert." It was this issue of human dignity that was the fulcrum of my dialogue with Pope John Paul II about the death penalty. "How can one possibly subject human beings to torture and death and yet respect their dignity?" I had asked the pope.

Here was Karla Faye, a woman who had transformed her life and would have been a source of healing love to guards and prisoners for as long as she lived, yet the iron protocol of retributive justice demanded that she be put to death. It was as if Bush and the pardons board had freeze-framed Karla Faye Tucker in the worst act of her life, then freeze-framed themselves into killing her. That's the way a machine works, relentless and preordained, with no room for the personal transcendence that conscience gives. It was all so mechanical, so unthinking, so *political*. That's why on the night of Karla Faye's killing, my anger at George W. Bush turned to outrage when Larry King aired Bush's press statement and I heard the way Bush invoked God to bless his denial of clemency. I already knew the substance of Bush's stance toward Karla Faye, but I had never heard the last sentence of his press statement: "May God bless Karla Faye Tucker and may God bless her victims and their families."

God bless Karla Faye Tucker?

Immediately after the statement, King turned to me for a response. When I heard Bush say, "God bless Karla Faye Tucker," I had to struggle mightily to keep a vow I made to reverence every person, even those with whom I disagree most vehemently. Inside my soul I raged at Bush's hypocrisy, but the broadcast was live and global. Not much time to rein myself in. I took a quick breath, said a fierce prayer, looked into the camera, and said, "It's interesting to see that Governor Bush is now invoking God, asking God to bless Karla Faye Tucker, when he certainly didn't use the power in his own hands to bless her. He just had her killed."

As governor, Bush certainly does not stand apart in his routine refusal to deny clemency to death row petitioners, but what does set him apart is the sheer number of executions over which he has presided. Callous indifference to human suffering may also set Bush apart. He may be the only government official to mock a condemned person's plea for mercy, then lie about it afterward, claiming humane feelings he never felt. On the contrary, it seems that Bush is comfortable with using violent solutions to solve troublesome social and political realities.

The aphorism "A hammer, when presented with a nail, knows to do only one thing" applies, par excellence, to George W. Bush. As governor of Texas, Bush tackled the social problem of street crime by operating the nation's busiest execution chamber in the country. At the time of the thirteen death row exonerations in Illinois, Bush stated publicly that although states such as Illinois might have problems with a faulty death penalty system, he was certain that in Texas no innocent person had ever been sent to death row, much less executed. That remains to be seen.

IV

In 2000, Senator Patrick Leahy of Vermont introduced to Congress a package of death penalty reforms called the Innocence Protection Act. The same year, U.S. senator Russell Feingold of Wisconsin introduced the first congressional bill to call for a nationwide moratorium on executions while the death penalty system is studied.[24] Recently, the American Bar Association issued stricter qualifications for defense counsel in capital cases, refurbishing its 1989 guidelines. And from legislative and blue-ribbon committees, recommendations pour in to make DNA testing mandatory for every defendant on trial for capital murder; provide access to DNA testing to death row inmates with probable claims of innocence; beef up qualifications of defense counsel at capital trials; establish funding and organization for a statewide system of indigent defenders; penalize prosecutors who hold back exculpatory evidence; tape not only confessions, but the entire interrogation of suspects by police detectives; be wary of jailhouse informers and take steps to reveal any deals they may have made with prosecution in exchange for testimony against a defendant; establish a state forensic laboratory independent of police and prosecutors; narrow the eligibility factors for capital punishment and exclude persons from execution who are mentally disabled; clear up jury instructions for both the guilt/innocence phase and the sentencing phase and make it mandatory that jurors are told of alternative sentences to death. The list of proposed reforms is long. But where is the political will to heed the recommendations and carry out the reforms?

In 2002, the Louisiana Legislature passed a resolution mandating that capital defendants on trial and death row inmates with issues of innocence have access to DNA testing. But the legislators allocated no funds for the testing. As a result, only a handful of defendants lucky enough to have aggressive and skilled advocates have been able to get DNA testing. Similarly, the Texas Legislature mandated DNA testing for capital defendants but put administration of the project into the hands of the overworked, bureaucratic, slow-moving court system. It is no surprise that only a few Texas death row inmates with innocence claims have managed to get DNA testing. Even so, DNA testing for every defendant accused of a capital crime is no magic bullet. Three in four homicides lack the biological evidence that DNA testing requires. After the defense has wrested funds from the state, the biological evidence may not have been preserved, or may be in a cardboard box somewhere in the back of a warehouse, or prosecutors may have deliberately destroyed it.

But one thing can be done: Improve the quality of defense. This is the central problem upon which practically everyone agrees, that attorneys appointed to defend poor people, especially in the southern states, are woefully inadequate. Speaking at a lawyers' conference, Supreme Court justice Sandra Day O'Connor said that poor people are at greatest risk of being wrongly put to death because of the defense they are likely to receive. Citing a study in Texas, O'Connor said that people with court-appointed attorneys were 28 percent more likely to be convicted and 44 percent more likely to be sentenced to death if convicted than people with resources to hire an attorney.

Testifying at the American Bar Association annual meeting in New York, Stephen Bright, a distinguished defense lawyer, decried the lamentable quality of indigent defense for capital defendants:

> A good example of the sad shape of the right to counsel is the recent argument made by Texas in the case of Calvin Burdine to the U.S. Fifth Circuit Court of Appeals. A Federal District Judge granted Burdine habeas corpus relief because the court-appointed defense lawyer slept through the trial. Texas appealed to the Fifth Circuit. I watched an assistant Solicitor General for Texas argue that the Fifth Circuit should reverse in that case and reinstate the conviction and the death penalty because *a sleeping lawyer is no different from a lawyer under the influence of alcohol, a lawyer under the influence of drugs, a lawyer with Alzheimer's, or a lawyer with mental illness.* All of those types of legal representation have been upheld as *not ineffective.* [emphasis mine, here and above] The judges actually engaged the Solicitor General in that argument, asking whether there wasn't a difference between a lawyer who's intoxicated but still functioning even though impaired, and a lawyer who is

completely unconscious because he is asleep. I was glad, as a member of the legal profession, that there wasn't a fifth grade class in that courtroom, because that argument and the fact that the court took it seriously is a disgrace to the legal profession. . . .

Luckily for Burdine, the Fifth Circuit, sitting en banc, disagreed with the three-judge panel's ruling [which upheld the prosecution's view that a sleeping lawyer was not ineffective]. The two votes of Judges Edith Jones and Rhesa Barksdale had outweighed Judge Fortunato Benavides' one dissenting vote.

Anyone close to the system realizes—and I think the public generally realizes—that you're better off in the courts today to be rich and guilty than to be poor and innocent. That's not equal justice. And if we can't do any better than what we are doing now, we should sandblast the words "Equal Justice Under Law" off the Supreme Court building.

Without adequate defense, fair trials are not possible. Defendants will be sentenced to death, not for committing the worst crimes, but for having the worst lawyers. With skilled attorneys, defendants accused of even the most heinous murders will be sentenced to death so rarely that capital punishment on that basis alone could be declared a violation of the constitutional requirement of "equal justice under law" and perhaps the Eighth Amendment's prohibition against "unusual punishment."

One story illustrates the point.

A journalist, Alex Kotlowitz, recently told of his interviews with jurors in Indiana, who had voted unanimously to spare the life of eighteen-year-old Jeremy Gross, even though they found him guilty of a truly egregious crime.[25] In fact, so brutal was Gross's crime, it seemed a foregone conclusion at the outset of the trial that the "death qualified" jury (in capital cases, jurors opposed to the death penalty are eliminated) must vote for death.

The crime had been recorded by four videocameras and was shown to jurors several times during the trial. Gross had entered a convenience store and shot and killed the cashier, Christopher Beers, in cold blood. The first shot hit Beers in the abdomen, the next in the chest. With Beers pleading, "Oh, God, please, no," and stumbling backward into the back office, Gross followed and, bending close, shot Beers in the face. Beers reached toward Gross, pleading, "Why, Jeremy, why?" and Gross told him to shut up, emptied the cash register, and fled. Jurors watched in horror as they witnessed the last agonizing moments of Beers's life, dragging himself to a pay phone to call for help, then collapsing by the receiver, his blood running in streams onto the floor, the receiver dangling above him. The jurors also heard an audiotape of Gross's confession. As the trial opened, the prosecutor said confidently, "There isn't a jury in this world . . . that would not recommend the ultimate penalty in this case, the death penalty." Surely if any murder met the Supreme Court's qualification of "worst of the worst," this was it.

But it didn't turn out that way, and the reason had everything to do with Jeremy Gross's defense. His forty-seven-year-old lawyer, Bob Hill, who had represented fourteen other men facing death sentences, stood before the jury and conceded that he had no case. He preempted the prosecutor and showed the videotape of the crime to the jury, openly admitting his own horror, which he knew the jurors must also feel. He recognized that during the sentencing phase of the trial, jurors are asked to sort out not only legal culpability, but moral blameworthiness. In his introduction, he told the jury, "There's no excuse for what Jeremy did, but I can explain how he gets to that convenience store. . . . You're talking about a coldhearted act, but you're not talking about a cold heart."

For the next five days, the jury heard from forty-one witnesses about Jeremy Gross's tortured young life, including testimony from his mother that Jeremy's father drank and beat her as Jeremy and his sister watched. Jurors saw photographs of Jeremy's mother with a welt on her neck, a gash on her scalp, and a blackened, bloodied eye. They heard that one of Jeremy's first memories was the sight of his drunken father slamming his mother's head against the refrigerator. They heard how Jeremy's mother would disappear for days while she drank and ingested prescription drugs and how she once poured lighter fluid on her drunken husband, asleep on the couch, and set him on fire as her children watched. Bob Hill had worked with mitigation specialists for a year and a half to prepare Jeremy's story. He unveiled two charts, called "chaos maps," which listed the twenty-seven addresses where Jeremy had lived by the time he was sixteen and the thirty-three schools he had attended. By the time Jeremy was eight and his sister was ten, they were taken by the state child welfare services.

Most of the jurors were parents. Some noticed that when Jeremy's mother testified, she made no eye contact with her son. Sometimes during the testimony, jurors cried. Some said they couldn't understand how a mother could be so uncaring. Some said they blamed Gross's parents even more than they blamed him. Gross had smoked marijuana immediately before going into the convenience store. Drugs were a sensitive issue for some jurors, whose children had struggled with addictions. One juror was a recovering cocaine and alcohol addict who knew firsthand how drugs could lead to violence. Once she had come close to robbing a convenience store herself, and on another occasion, drugged and furious, she had fired a gun at her husband but missed. For the defense, such moments of identification between jurors and defendant are what the mitigation portion of the trial is all about. Defense lawyers hope that jurors will see the humanity of their client no matter how horrific the crime and, even more, that jurors will come to the startling recognition "There but for the grace of God go I."

Jeremy Gross was fortunate to be defended by Bob Hill. Presenting childhood abuse as mitigation is tricky. As prosecutors will point out, not everyone who has a wretched childhood kills. Hill knew that he couldn't present Jeremy simply as an abused and broken individual. If the jury felt he was too far gone, they could easily decide to end his miserable life. Hill had to persuade them that there was something in Jeremy Gross worth saving. So he found the foster parents who for one short year had rescued Jeremy and his sister from their misery, surrounding them with love and kindness. They had enrolled Jeremy in the Boy Scouts, given him and his sister chores to do, and sat with them every night at dinner to talk about the day—like a family. Jeremy began to do well in school and played Little League baseball. "I was very proud of him, like he was my own son," his foster father testified, and choked up when he talked about how he and his wife had wanted to adopt Jeremy and his sister but were prevented by child welfare services, who returned the children to their mother. The jurors noticed that his foster father was the only witness with whom Jeremy Gross made eye contact.

The jurors voted unanimously for Jeremy Gross to live, which surprised even them. Going into the trial, all of them thought that justice would demand death. One juror remembers thinking, *This is pretty easy. This won't take long. Guilty. And death.*

I remember Millard Farmer teaching me the importance of the sentencing phase in capital trials. "Most defense lawyers put all their efforts into the guilt/innocence phase," he said, "and next to nothing into the sentencing phase. But showing the jury that your client is a human being with a human story is everything."

Bob Hill spent *eighteen months* preparing his argument for Jeremy Gross. He had to telephone and visit Jeremy's mother ten times before she would consent to testify. It is not easy for a mother in public to admit to gross negligence. In glaring contrast, Dobie Williams's lawyer presented such scant mitigation, a federal judge held that it was as if Dobie had had no lawyer at all. And Joseph O'Dell, representing himself, had expended most of his energies trying to gain acquittal; when he was found guilty, he was devastated and had neither skill nor money to assemble mitigation witnesses. He also had to contend with the prosecution's misleading the jury into believing that if they were to sentence him to life imprisonment, he could get out on parole and kill again. It wasn't true, but the jury didn't know that, and they did what they felt they had to do to protect the community.

To reform the death penalty system, the defense of Jeremy Gross must be the rule, not the exception.

Colorado's Office of the State Public Defender, led by David Wymore, chief trial deputy, is one of the best public defender systems in the nation and is the reason that Colorado has only one person on death row.

I met Dave Wymore in Boulder, Colorado, in 2003 at the University of Colorado, and he explained to me how public defense in Colorado works. In Louisiana, defenders of the indigent typically struggle under caseloads of hundreds of clients facing felony charges, some of them indicted for capital crimes. Wymore, who has been a public defender for twenty-nine years, told me the first thing he did was to travel to rural counties where the defenders were "getting the stuffing kicked out of them" on capital cases. "So I'd go in and handle the capital cases myself, and there was none of the 'good ol' boy' stuff that can go on between defenders and prosecutors. When I sit down with the prosecutor, I lay out the choice: the velvet glove or the whip."

Wymore begins each case by preparing the defendant to accept responsibility for his or her actions (when evidence warrants this). He has a set goal: a life sentence without a trial. He offers the prosecutor the velvet glove: My client will plead guilty and you win the case if you "are willing to take death off the table." But if the prosecutor wants death, Wymore tells him that he's not going to let the state kill his client, and if they lie or cheat by coaching eyewitnesses or hiding evidence or try another trick, he'll expose them and hold them accountable.

The Office of the State Public Defender in its existing form began in 1970 when county-funded public defenders' offices got together and lobbied for money from the legislature, arguing that a statewide public defender program would be cheaper and more efficient and would guarantee uniformity in the quality of defense across the state—all of which proved to be true. The legislature prefers to fund the defenders than to have judges appoint attorneys to overflow cases, which costs more because, as Wymore says, "private attorneys bill the hell out of the system."

Wymore thinks the defenders have been successful because they do not hire attorneys wishing to spend a couple of years in the office merely to get litigation experience. They hire only lawyers who seek a career in public defense.

What impressed me most is the thorough way Wymore trains defense attorneys to select a jury. He says that it's up to the defense attorney to expose the inherent bias in the courtroom, laying it on the table for the judge, the prosecutor, and the potential jurors to see. "You have to aggressively weed out what we call 'automatic death jurors,'" he says, explaining that most jurors presume death is the appropriate sentence and that it is up to defense to demonstrate that a life sentence is warranted. Not so, he says. "Constitutional law states that life is presumed and the burden is on the prosecution to prove that death is warranted." He teaches attorneys to ask jurors directly if they could ever vote for a life sentence even after convicting the defendant of cold-blooded, premeditated murder. Also, he urges defenders to object if prosecutors ask if jurors could "vote for" the death penalty given the right circumstances, then ask if they could "consider" mitigating evidence. Wymore says that defense attorneys must learn whether jurors are "ready, willing, and able to give positive value" to mitigating circumstances; and he presses them to strip away camouflages jurors use to disguise a deeply felt conviction that the death penalty is the only appropriate sentence for intentional murder. He unabashedly urges jurors to embrace what he calls "the jury bill of rights," explaining that one lone juror can prevent death, that any juror can make the decision to grant mercy, not because the defendant deserves mercy, but because mercy arises from the juror's own values or common sense. Perhaps most of all, Wymore urges jurors to respect each juror's decision but also to respect themselves by standing by their decision and not "caving in" to pressure from other jurors.

V

We read a newspaper account about a man kidnapped and held captive in an abandoned farmhouse. Although his abductor supplied the captive with food and water, he would periodically put a revolver to the defenseless man's head, cock the gun, and say, "Die," but the gun would click and the man would live to see another day. Sometimes the abductor would tell his captive to prepare himself, that he had one more month to live. But the appointed day of death would come and go, and the captive was still alive. When, at last, law enforcement officials located the house in which the captive was held, the abductor had fled, leaving the captive's body strapped to a bed, a dried trickle of blood coming from the bullet wound in his temple.

Anyone can tell the victim was tortured. The essential elements are there: The captive was defenseless and terrorized by the threat of immediate death. The crux of a newly framed constitutional argument that the death penalty, by its very nature, is torture involves these two elements. Amnesty International defines torture as an "extreme mental or physical assault on a person who has been rendered defenseless." Mental torture is harder to see than physical torture but is nonetheless real. Half a century of research has taught us that mental torture may cause more suffering than physical pain.

On the album of *Dead Man Walking* (Sony), Johnny Cash sings: "In your mind, in your mind . . . it all goes down in your mind. . . ."

Abuse of Iraqi detainees by U.S. personnel in Abu Ghraib prison has brought the subject of torture to the fore of public discourse.

Photographs of naked Iraqi prisoners stacked in a human pyramid and a naked man crawling with a leash attached to his neck shocked us. Seeing American soldiers pointing toward their captives and mocking them shocked us even more. The photographs made torture visible. But the mental torture of the death penalty is invisible, and so far the U.S. Supreme Court has refused to see it. In *Furman* and *Gregg,* the Court said that the intentional killing of human beings rendered defenseless is not an act of cruelty. The fact that Dobie Williams was brought to the brink of death three times before he was finally killed did not, in the Court's opinion, constitute torture. Nor did the mental anguish of Joseph O'Dell, who watched as two prisoners, one of them a close friend, were showered and led to execution a few feet away from his cell. He thought he was next. But his tears and the cry "They almost killed me" evoked no compassion in the Supreme Court. Neither did the cries of Betty Williams and the other mothers whose sons and daughters are killed by the state. Nor is the Supreme Court willing to acknowledge the slow, corrosive torture the condemned endure for ten or twenty years, confined in cells the size of a small bathroom (U.S. death row cells are smaller by a foot than the cells in Abu Ghraib).

The death penalty, the Supreme Court claims, is an act of retribution; so whatever suffering the condemned endure is part of the price they pay for their crimes. Punishment, after all, is meant to inflict pain. And while the Court disapproves of any form of physical abuse of prisoners (such as beatings, prolonged sleep deprivation, or withholding food and water or necessary medications), thus far it has ignored mental suffering endured by men and women condemned to death. In the Court's reasoning, even though life sentences without parole are available, only a "death for a death" will do. In *Gregg,* the Court says: "Retribution is an expression of the community's belief that certain crimes are themselves so grievous an affront to humanity that the only adequate response may be the penalty of death." And, as I noted in my letter to Pope John Paul II, the U.S. Supreme Court has ruled that killing human beings is not an assault on their dignity. Thus, by legalizing premeditated homicide, the Supreme Court legalizes torture. Morally speaking, this is dangerous, for it presupposes that a system of justice can in all cases identify the truly guilty with a degree of certainty that, we know, cannot be obtained. This ruling also seems oblivious to the corrosive effects on the souls of those who carry out the killings. "Afterward, when I get home I sit up in my La-Z-Boy chair the rest of the night. I can't sleep, can't eat," Major Kendall Coody told me after partici- pating in his fifth execution in the Louisiana death chamber. And his participation in the killings wasn't even direct. After prisoners were executed, his job was to collect their personal belongings to send to their families.

When the Abu Ghraib scandal first broke, government officials tried to confine blame to a few rogue soldiers, but inquiries revealed that the soldiers were working within a climate of abuse that had raised questions all the way up to the White House. Memos docu- mented that government officials first sought legal advice before ordering torture tactics against terrorist suspects. The question of Pentagon and Defense Department officials to their lawyers is shock- ing in its callous simplicity: "The Geneva Conventions prohibit us from torturing or humiliating prisoners of war; how might we legally circumvent those prohibitions so we can inflict pain on detainees during interrogation and not be held legally accountable?" The response was to replace the designation "prisoners of war" with "enemy combatants." "Prisoners of war" have human rights pro- tected by international agreements. There is little consensus on the legal rights, if any, of "enemy combatants." Terrorist suspects detained in U.S. bases in Afghanistan, Guantánamo Bay, Cuba, and in Abu Ghraib and other bases in Iraq may be held indefinitely with- out charge and without legal counsel as long as their captors see fit.[26] International human rights groups have been barred from the camps. As of June 2004, more than five thousand foreign nationalists have been jailed and stripped of their civil liberties in the United States, Guantánamo, or Iraq since September 11, in antiterrorism "preven- tion detention" measures. Military intelligence officers told the Red Cross that 70–90 percent of the people locked up in Iraq have been arrested by mistake.

Torture was legalized under Nazi Germany's Nuremberg Laws, which "redefined" Jews as non-citizens and non-human. By the same legal logic, the Louisiana Legislature legalized cockfighting by designating roosters as "fowl," not "animals," thus circumventing the state's prohibition against cruelty to animals.[27]

President Bush's legal counsel, Alberto Gonzales, remarked that the nature of the war on terror "renders obsolete Geneva's strict limitations on questioning of enemy prisoners and renders *quaint* [italics added] some of its provisions." Gonzales, you may recall, gave legal guidance to Governor Bush, who dispatched 152 persons to the Texas death chamber.

But the Pentagon's list of approved "stress and duress" interrogation techniques, which includes throwing suspects against walls, hooding them, depriving them of sleep for days at a time, and binding them in painful positions, forbids "extreme" mental torture, such as *"threatening detainees with immediate death."* (italics added)

The Convention Against Torture and Other Cruel, Inhumane or Degrading Treatment or Punishment (wording from Article 5 of the UN Universal Declaration of Human Rights), which has been ratified by the U.S. Senate, holds us to a higher standard of moral conduct than we have been able to achieve on our own. By signing on to the Convention Against Torture, we have committed ourselves never to engage in "any act by which severe pain or suffering, whether physical or mental, is intentionally inflicted."

The concept of severe "mental" suffering is revolutionary. It reveals an "evolving standard of decency" of human rights never before embraced by the United States. With these words, the United States Supreme Court and its people face a new reality about the death penalty: There is simply no way that we are ever going to figure out how to preordain the killing of a human being without inflicting severe mental suffering.

The defenselessness of persons under the control of their captors is central to understanding torture. If someone can resist an aggressor, we don't call it torture. It is the defenselessness of the victim that makes us loathe torturers and cringe when we see the photographs of our soldiers smiling and giving a thumbs-up at the plight of suffering Iraqi prisoners.

I was glad when the Supreme Court consulted the wisdom and experience of the world community in *Atkins* and ruled that executing mentally retarded persons is an act of cruelty. Most of our democratic allies stopped killing mentally handicapped persons long ago, though Justice Scalia, as we have seen, dissented in *Atkins,* scornfully refusing to consider international moral standards of cruelty. "[Other countries'] notions of justice are (thankfully) not always those of our people," he said.

Justices Scalia and Clarence Thomas and Chief Justice Rehnquist were the only dissenters in *Atkins*. Perhaps they were trying to hold the line against the Court's "slippery slope" for fear that by declaring the execution of the mentally retarded a violation of the Eighth Amendment's prohibition against cruelty, the Court might eventually forbid the execution of juveniles. Their fears are justified. Some of their colleagues are signaling that they intend to do precisely that. Right after *Atkins*, John Paul Stevens, Ruth Bader Ginsburg, and Stephen Breyer expressed grave reservations about the moral decency of executing juveniles, pointing out that only a handful of nations—Iran, Nigeria, Pakistan, and Saudi Arabia—still kill children. In a public speech in Atlanta recently, Justice Sandra Day O'Connor said, "I suspect over time we will rely increasingly [on], or take notice of, international and foreign law in resolving domestic issues." She added that when 30 percent of the U.S. gross national product is derived internationally, "no institution of government can afford to ignore the rest of the world." Only the United States and Somalia have refused to sign the Covenant on the Rights of the Child. U.S. officials have admitted that a major obstacle lies in the covenant's prohibition of juvenile executions.

I wonder what the Framers of the Constitution would think of how the United States holds on to the death penalty while so many of our allies have abandoned it over the last fifty years. The Framers wrote the best Constitution they could, incorporating the best ideas and values from other countries. They very much wanted the new Republic to stand tall among other nations in its respect for the human person against the massive powers of the state. I think they would be appalled by the way constitutional protections of defendants have been ignored or abused in the administration of the death penalty. In the absence of those protections, they would not be surprised that so many innocents have been caught up in the system. I think they'd be shocked at the legalistic quagmire the courts have created and immensely saddened by the Supreme Court's heavy emphasis on procedure over law. With long-term imprisonment available, as it was not in their day, they'd be quick to see that capital punishment was no longer necessary or desirable. And I think they'd take Senate ratification of the UN Convention Against Torture very seriously, embracing its prohibition against mental and physical cruelty. I can see them proudly holding high the United

Nations Universal Declaration of Human Rights on which the torture convention was based.

I end this book with two cries of the heart: one from a father whose daughter was murdered, the other from a prisoner gassed to death in North Carolina.

Bud Welch lost his daughter, Julie, in the Oklahoma City bombing on April 19, 1995. He's told me that when the day of Timothy McVeigh's execution arrived, after six years of waiting, most of the 168 victims' families had figured out that whether he was executed or sentenced to a hundred lifetimes of imprisonment had become irrelevant. "Whatever happened to McVeigh," Bud said, "really had nothing to do with my spiritual task. I have to reconcile myself to the empty chair, where once our precious Julie sat. I have to deal with the fact that I am never going to have lunch with her on Wednesdays again. I'll never hear her laugh again. Never hear her voice on the phone. So, I get to watch McVeigh die? I get to wait and see if he offers me a crumb of remorse? Even if Timothy McVeigh were to have an incredible conversion and knelt before me and wept and begged my forgiveness, that wouldn't restore my loss. It doesn't bring my Julie back. The chair is still empty. It doesn't tuck her into my arms again. I've met Bill McVeigh, Tim's father. He's suffering more than I am. I'm proud of Julie. I brag about her to everyone I meet, but what can Bill McVeigh say about his son? The thought that his son killed 168 human beings must evoke the most unspeakable sorrow in him and guilt that he failed his son in the most terrible way. I'd rather be me than him any day. For the first few months after Julie's death, all I could think about was getting McVeigh. It was good that when they brought him from the jail to the courthouse they put a lead vest on him, because I would have easily, gladly, taken a shot at him. I was consumed with anger. I was smoking five packs of cigarettes a day and drinking heavily. But my epiphany came one day when I was in my car and reached to turn on the radio, and it hit me. I remembered when Julie and I were driving and the news was on, telling about an execution in Texas, and Julie turned to me and said, 'Dad, the death penalty is nothing but vengeance; it just fuels hate.' And I got it. I realized that killing McVeigh would only dishonor Julie. I'm Catholic. I believe in the sanctity of all life, not just innocent life, but mass murderers, too. Julie was one amazing young woman, and I'll never stop bragging about her. But there's not a night I put my head on the pillow that I don't think of her. I'll never get over it that she's been taken from us."

Bud Welch is a member of Murder Victims' Families for Human Rights. He gives hundreds of talks a year, sharing about Julie and how he manages to "get off the train of hatred."

The execution chamber in Central Prison, Raleigh, North Carolina, is airtight. A wooden chair with a high back, armrests, and footrest is mounted against the chamber's back wall. Under the chair a metal container contains cyanide, and under the cylinder is a metal canister filled with a sulfuric acid solution. When executioners turn three keys in the control room, an electric switch causes the bottom of the cyanide container to open, dropping the cyanide into the acid, which produces the lethal gas. A heart monitor, which can be read in the control room, is attached to the chest of the condemned. After the warden pronounces the prisoner dead, ammonia is pumped into the chamber to neutralize the gas, and exhaust fans pump the inert fumes from the chamber. Members of the prison staff then enter the chamber and remove the body for release to the county medical examiner. Leather belts, strapped across chest, arms, and legs, affix the condemned to the chair, and a leather mask with small holes near the nose and mouth is attached to the face.

In 1983, the General Assembly of North Carolina gave the condemned the option to choose death by lethal injection. Under this provision, the warden must be notified in writing by the condemned at least five days before the execution that he or she would prefer death by lethal injection.

David Lawson chose to die in the gas chamber. He said he wanted the people of North Carolina to know they were killing a man. He tried to have his execution videotaped and broadcast, but state and federal courts denied his request, arguing that he did not have a constitutional right to make his death public.

In a last appeal to the U.S. Supreme Court, David Lawson's lawyers requested a stay of execution, arguing that execution by gas was a form of cruel punishment and in violation of the Eighth Amendment, but the Court refused to hear the petition.

On June 15, 1994, David Lawson was killed by the state of North Carolina for the murder of Wayne Shinn, whom he had shot during a burglary in 1980. It took thirteen minutes for the gas to kill him.

Lawson, wearing only socks and boxer shorts over a diaper, sat in the chair and watched as guards strapped his chest, arms, and legs to the chair and hooked up an electrode over his heart. Guards then placed a leather mask over his face. Soon after 2:00 a.m., the cyanide was dropped into the acid and the lethal fumes began to rise. Lawson, choking and gasping and straining against the straps, took short breaths and cried out, "I am human. I am a human being." He pushed up on his feet and kicked his legs. His hands gripped the ends of the armrests. Drool and tears slid from under the mask. A few deep breaths of the gas would have killed him sooner, but David Lawson continued to take short breaths and despite paroxysms of choking cried out until his voice was but a whisper: "I . . . am . . . a human . . . being."

EPILOGUE

The journey continues.

In April 2004 Susan Sarandon telephoned to tell me that James Allridge, a man on death row in Texas with whom she had been corresponding, had a date of execution of August 26, and she felt the date was real. She was shaken. I could hear it in her voice. She had written to James for eight years and come to know him as a person, alive and filled with insight, allowing the alchemy of seventeen years on death row to transform his life. On several occasions when I visited Susan in New York, she had shown me James's art. Using ordinary colored pencils, he had found a most amazing way to draw light out of flowers.

"What should I do?" she asks.

"Just what you've been doing," I answer. "Be his friend. You give him dignity."

She said that she'd visit him, but try to keep it quiet. (Which proved to be impossible. Media awaited her when she arrived at the prison.)

One month later when Susan and I talked, she dropped a bomb-shell: "James wants you to be with him if he's killed."

I said, "Oh no, Susan, you should be with him. You've been his friend for eight years."

She said, "No, no, Helen, you saw the film, this is what *you* do."

I thought, What is this? Life imitating art imitating life?

That's how it came about that on August 26 when James Allridge became the 325th person killed by the state of Texas, I was with him as his spiritual adviser. His appeals lawyer, Jim Marcus of the Texas Defender Service, and his hardworking team* did their utmost to save James's life. They had a video made of James's transformed life and sent it to the six members of the Texas Board of Pardons and Paroles, hoping to convince them to grant clemency, and in the petition to the appeals court and the U.S. Supreme Court James's legal team presented two new constitutional issues:

The first asked, Does the Eighth Amendment prohibit the state of Texas from incarcerating a prisoner for seventeen years, rehabilitating him into a model inmate, who enhances the safety and stability of the prison society, and then executing him based on the erroneous prediction that he would pose a threat to society if sentenced to life in prison? As had happened in the case of Karla Faye Tucker, James Allridge once again raised the question: Why kill a person who is rehabilitated?

The second questioned the constitutionality of the Texas capital sentencing statute, which, though demanding that a jury find proof *beyond reasonable doubt* for guilt (a requirement of "due process"), drastically reduced the standard for determining punishment. The Texas statute requires that for a sentence of death to be imposed a jury only need determine the *probability* that a defendant would continue to pose a threat of future dangerousness to society. The injection of the word *probability*, however, drains the "beyond a reasonable doubt" of any meaning (it would be like telling the jury it could convict if they believed—beyond a reasonable doubt—that the defendant *might* be guilty. When Jim told me of the "future dangerousness" argument, I couldn't help but wonder that if jurors in capital cases

*Assisted by Peter M. Friedman and Lisa R. Fine of Weil, Gotshal & Manges LLP, a civil law firm in Washington, D.C.

already face the impossible task of analyzing people's *past* actions to determine the "worst of the worst" murders, how on God's green earth can they be expected to predict how human beings might act in the *future*? At least past actions yield tangible evidence that can be examined; but what is the content, the raw matter for predicting future actions? Doesn't it fly in the face of "due process of law" to punish people for what they *might* do in the future? The issue of "future dangerousness" raises a constitutional challenge particularly for Texas, which is one of only three states to allow this highly speculative consideration to play a crucial role in life and death decisions made by juries.

Unsurprisingly, the Texas Defender Service's (TDS) study of 155 Texas capital cases in which prosecutors hired experts to predict defendants' future dangerousness revealed that the so-called experts' predictions were wrong 95 percent of the time. (The study, "Deadly Speculation: Misleading Texas Capital Juries with False Predictions of Future Dangerousness" is available at: www.texasdefender.org/publications.htm.)

That's a stunning number of wrong predictions, but what else can be expected of a process based on sheer speculation? As the TDS study points out, "Beginning in the early 1980s researchers and professionals concluded that 'mental health professionals cannot predict dangerousness,' " and the American Psychiatric Association states, "the unreliability of psychiatric predictions of long-term dangerousness is by now an established fact within the profession." Predictably, prognostications of future dangerousness, are fertile fields for racial prejudice to insinuate itself. In at least seven death cases reviewed by the TDS a licensed psychologist, hired by the state, testified that, in his opinion, being a member of a minority race makes a defendant more dangerous.

As is their pattern, neither the Texas Court of Criminal Appeals nor the U.S. Supreme Court agreed to consider the constitutional issues raised in James Allridge's petition. The U.S. Supreme Court did not give a reason for not hearing James's case (it rarely does). The Texas Court of Criminal Appeals (the Texas supreme court for criminal cases) stated that it would not allow consideration of James's claims because they should have been raised by James's previous lawyers. (In other words, Sorry, Mr. Allridge. It looks like, even though you have provocative and interesting constitutional challenges, you're petitioning too late. It's regrettable that your previous lawyers did not have the smarts and creativity to raise the issues within the timeframe we've mandated. So, it looks like you die, Mr. Allridge.)

So, once more we see the machinery of death at work in the courts: procedural requirements valued over substance, legal mechanisms trumping what Jesus called the "weighty matters of justice and mercy."

I hope I go to my death with a tiny fraction of the poise and grace James Allridge possessed as he stepped into eternity. He asked pardon of the victim's family, thanked family and friends for loving him, and as calmly as if he were talking about going on an errand, departed with the words: "I came into this world in love and I leave it in love." And once again I found myself standing as mute witness to the protocol of death, this time in the busiest killing chamber in the United States. The night before James was killed by the state of Texas, another man, Jasen Shane Busby, had been killed, and Jim Marcus predicted fifteen more executions before the end of January 2005. As of September 27, the state of Texas accounted for half of the total number of U.S. executions in 2004. Regional disparity in the application of the death penalty could not be more pronounced, and the Fourteenth Amendment's promise of "equal protection of law" could not be more flagrantly ignored. Yet the official guardians of the Constitution continue to allow procedural requirements to shield them from taking a fresh look at the constitutional challenges that continue to arise in death cases. Justices' rigid adherence to stay the course of their own legal precedents, no matter how wrongheaded, renders them unwilling to admit, as did Justice Harry Blackmun, that "the death penalty experiment has failed." And so the southern machinery of death clanks on, for that is what it truly is, a predominantly southern practice that goes back to the days of slavery.

The last cry of the heart is my own.

I invite you to join me in the struggle to end the death penalty in the United States and around the world. Its practice demeans us all.

A page of resources follows. For a jump start go to www. moratoriumcampaign.org. For photos of Dobie Williams, Joseph

O'Dell, and Lori Urs and me with Pope John Paul II, go to www. deathofinnocents.com and www.sisterhelen.org.

Now that this book is finished, I'll once again be on the speaking circuit. It means leaving the quiet writing haven and getting on airplanes again.

See you on the road.

AUTHOR'S NOTE ON RESOURCES

Groups across the country are working to stop the injustices of our nation's broken machinery of death. Contact any of the groups below for more information and for ways to get involved.

Death Penalty Information Center: A source of comprehensive, well-researched information on the death penalty in the U.S.; school study guides available. Visit www.deathpenaltyinfo.org.

The Moratorium Campaign: The home of Sister Helen Prejean's national moratorium petition drive calling for a freeze on state and federal executions. Visit www.moratoriumcampaign.org.

Equal Justice USA/Quixote Center: Working state by state for a moratorium on executions. Visit www.quixote.org/ej.

National Coalition to Abolish the Death Penalty: A national group with state affiliates that publishes information about upcoming executions. Visit www.ncadp.org.

Amnesty International USA: A worldwide human rights organization that works to end the death penalty. Visit www.aiusa.org.

Restorative Justice: A movement that emphasizes healing the wounds of victims, offenders, and communities caused by crime. For general information visit www.restorativejustice.org.

Murder Victims' Families for Human Rights: A national group of family members who have lost loved ones to murder and who oppose the death penalty. Visit www.murdervictimsfamilies.org.

Bridges to Life: A project begun by John Sage, a murder victim's family member, who has found a way to bring victims and incarcerated prisoners together to promote healing and to prevent recidivism. Visit www.bridgestolife.org.

NOTES

CHAPTER ONE: DOBIE GILLIS WILLIAMS

1. The others were Robert Lee Willie in 1984, Willie Celestine in 1987, and Joseph Robert O'Dell in 1997.

2. Donald A. Cabana, *Death at Midnight: The Confession of an Executioner* (Boston: Northeastern University Press, 1996), p. 172.

3. Stuart James, Forensic Consultants, Inc., Ft. Lauderdale, Florida.

4. This figure is current as of October 1, 2004. For a complete (and updated) list, see www.deathpenaltyinfo.org and click on "innocence."

5. *Brady v. Maryland,* 373 U.S. 83 (1963).

6. See Michael L. Radelet, Hugo Adam Bedau, and Constance E. Putnam, *In Spite of Innocence* (Boston: Northeastern University Press, 1992).

7. An example is Roger Keith Coleman, electrocuted in Virginia on May 20, 1992. He forfeited his appeal because his attorneys filed the papers one day late. See John C. Tucker, *May God Have Mercy* (New York: W. W. Norton, 1997), pp. 110–16; *Coleman v. Thompson,* 501 U.S. 722 (1991) (in which the Supreme Court said that Coleman's "Notice of Appeal" was filed three days late but nonetheless affirmed an order by a federal court dismissing the appeal).

8. Thomas Fraser, John Koneck, and Clinton Cutler of Fredrikson and Byron P.A. in Minneapolis, Minnesota, who would describe their experience in a paper entitled "Death Penalty in Louisiana" in the *University of Toledo Law Review* 35 (2004): 617–24. They are civil litigators, and it was the first time they had ever worked on a death penalty case. They had visited Dobie's home, talked to his family, and become much more involved than they had expected to.

CHAPTER TWO: JOSEPH O'DELL

I

1. See, for instance, Trip Gabriel, "Freedom Fighter," *The New York Times,* May 10, 1992, Section 6, p. 24. Centurion Ministries is located at 221 Witherspoon St., Princeton, N.J. 08542; (609) 921-0334. Website: www.centurionministries.org.

2. As of October 1, 2004, Texas had executed 326 prisoners since 1972; Virginia had executed 91. Up-to-date execution figures can be found on the website of the Death Penalty Information Center, www.deathpenaltyinfo.org.

3. Blood contains two proteins, called antigens, used to determine blood type. The antigens are called A and B. If the A antigen is present on the surface of the red blood cells, then the blood type is A; if the B antigen is present, the blood type is B; if both A and B antigens are present, the blood type is AB; if neither is present, the blood type is O. In addition to AB blood grouping, another antigen is used to determine the Rh blood group. The most common Rh antigen is called D. If it is present, then the blood type is Rh+; if it is absent, the blood type is Rh–. According to the American Association of Blood Banks, blood types in the U.S. population are A+ (34 percent); A– (6 percent); B+ (9 percent); B– (2 percent); AB+ (3 percent); AB– (1 percent); O+ (38 percent); O– (7 percent).

4. Trial transcript, *Commonwealth v. O'Dell,* 364 S.E.2d 491 (Va. 1987) p. 135.

5. Dated November 1, 1985.

6. According to the American Psychiatric Association, predicting future dangerousness is impossible, and physicians should not attempt to do so. In 1981, the American Psychiatric Association presented an amicus curiae brief to the U.S. Supreme Court stating that "psychiatric prediction of dangerousness, whatever its basis, is of such low reliability as to confound the fact-finding process and to warrant exclusion of such predictions as a matter of law." Paul S. Appelbaum, "Psychiatrists' Role in the Death Penalty," *Hospital and Community Psychiatry* 32 (1981): 761–62.

7. According to the Department of Justice, the average age of those on death row at the time of their arrest is twenty-eight. See www.ojp.usdoj.gov/bjs/cp.htm.

8. Denny LeBoeuf is director of the Capital Post-Conviction Project of Louisiana, which provides postconviction representation for people sentenced to death.

9. Michael Graham's testimony may be found at http://judiciary.senate.gov/oldsite/te062701Gra.htm.

10. Sara Rimer, "Two Death-Row Inmates Exonerated in Louisiana," *The New York Times,* January 6, 2001, p. 8.

11. Joe Jackson and June Arney, "Controversies Trail Alberi in His Quest for Judgeship," *Virginian-Pilot* (Norfolk), March 3, 1996, p. A1.

12. Richard Reynas was the investigator hired by Centurion Ministries who worked with Lori Urs.

13. Clifford S. Zimmerman, "From the Jailhouse to the Courthouse: The Role of Informants in Wrongful Convictions," pp. 77–98, in Saundra D. Westervelt and John Humphrey, eds., *Wrongly Convicted: Perspectives on Failed Justice* (New Brunswick, N.J.: Rutgers University Press, 2001).

14. O'Dell trial transcript, p. 138.

15. *Giglio v. U.S.,* 405 U.S. 150 (1972).

16. See, for instance, Westervelt and Humphrey, eds., *Wrongly Convicted: Perspectives on Failed Justice;* Radelet et al., *In Spite of Innocence.*

17. Such as Michael Small in Louisiana and Millard Farmer in Georgia. Farmer, when representing a black man named Thomas Grant accused of raping and robbing a white female, attempted to ask jurors during the voir dire examination if they were prejudiced against African Americans. For no more than that, the judge held him in contempt and sentenced him to jail without bond. When the court of appeals reversed the judge's decision (*Farmer v. Knox,* 137 Ga. App. 478, 224 S.E.2d 123 [1976]), the judge stated to the local newspaper in Brunswick, Georgia, that he would not allow Millard in his court again. Millard refused to leave the case, which was eventually dismissed when his client passed a lie detector test and the prosecution witness confessed to falsely reporting a crime.

18. See, for instance, James S. Liebman, Jeffrey Fagan, and Valerie West, "A Broken System: Error Rates in Capital Cases, 1973–1995," available at justice.policy.net/jpreport.finrep.PDF (March 13, 2001).

19. From Lori Urs's article: "*Commonwealth v. Joseph O'Dell:* Truth and Justice or Confuse the Courts?; The DNA Controversy," *New England Journal of Criminal and Civil Confinement* 25 (1999): 311, 315–17. "After proceeding pro se through a six week trial, after which he was convicted, O'Dell appealed to the Supreme Court of Virginia, which affirmed the judgment of the trial court. On April 1, 1988, the Virginia Supreme Court decided an issue on rehearing that was previously held to be procedurally barred. The court, however, affirmed the conviction, but left a viable issue open for appellate review. The United States Supreme Court denied O'Dell certiorari to hear the appeal.

"O'Dell filed a Petition for a Writ of Habeas Corpus in the [state] Circuit Court of Virginia Beach. The majority of his claims were dismissed without an evidentiary hearing, with the remainder of the claims dismissed after a limited evidentiary hearing on O'Dell's competency and forensic claims.

"O'Dell appealed the dismissal of his state habeas petition. The Virginia Supreme Court dismissed the appeal since O'Dell was procedurally barred on all of his claims due to an error in the filing procedure. In 1991 O'Dell, with no other alternatives, petitioned the United States Supreme Court for a Writ of Certiorari, which was denied. While the Court declined to hear his case, Justice Blackmun, along with Justices Stevens and O'Connor, issued a rare statement expressing concern over his procedural bar and urged the court to hear his federal claims. Justice Blackmun stated that:

" 'There are serious questions as to whether O'Dell committed the crime or was capable of representing himself—questions rendered all the more serious by the fact that O'Dell's life depends upon their answers. Because of the gross injustice that would result if an innocent man were sentenced to death, O'Dell's substantial federal claims can, and should, receive careful consideration from the federal court with habeas corpus jurisdiction over the case.'

"On July 23, 1992, O'Dell filed a Petition for a Writ of Habeas Corpus in the Federal District Court of Virginia. In light of the concerns expressed by the three U.S. Supreme Court Justices, the court entertained O'Dell's actual innocence claim pertaining to the DNA evidence at the federal evidentiary hearing on August 2, 1994.

"Although the DNA evidence did establish the 'fair probability' that, in light of all probative evidence available at the time of his federal evidentiary hearing, 'the trier of the facts would have entertained a reasonable doubt of his guilt,' O'Dell, failed to meet the higher actual innocence standard and failed to establish that 'no rational trier of fact could [find] proof of guilt beyond a reasonable doubt.' The District Court ruled favorably for O'Dell on a more technical issue and vacated his death sentence.

"After O'Dell appealed to the Fourth Circuit Court of Appeals, on September 10, 1996, the court, sitting en banc, entered judgment reversing the District Court's order to the extent it granted habeas relief to O'Dell, and reinstated the death sentence. The court found that O'Dell's claim of actual innocence was 'not even colorable.' In its ruling, the court misstated a number of facts that, in order to correct, required an entire appendix to the U.S. Supreme Court Petition.

"On November 26, 1996, O'Dell appealed to the U.S. Supreme Court. The Court granted certiorari, but refused to hear argument on actual innocence. Even though the Court conceded that O'Dell's 1986 sentencing proceeding was plainly unconstitutional under a 1992 decision by the Court, in a 5–4 decision, it refused to apply the law retroactively to O'Dell. Justice Scalia, however, ignored the factual finding of the District Court and misstated that the blood on O'Dell's jacket 'matched' the victim. This error illustrates how DNA results can be, and sometimes are, manipulated, misapplied, or misunderstood by the courts."

20. The United States Constitution, Article I, Section 9, Clause 2.

21. See, for example, Marshall J. Hartman and Jeanette Nyden, "Habeas Corpus and the New Federalism After the Anti-Terrorism and Effective Death Penalty Act of 1996," *John Marshall Law Review* (Winter 1997): 337; and Andrea D. Lyon, "New Opportunities for Defense Attorneys: How Record Preservation Requirements After the New Habeas Bill Require Extensive and Exciting Trial Preparation," *John Marshall Law Review* (Winter 1997): 389.

22. Leading that team was Leon Friedman, who is now the Joseph Kushner Distinguished Professor of Civil Liberties Law at Hofstra University School of Law and has a long history of activity in the civil rights arena.

23. See James S. Hirsch, *Hurricane: The Miraculous Journey of Rubin Carter* (Boston: Houghton Mifflin, 2000); and Paul B. Wice, *Rubin "Hurricane" Carter and the American Justice System* (New Brunswick, N.J.: Rutgers University Press, 2000).

24. *O'Dell v. Thompson,* 502 U.S. 995 (1991).

25. During his eleven years of pleadings in state and federal courts, O'Dell petitioned the U.S. Supreme Court three times and was denied, the Virginia Supreme Court twice and was denied, the Fourth Circuit once and was denied. His only break came from a federal district court, which temporarily vacated his death sentence, but that was short-lived when the Fourth Circuit sided with the prosecution and summarily overturned the lower court's decision.

II

26. *Simmons v. South Carolina,* 512 U.S. 154, 161 (1994).

27. The death penalty today is authorized in thirty-eight states and by the federal government. In thirty-six of those thirty-eight states, and in the federal jurisdiction, defendants who are eligible for the death penalty but not sentenced to death are sentenced to life imprisonment with no chance for parole. The exceptions are New Mexico and Texas. For more information, see www.deathpenaltyinfo.org and click on "Life Without Parole."

28. Peter Finn, "Given Choice, Virginia Juries Vote for Life: Death Sentences Fall Sharply When Parole Is Not an Option," *The Washington Post,* February 3, 1997, p. A1.

29. The defendant was John Brooks, a mentally ill and severely mentally handicapped African American man.

30. Michelle Millhollon, "Death Penalty Dinners: D.A. Doug Moreau Uses Public Funds for Lavish Meals for Staff Members After Successful Death Penalty Trials," *Sunday Advocate* (Baton Rouge), September 12, 1999, p. 1.

31. The scientific debate revolved around the controversial use of monomorphic probes to achieve the results, and the National Research Council had judged that the probes produced inaccurate results—which led the judge to conclude that the blood on the jacket should be declared inconclusive.

32. See Stephen B. Bright, Charles F. Baird, Penny J. White, George H. Kendall, Stephen F. Hanlon, and Charles J. Ogletree Jr., "Breaking the Most Vulnerable Branch: Do Rising Threats to Judicial Independence Preclude Due Process in Capital Cases?" *Columbia Human Rights Law Review* (Fall 1999): 123–73.

33. Millard Farmer was the attorney hero in my book *Dead Man Walking.*

34. The decision was *O'Dell v. Netherland,* 95 F.3d 1214 (1996). Before Wilkinson, chief judge, and Russell, Widener, Hall, Murnaghan, Ervin, Wilkins, Niemeyer, Hamilton, Luttig, Williams, Michael, and Motz, circuit judges. Judge Luttig wrote the opinion, in which Chief Judge Wilkinson and Judges Russell, Widener, Wilkins, Niemeyer, and Williams joined. Judge Ervin wrote an opinion concurring in part and dissenting in part, in which Judges Hall, Murnaghan, Hamilton, Michael, and Motz joined.

35. An example of a case where a defendant was sentenced to death despite the fact that the defense attorney slept during significant portions of the trial is Calvin Burdine in Texas. Eventually, the death sentence was thrown out by a federal court and Burdine was resentenced to life imprisonment. Lisa Teacher, "Convicted Killer

Avoids Death Row: Notorious 'Sleeping Lawyer Case' Ends in Plea Agreement," *The Houston Chronicle,* June 20, 2003, p. 29.

36. After Burdine won a new trial in federal district court in 1999, the state of Texas appealed, asking a federal circuit court to reinstate the death penalty despite the sleeping lawyer. In October 2000, a three-judge panel of the Fifth Circuit Court of Appeals reinstated the death sentence. The two judges in the majority, Rhesa H. Barksdale and Edith H. Jones, ruled that it was impossible to determine if the sleeping lawyer actually harmed Burdine's case. "We cannot determine whether Cannon slept during a 'critical stage' of Burdine's trial," the judges wrote. Eventually this ruling was overturned by the full court. Henry Weinstein, "Attorney's Dozing at Center of Texas Murder Case Challenge: Defendant Facing the Death Penalty Contends His Lawyer in 1984 Trial Was No More 'Than a Potted Plant,' " *Los Angeles Times,* January 23, 2001, p. 1.

37. Laura Lafay, "U.S. Supreme Court Halts Virginia Execution: O'Dell Is a Cause Célèbre for Italians, Who Largely Oppose the Death Penalty," *Virginian Pilot,* December 18, 1996.

38. On February 4, 1999, Sean Sellers was executed in Oklahoma for a murder he committed when he was sixteen years old. Not until 2002 did the Supreme Court rule that the death penalty could not be imposed on mentally retarded defendants. *Atkins v. Virginia,* 536 U.S. 304 (2002).

39. Between January 1, 1977, and November 2, 2004, there were 938 executions in the United States.

40. Sara Rimer, "Working Death Row," *The New York Times,* December 17, 2000, p. 1.

41. Donald A. Cabana, *Death at Midnight: The Confession of an Executioner* (Boston: Northeastern University Press, 1996).

42. Bill Pelke, *Journey of Hope* (Philadelphia: Xlibris Corporation, 2003).

43. See www.ncadp.org.

44. Dorothy Day was born in Brooklyn in 1897. In 1933, she founded *The Catholic Worker,* a publication that reflected her belief in an "economy based on human needs, rather than the profit motive" and unashamedly promoted neutral pacifism. She also ran the House of Hospitality in the slums of New York and continued her work for social justice throughout her life. See www.mcs.drexel.edu/~gbrandal/Illum_html/Day.html.

45. *Summa Theologica,* II-II, Ques. 64, a.2, and 3. E. Christian Brugger, *Capital Punishment and Roman Catholic Moral Tradition* (Notre Dame, Ind.: University of Notre Dame Press, 2003), pp. 65–79.

46. This I am learning from Northern Cheyenne friends, who are teaching me to recognize the Great Spirit in everything—land, trees, rivers, animals.

47. According to Amnesty International, eighty countries now have no death penalty whatsoever. Another fifteen have no death penalty for "ordinary crimes," while a further twenty-three are "abolitionist in practice." See "Abolitionist and Retentionist Countries," web.amnesty.org/pages/deathpenalty-countries-eng.

48. This refusal by members of the European Union to extradite criminals to death

penalty countries is playing a dramatic role in the initiatives against terrorism launched worldwide in the wake of the September 11, 2001, terrorist attack. Currently, none of the one thousand or so suspected terrorists in the attack who have been arrested by members of the EU will be extradited to the United States unless there is a formal written assurance that the death penalty will not be sought.

49. See Edith Coron, "Post-Communist Russia Meets World," *The Christian Science Monitor,* November 28, 1997.

50. "A New Springtime of Faith," *St. Louis Post-Dispatch,* January 28, 1999.

51. See www.santegidio.org/pdm/news/09_07_01.htm.

III

52. *O'Dell v. Netherland,* 521 U.S. 151 (1997).

53. Barry Scheck, Peter Neufeld, and Jim Dwyer, *Actual Innocence: Five Days to Execution and Other Dispatches from the Wrongly Convicted* (New York: Doubleday, 2000).

54. Figures from the Innocence Project. See www.innocenceproject.org.

55. See Spencer S. Hsu, "Allen Denies Death-Row Inmate's Request for DNA Test," *The Washington Post,* July 12, 1997.

56. The evidence was destroyed on March 30, 2000, when Virginia Beach Circuit Court deputy clerk Jaime C. Reyes tossed two bags and a package containing DNA evidence into the city incinerator at the Bureau of Animal Control.

CHAPTER THREE: THE MACHINERY OF DEATH

I

1. Antonin Scalia, "God's Justice and Ours," *First Things: The Journal of Religion and Politics* 123 (May 2002): 17–21.

2. *O'Dell v. Netherland,* 521 U.S. 151 (1997) (Scalia, J., joining Court's denial of O'Dell's petition); *Williams v. Cain,* 525 U.S. 859 (1998) (denying certiorari).

3. *O'Dell v. Netherland,* 521 U.S. 151 (1997) (Justice Scalia voted in the five-vote majority to deny O'Dell's petition).

4. Letter from Sister Helen Prejean to Pope John Paul II, January 1, 1997, copy on file with the author.

5. Conference, A Call for Reckoning: Religion and the Death Penalty, University of Chicago Divinity School, January 25, 2002 (presented by the Pew Forum on Religion and Public Life).

6. See, for instance, James Warren, "A Feisty Scalia Tackles the Death Penalty," *Chicago Tribune,* January 28, 2002.

7. See Anne Thompson, "Scalia: Stuck in the Past," *The Washington Post,* February 26, 2002 (op-ed by student who questioned Justice Scalia).

8. John Paul II, *Evangelium Vitae* (*Gospel of Life*), issued March 30, 1995 (English translation in *Origins* 24, no. 42 [1995].

9. *The Catechism of the Catholic Church* (September 1997) ("the cases in which the execution of the offender is an absolute necessity 'are rare, if not practically nonexistent,' " p. 2267).

10. Thompson, "Scalia: Stuck in the Past."

11. Scalia, "God's Justice and Ours."

12. U.S. Constitution, Fifth Amendment.

13. U.S. Constitution, Fourteenth Amendment.

14. Scalia, "God's Justice and Ours" (discussing the fallacy of considering the Constitution as a "living document").

15. See *Callins v. Collins,* 510 U.S. 1141 (1994) (Scalia, J., concurring in denial of a writ of certiorari).

16. *Gregg v. Georgia,* 428 U.S. 153 (1976).

17. *Callins v. Collins,* 510 U.S. 1141 (1994) (Blackmun, J., dissenting from a denial of a writ of certiorari).

18. William Faulkner, Banquet Speech, receiving the 1949 Nobel Prize for Literature, December 10, 1950; see www.nobel.se/literature/laureates/1949/faulkner-speech.html (visited February 3, 2004).

19. For a discussion of some of these conflicts, see Helen Prejean, CSJ, *Dead Man Walking: An Eyewitness Account of the Death Penalty in the United States* (New York: Random House, 1993), esp. chapter 11.

20. Scalia, "God's Justice and Ours."

II

21. Ibid.

22. Ibid.

23. See, for example, United States Catholic Bishops' Pastoral Letter, "Living the Gospel of Life: A Challenge to American Catholics" (1998).

24. James J. Megivern, *The Death Penalty: A Historical and Theological Survey* (Mahwah, N.J.: Paulist Press, 1997), p. 18.

25. See *The Complete Word Study New Testament with Greek Parallel* (King James Version), compiled and edited by Spiros Zodhiates (Iowa Falls, IA: World Bible Publishers, 1992).

26. See Somini Sengupta, "Facing Death for Adultery, Nigerian Woman Is Acquitted," *The New York Times,* September 26, 2003, p. A3.

27. *Callins v. Collins,* 510 U.S. 1141 (1994) (Scalia, J., concurring in denying a writ of certiorari).

28. See, for instance, St. Anselm, *Proslogium; Monologium: An Appendix in Behalf of the Fool by Gaunilo;* and *Cur Deus Homo,* translated from the Latin by Sidney Norton Deane, with an introduction, bibliography, and reprints of the *Opinions of Leading Philosophers and Writers on the Ontological Argument* (Chicago: Open Court Publishing Company, 1903, reprinted 1926).

29. Scalia, "God's Justice and Ours."

30. Ibid.

III

31. See Marc Mauer and Tracy Huling, "Young Black Americans and the Criminal Justice System: Five Years Later" (Washington, D.C.: The Sentencing Project, 1995). ("Almost one in three [32.2 percent] young black men in the age group 20–29 is under criminal justice supervision on any given day—in prison or jail, on probation or parole.")

32. See Jeremy Travis, Amy L. Solomon, and Michelle Waul, *From Prison to Home: The Dimensions and Consequences of Prisoner Reentry* (Washington, D.C.: The Urban Institute, 2001). ("Further, although the majority of prison inmates enter prison with substance abuse problems, only 10 percent of state inmates in 1997 reported receiving professional substance abuse treatment, down from 25 percent in 1991. Of the soon-to-be-released population, 18 percent of those with a substance abuse problem received treatment while incarcerated." At p. 18.)

33. Sixty-seven percent of the 2002 federal drug control budget was dedicated to supply reduction, and only 33 percent was dedicated to demand reduction, or treatment. In this sense, two thirds of the budget went toward punishment rather than treatment. These figures can be found in table 1.13, p. 17, in *The Sourcebook of Criminal Justice Statistics 2001,* by Ann L. Pastore and Kathleen Maguire, eds. (2002), U.S. Bureau of Justice Statistics, Washington, D.C.: USGPO.

34. Redlining is the practice of automatically denying someone a loan.

IV

35. See conference A Call for Reckoning. Transcript at pewforum.org/deathpenalty/resources/transcript3.php3 (visited September 24, 2004).

36. See *Furman v. Georgia,* 408 U.S. 238, 257 (1972) (Brennan, J., concurring).

37. *Glass v. Louisiana,* 471 U.S. 1080 (1985) (Brennan, J., dissenting from denial of a writ of certiorari).

38. *Furman v. Georgia,* 408 U.S. 238 (1972).

39. *Gregg v. Georgia,* 428 U.S. 153 (1976).

40. See *Coker v. Georgia,* 433 U.S. 584 (1977).

41. *Thompson v. Oklahoma,* 487 U.S. 815 (1988).

42. See *Walton v. Arizona,* 497 U.S. 639 (1990) (Scalia, J., concurring in part and stating his disagreement with the decision in *Lockett v. Ohio,* 438 U.S. 586 [1978]).

43. *Atkins v. Virginia,* 536 U.S. 304 (2002).

44. *Atkins v. Virginia,* 536 U.S. 304, 337–54 (2002) (Scalia, J., dissenting).

45. See Human Rights Watch, *Beyond Reason: The Death Penalty and Offenders with Mental Retardation* (March 20, 2001).

46. See Denis Keyes, William Edwards, and Robert Perske, "People with Mental Retardation Are Dying Legally," *Mental Retardation* 35 (February 1997): 59–63.

47. Bill Montgomery, "Retarded Man's Execution Stirred Protest Worldwide," *The Atlanta Constitution,* October 13, 1986.

48. *Penry v. Lynaugh,* 492 U.S. 302 (1989).

49. *Atkins v. Virginia,* 536 U.S. 304, 345 (2002) (Scalia, J., dissenting).

50. Scalia, "God's Justice and Ours."

51. See Bureau of Justice Statistics, *Capital Punishment 2002* (November 2003).

52. *Plessy v. Ferguson,* 163 U.S. 537 (1896).

53. *Brown v. Board of Education,* 347 U.S. 483 (1954).

54. *McCleskey v. Kemp,* 481 U.S. 279 (1987).

55. Marc Mauer, *The International Use of Incarceration, 1992–1993.* (Washington, D.C.: The Sentencing Project, September 1994).

56. Warren, "A Feisty Scalia Tackles the Death Penalty."

V

57. "Killer Executed in Louisiana as Appeals Fail," *Los Angeles Times* (from wire services), April 5, 1984 (noting that Eddie Sonnier's sentence was reduced to life).

58. See, for instance, FBI Uniform Crime Reports: 14,054 people were murdered in 2002; according to the Bureau of Justice Statistics, 159 people were sentenced to death in the same year; *Capital Punishment 2002* (November 2003).

59. See, for instance, Death Penalty Information Center, Costs, at www.deathpenalty-info.org/article.php?did=108&scid=7 (visited September 24, 2004).

60. See, for example, Death Penalty Information Center (DPIC), Life Without Parole, at www.deathpenaltyinfo.org/article.php?did=555&scid=59 (visited September 24, 2004). According to the DPIC, New Mexico and Texas, the only two death penalty states without a sentence of life without parole, have life sentences with lengthy periods before the defendant is even eligible for parole.

61. See, for instance, Death Penalty Information Center, Public Opinion, at www.deathpenaltyinfo.org/article.php?did=209&scid=23 (visited September 24, 2004).

62. Millard Farmer has been an innovator and defense attorney in death penalty cases for many years. See, for instance, David Frey, "Death Row Attorney Honors King's 'Birthnight,' " *Aspen Daily News,* January 19, 2004.

63. Robert Wayne Williams was executed on December 14, 1983.

64. John Taylor was executed on February 29, 1984.

65. Many of these are federal constitutional rights found in the Bill of Rights and subsequent amendments, such as the Fourth (search and seizure protections), Sixth (right to a trial and a lawyer), and Fourteenth (rights to due process and equal protection).

VI

66. As of September 24, 2004, there have been 929 executions and 116 people freed from death row after their convictions were overturned. Death Penalty Information Center, www.deathpenaltyinfo.org.

67. *McGautha v. California,* 402 U.S. 183 (1971).

68. *Furman v. Georgia,* 408 U.S. 238 (1972).

69. *Gregg v. Georgia,* 428 U.S. 153 (1976).

70. *Jurek v. Texas,* 428 U.S. 262 (1976).

71. *Proffitt v. Florida,* 428 U.S. 242 (1976).

72. *Gregg v. Georgia,* 428 U.S. 153 (1976).

73. *McGautha v. California,* 402 U.S. 183, 204 (1971).

74. *Furman v. Georgia,* 408 U.S. 238 (1972).

75. See Stuart Banner, *The Death Penalty: An American History* (Cambridge: Harvard University Press, 2002), p. 266; Michael Meltsner, *Cruel and Unusual* (New York: Random House, 1973), p. 291.

76. See Jeffrey M. Jones, "Support for the Death Penalty Remains High at 74%, Slight Majority Prefers Death Penalty to Life Imprisonment as Punishment for Murder," Gallup News Service, May 19, 2003 (listing earlier poll results).

77. *Witherspoon v. Illinois,* 391 U.S. 510, 520 (1968).

78. See James W. Marquart and Jonathan R. Sorenson, "A National Study of the Furman-Commuted Inmates: Assessing the Threat to Society from Capital Offenders," *Loyola of Los Angeles Law Review* 23 (1989): 5–28.

79. Charles W. Ehrhardt and L. Harold Levinson, "Florida's Legislative Response to Furman: An Exercise in Futility?" *Journal of Criminal Law and Criminology* 64 (1973): 10–21.

80. See *Proffitt v. Florida,* 428 U.S. 242 (1976).

81. *State v. Dixon,* 283 So.2d 1, 22 Florida (1973).

82. Michael Mello, "Florida's 'Heinous, Atrocious or Cruel' Aggravating Circumstance: Narrowing the Class of Death-Eligible Cases Without Making It Smaller," *Stetson Law Review* 13 (1984): 523–54; Robert Sherrill, "Death Row on Trial," *The New York Times Magazine* (November 13, 1983): 80–83.

83. Ramsey Clark, "Spenkelink's Last Appeal," pp. 224–33, in Hugo Adam Bedau, ed., *The Death Penalty in America,* 3rd ed. (New York: Oxford University Press, 1982).

84. As of September 24, 2004, there have been 929 executions in the United States. Of those 929, 758 (81.6 percent) were convicted of killing whites. See www.deathpenaltyinfo.org.

85. *Lockett v. Ohio,* 438 U.S. 586 (1978).

86. Audio program at Sound Portraits, www.soundportraits.org/on-air/parents_at_an_execution (visited September 24, 2004; transcript available from Sound Portraits). National Public Radio, *All Things Considered,* March 11, 2003.

87. In March 2003, Delma Banks was granted a stay by the U.S. Supreme Court just ten minutes before his scheduled execution. *Banks v. Cockrell,* 583 U.S. 917 (2003).

In February 2004, the Supreme Court threw out his death sentence and remanded the case back to trial court for further proceedings. *Banks v. Dretke*, 124 S.Ct. 1256 (2004); see also Linda Greenhouse, "Man on Death Row 24 Years Seems to Gain Before Justices," *The New York Times*, December 9, 2003.

88. Ilene Phillipson, *Ethel Rosenberg: Beyond the Myths* (New York: Franklin Watts, 1988), p. 303.

89. See H. Reske, "Courts Battle over Harris Execution," *ABA Journal* (July 1992): 26.

90. *Strickland v. Washington*, 466 U.S. 668 (1984).

91. See Ronald J. Tabak et al., "Judicial Activism and Legislative 'Reform' of Federal Habeas Corpus: A Critical Analysis of Recent Developments and Current Proposals," *Albany Law Review* 1 (1991): 10, note 24.

92. See Associated Press, April 10, 2001.

93. See, generally, Stephen Bright, "Counsel for the Poor: The Death Sentence Not for the Worst Crime but for the Worst Lawyer," *Yale Law Journal* 103 (1994): 1835.

94. *Burdine v. Johnson*, 262 F.3d 336 (2001); *Cockrell v. Burdine*, 122 S.Ct. 2347 (2002).

95. Diane Jennings, et al., "Defense Called Lacking for Death Row's Poor," *Dallas Morning News*, September 11, 2000. (One in four condemned inmates are represented at trial or on appeal by court-appointed attorneys who have been disciplined for misconduct at some point in their careers.)

96. *Burdine v. Johnson*, 231 F.3d 950 (2000). Judges Edith H. Jones and Rhesa Hawkins Barksdale formed the majority, while Judge Fortunato P. Benavides dissented.

97. *Cockrell v. Burdine*, 122 S.Ct. 2347 (2002). The U.S. Supreme Court declined to decide an appeal by the state of Texas of a Fifth Circuit Court of Appeals ruling that granted Texas death row inmate Calvin Burdine a new trial on the basis of ineffective counsel. According to several witnesses, Burdine's attorney dozed repeatedly during his original trial. The circuit court held that "unconscious counsel equates to no counsel at all" and that Burdine was therefore "denied counsel at a critical stage of his trial." *The New York Times*, June 4, 2002.

98. *Stanford v. Kentucky*, 492 U.S. 361 (1989).

99. Between 1990 and September 24, 2004, there were thirty-eight juveniles around the world who were executed. Nineteen of them were executed in the United States. See web.amnesty.org/pages/deathpenalty-children-eng. See also Roger Hood, *The Death Penalty: A Worldwide Perspective*, 3rd ed. (New York: Oxford University Press, 2002), pp. 114–19.

100. See, for instance, Dorothy Otnow Lewis, Jonathan H. Pincus, Marilyn Feldman, Lori Jackson, and Barbara Bard, "Psychiatric, Neurological, and Psychoeducational Characteristics of 15 Death Row Inmates in the United States," *American Journal of Psychiatry* 143 (July 1986): 838–45.

101. *Ford v. Wainwright*, 477 U.S. 399 (1986).

102. Patterson was executed May 18, 2004. See Scott Gold, "Mentally Ill Killer Is Put

to Death in Texas"; and "Gov. Perry Disregards a Prison Board's Recommendation That the Schizophrenic Man's Sentence Be Commuted to Life in Prison," *Los Angeles Times,* May 19, 2004, p. A14.

103. *Singleton v. Norris,* 319 F.3d 1018 (2003); *Singleton v. Norris,* 124 S.Ct. 74 (2003); Tracy Shurley, "Singleton Dies," *Arkansas Democrat-Gazette* (Little Rock), January 7, 2004, p. 11.

104. *Herrera v. Collins,* 506 U.S. 390 (1993).

105. *Keeney v. Tamayo-Reyes,* 504 U.S. 1 (1992).

106. *Murray v. Giarratano,* 492 U.S. 1 (1989).

107. See 22 U.S.C. §2244(d); see also, for instance, *Williams v. Cain,* 125 F.3d 269 (1997).

108. *McCleskey v. Kemp,* 481 U.S. 279 (1987).

109. See Marvin E. Wolfgang and Marc Riedel, "Racial Discrimination, Rape, and the Death Penalty," pp. 194–205, in Bedau, ed., *The Death Penalty in America,* p. 197.

110. *Coker v. Georgia,* 433 U.S. 584 (1977).

111. David C. Baldus, George G. Woodworth, and Charles A. Pulaski Jr., *Equal Justice and the Death Penalty: A Legal and Empirical Analysis* (Boston: Northeastern University Press, 1990).

112. General Accounting Office, *Death Penalty Sentencing: Research Indicates Pattern of Racial Disparities* (GGD-90-57) (Washington, D.C.: General Accounting Office, 1990).

113. The vote in the *McCleskey* case was 5–4. Interestingly, the decision was written and the deciding vote cast by Justice Lewis Powell, who was then serving his last year on the Court. Four years later, Powell's biographer asked the retired justice if he wished he could change his vote in any single case. Powell replied, "Yes, *McCleskey v. Kemp.*" Powell, who voted in dissent in *Furman* and in his years on the Court remained among the justices who regularly voted to sustain death sentences, had changed his mind. "I have come to think that capital punishment should be abolished . . . [because] it serves no useful purpose." See J. C. Jeffries Jr., *Justice Lewis F. Powell, Jr.: A Biography* (New York: Charles Scribner's Sons, 1994), pp. 451–52.

114. *Batson v. Kentucky,* 476 U.S. 79 (1986).

115. Editorial, "How Large a Fig Leaf?" *The Washington Post,* October 27, 2002, p. B6 (quoting a 1963 prosecutor training manual).

116. William Bradford Huie, "The Shocking Story of Approved Killing in Mississippi," *Look* magazine, January 24, 1956.

117. Between 1976 and September 24, 2004, there were 929 executions in the United States. Of them, 313 involved black defendants, 194 of whom (62 percent) were convicted of killing whites. Death Penalty Information Center: www.deathpenaltyinfo.org.

118. See, for instance, Paige M. Harrison and Jennifer C. Karberg, *Prison and Jail Inmates*

at Midyear 2003 (Washington, D.C.: U.S. Department of Justice, Bureau of Justice Statistics, May 2004); and Marc Mauer, *The International Use of Incarceration, 1992–1993* (Washington, D.C.: The Sentencing Project, September 1994).

119. See Bryan Stevenson, "Close to Death: Reflections on Race and Capital Punishment in America," in Hugo Adam Bedau and Paul G. Cassell, eds., *Debating the Death Penalty: Should America Have Capital Punishment?* (New York: Oxford University Press, 2004), pp. 89, 92.

120. *Williams v. Taylor,* 529 U.S. 362 (2000).

121. *Atkins v. Virginia,* 536 U.S. 304 (2002).

122. *Ring v. Arizona,* 536 U.S. 584 (2002).

123. *Miller-el v. Cockrell,* 537 U.S. 322 (2003).

124. *Banks v. Dretke,* 124 S.Ct. 1125 (2004).

125. *Wiggins v. Smith,* 539 U.S. 510 (2003).

126. *Plessy v. Ferguson,* 163 U.S. 537 (1896).

VII

127. *Callins v. Collins,* 510 U.S. 1141, 1145 (1994) (Blackmun, J., dissenting from a denial of a writ of certiorari).

128. *Coleman v. Thompson,* 501 U.S. 722, 758–59 (1991) (Blackmun, J., dissenting).

129. *Sawyer v. Whitley,* 505 U.S. 33 (1992).

130. *Herrera v. Collins,* 506 U.S. 390, 446 (1993) (Blackmun, J., dissenting).

131. *Callins v. Collins,* 510 U.S. 1141, 1153 (1994) (Blackmun, J., dissenting from a denial of a writ of certiorari).

VIII

132. Conference, A Call for Reckoning. Transcript at pewforum.org/deathpenalty/resources/transcript3.php3 (visited September 24, 2004).

133. Ibid.

134. An April 2002 Zogby International poll of likely voters in Illinois found that 64 percent of respondents supported Governor George Ryan's moratorium on executions. See *St. Louis Post-Dispatch,* April 29, 2002, p. A5.

135. Press release, DePaul University, January 10, 2003, at http://sherman.depaul.edu/media/webapp/mrNews2.asp?NID=932&ln=true (visited September 24, 2004).

CHAPTER FOUR: THE DEATH OF INNOCENCE

I

1. Bureau of Justice Statistics: Capital Punishment Annual Reports.

2. Statistics from the Death Penalty Information Center (DPIC), www.deathpenaltyinfo.org. DPIC is an excellent source of information for anyone wanting the latest statistics and news about the death penalty. And for an in-depth

international perspective on the death penalty, see Amnesty International's Death Penalty Campaign Information Center at www.amnesty.org/pages/deathpenalty-index-eng.

3. According to Robert B. Dunham, the director of training in the Philadelphia office of the Federal Defenders Association, Capital Habeas Corpus Unit, Lynne Abraham has attempted to downplay the rate at which her office continues to seek the death penalty, in the face of a city council that has passed a death penalty moratorium resolution in 2000 and again in 2004.

4. Those five districts were Puerto Rico, eastern Virginia, eastern New York, southern New York, and all of Maryland. Statistics gathered by the U.S. Department of Justice, September 12, 2000.

5. See, for instance, Karen Branch-Brioso, "Ashcroft Takes Proactive Stance on Death Penalty," *St. Louis Post-Dispatch,* February 6, 2003; Dan Barry, "Ashcroft and Prosecutors at Odds over Role of I.Q. in Murder Case," *The New York Times,* March 18, 2003; Benjamin Weiser and William Glaberson, "Ashcroft Pushes Executions in More Cases in New York," *The New York Times,* February 6, 2003; and Jen McCaffery, "Spurt of Acquittals Raises Concerns," *Roanoke Times,* April 18, 2004.

6. Death Penalty Information Center, *A Guide to the Death Penalty,* pp. 67–68.

7. Howard Witt, "Texas Grimly Efficient in Executions," *Chicago Tribune,* March 15, 2004.

II

8. Barry Scheck, Peter Neufeld, and Jim Dwyer, *Actual Innocence: Five Days to Execution and Other Dispatches from the Wrongly Convicted* (New York: Doubleday Books, 2000).

9. See www.innocenceproject.org/about/other_projects.php for a list of state Innocence Projects. As a volunteer at one such project, Lori Urs responded to Joseph O'Dell's plea for help and, after O'Dell was killed, founded an Innocence Project at Rutgers School of Law while a student there.

10. *State v. Timmendequas,* 773 A.2d 18, 50 (N.J. 2001) (Long, J., dissenting).

11. Rakoff's opinion was overturned but is on appeal to the U.S. Supreme Court. *U.S. vs. Quinones,* 205 F.Supp.2d 256 (S.P.N.Y. 2002) (emphasis added), rev'd by 313 F.3d 49 (2d Cir. 2002).

12. David C. Baldus, George Woodworth, Gary L. Young, and Aaron M. Christ, *The Disposition of Nebraska Capital and Non-Capital Homicide Cases (1973–1999): A Legal and Empirical Analysis,* July 2001.

13. Speaking about his intention to introduce a death penalty abolition bill, *Richmond Times-Dispatch,* November 14, 2000.

14. George F. Will, "Innocent on Death Row," *The Washington Post,* April 6, 2000.

15. Largely through the tireless efforts to educate citizens by People of Faith Against the Death Penalty, currently under the leadership of Stephen Dear. Online at www.pfadp.org; e-mail at info@pfadp.org.

16. See Death Penalty Information Center, www.deathpenalty.org/article.php? scid=23&did=210 and www.deathpenaltyinfo.org/article.php?scid=23&did=592.

17. Lewis Williams, age forty-five, was executed by lethal injection on January 14, 2004, at 10:07 a.m. at the Southern Ohio Correctional Facility in Lucasville. Twenty years earlier, he had been sentenced for murdering Leoma Chmielewski, age seventy-six, during a robbery in her Cleveland home. Mary McCarty, "Execution Exposes Inhumanity of Death Penalty," *Dayton Daily News,* January 15, 2004.

18. Helen Prejean, CSJ, *Dead Man Walking: An Eyewitness Account of the Death Penalty in the United States* (New York: Random House, 1993), pp. 101–105.

III

19. Amnesty International press release, "Death Penalty: Latest Worldwide Statistics Released," AI Index: ACT 50/012/2004, Geneva, April 2004. Amnesty International indicated that at least 726 people were executed in China in 2003, but the true figure was believed to be much higher. A senior Chinese legislator suggested in March 2004 that China executes "nearly 10,000" people each year. Also, according to Craig S. Smith, "Chinese Fight Crime with Torture and Executions," *The New York Times,* September 9, 2001, as many as 191 people were executed in a single day. "Since President Jiang Zemin announced the crackdown in April, at least 3,000 people have been executed. . . . With increasing frequency, prisoners are formally arrested or sentenced at public rallies. Nearly two million people attended such rallies in Shaanxi Province in April and May. On June 25, more than 5,000 people attended a rally in Hubei Province, at which 13 people were sentenced to death, 8 of whom were executed immediately. The condemned are normally paraded through town on the beds of open trucks, before being driven to the execution ground, often trailed by a caravan of onlookers."

20. *People v. LaValle* (2004). For the full story, see W. Glaberson, "A 4–3 Ruling Effectively Halts Death Penalty in New York," *The New York Times,* June 25, 2004.

21. Prejean, *Dead Man Walking,* pp. 169–74.

22. Alan Berlow, "The Texas Clemency Memos," *The Atlantic Monthly,* July/August 2003.

23. Tucker Carlson, "Devil May Care," *Talk* magazine, September 1999, p. 106.

IV

24. Senator Feingold introduced the National Death Penalty Moratorium Act in 2000.

25. Alex Kotlowitz, "In the Face of Death," *The New York Times Magazine* (July 6, 2003).

V

26. Recent Supreme Court decisions have found this unacceptable. See, for instance, *Rasul v. Bush,* 124 S.Ct. 2686, 72 USLW 4596, 4 Cal. Daily Op. Serv. 5693, 2004 Daily Journal D.A.R. 7777, 17 Fla. L. Weekly Fed. S 457 (2004).

27. It gets better. Probably because of people's affection for pets, ten birds in the state have been allowed to remain animals. The law reads, "Fowl shall not be defined as

animals. Only the following birds shall be identified as animals for purposes of this Section: parrots, parakeets, lovebirds, macaws, cockatiels or cockatoos, canaries, starlings, sparrows, flycatches [*sic*], mynah or myna." This gem of southern culture comes from my friend Julia Reed's book, *Queen of the Turtle Derby and Other Southern Phenomena*.

INDEX

ATHE keynote — "I started out as a regular nun."

Dead Man Walking play / theatre project

school project
university

Cover the face to protect the witness

|"we mask death"

protocol of death

"nobody is gonna see this..."

"nuns have not done well in films"

"it's even got dead in the title"

"we need theatre in this country"

"the film plows the ground and the book tills the soil ..."

103 schools have perf.
pilot prog.
in Jesuit schools

Vocation of acting is ~~free will~~ enforced of compulsion

S. Sarandon

keeping it in "the schools"

royalties go to Actor's Gang

DOC theatre

Our Children's Place

has gotten large grants to do a year

(univ, "some" high schools)

UNC – death of penalty events

I cannot do this play w/out open the conversation this play into prisons in general

ALSO BY SISTER HELEN PREJEAN

*"This arresting account should do for the debate over capital
punishment what the film footage from Selma and
Birmingham accomplished for the civil rights movement:
turn abstractions into flesh and blood."*
—Bill McKibben

DEAD MAN WALKING

In 1982, Sister Helen Prejean became the spiritual advisor
to Patrick Sonnier, the convicted killer of two teenagers
who was sentenced to die in the electric chair of Louisiana's
Angola State Prison. In the months before his death, the
Roman Catholic nun came to know a man who was as terrified as he had once been terrifying. At the same time, she
came to know the families of the victims and the men
whose job it was to execute Sonnier—men who often harbored doubts about the rightness of what they were doing.
Out of that dreadful intimacy comes a profoundly moving
journey through our system of capital punishment. Confronting both the plight of the condemned and the rage of
the bereaved, the needs of a crime-ridden society and the
Christian imperative of love, *Dead Man Walking* is an
unprecedented look at the human consequences of the
death penalty.

Current Affairs/0-679-75131-9

VINTAGE BOOKS
Available at your local bookstore, or call toll-free to order:
1-800-793-2665 (credit cards only).

a "live" event   Tim
"share an experience"   Robbins
potent   pre-
viseral, "real"   audience dress
                  equal
  g   participant

- emotion-first process   mentions
    → prevents slip   Exonerated
       into propoganda
    ↓
leads to discussion — "spirit ⟩ draws
                    to satire/ people
                       humor in

there is a (public)
  who want "free expression"

"to hear music
 (many out of
 (that city [New Orleans]
 ... is the music of the
     ages"